D1214183

CENSORSHIP: THE IRISH EXPERIENCE

Censorship: the Irish experience

MICHAEL ADAMS

KDK
1262
.A3

UNIVERSITY OF ALABAMA PRESS
University, Alabama

WITHDRAWN

INDIANA
UNIVERSITY
LIBRARY
OCT 1 3 1981

SOUTH BEND

lw
10-12-81

Technical information

Published, 1968, in the United States
and Canada, by the
UNIVERSITY OF ALABAMA PRESS.
© Michael Adams 1968.
Printed in the Republic of Ireland.
This book is set in 10 on 12pt
Monotype Plantin and was printed
by O'Gorman Ltd., Printinghouse,
Galway, Ireland.
Library of Congress Catalog Card
Number 68-22681

Contents

Acknowledgements

This book would never have come to be without the encouragement and help of Professor Howard Warrender and Dr Cornelius O'Leary of the Political Science Department of the Queen's University of Belfast who guided its original elaboration as a university thesis. I realise I cannot adequately express my gratitude to them.

From another point of view it owes a great deal to all those who gave me access to private papers and so amicably tolerated my interviews or questions. In particular I must mention Miss Emma Bodkin, Mr Gerald Boland, the Right Reverend Mgr Patrick Boylan, PP, VG, Fr Peter Connolly, His Honour Judge J. C. Conroy, Mr P. F. Donovan, Mr Andrew Ganly, Mr Justice Kevin Haugh, Miss Mary Lavin, Mr Brian MacMahon, Mr Louis McRedmond, Mr Justice T. C. Kingsmill Moore, Miss Mairin O'Byrne, Mr T. J. O'Connell, Mr Dermot J. O'Flynn, Mrs J. J. Pigott, Fr Roland Burke Savage, SJ, Dr Owen Sheehy Skeffington, Dr Michael Tierney, the Editor of the *Irish Times* (for access to its files of press cuttings) and also the officials of the Department of Justice and the Censorship of Publications Office, who gave of their time to answer numerous letters concerning their work.

Naturally I alone am responsible for any assessments or judgements made on the basis of this evidence.

A final and special word of thanks must go to the Staff of the National Library of Ireland where I have worked intermittently over a number of years, and to Mrs Olive Cotter who so patiently helped me with the final preparation of the typescript.

MICHAEL ADAMS
20 February 1967

Foreword

Almost forty years have passed since censorship of publications in Ireland was inserted in a legal and political structure and for this reason alone it does seem to offer a useful subject for an exercise in political science. This present study is little more than a chronicle of the Irish experience during that period; it recalls the original reasons for the introduction of a system which many people even in the 1920's saw as a sinister attempt to mould the mind of a young nation; it examines the application of the law over the years, avoiding wider constitutional and philosophical questions which might also be asked, and skirting literary and moral aspects with which I am not competent to deal; and in particular it indicates the extra-legal, social influences which have in various ways modified the behaviour of the censors. It deals with the more influential side of formal censorship, making no more than passing reference to the censorship of films; and it is only a partial contribution to the more general subject of Irish grundyism.

It is difficult to avoid taking sides on any social issue—it is virtually impossible when the subject of study is one which affects the entire intellectual life of one's country. Yet I feel I will not be accused of tilting the balance and giving an unfair advantage to one party to a perennial Irish quarrel: indeed the criticism may be that I have *not* been partisan, that integrity calls for a commitment in the form of a series of judgements on the rightness and wrongness of censorship decisions. My unsatisfactory reply is that years of intermittent research into this question have taught me to be less categorical than I might otherwise have been: whereas principles of social action may be clear to many people and to myself the application of these principles is never absolute except for those whose social involvement is inspired by a more or less unconscious desire to force the freedom of others: at any rate this is a paternal teaching to which I wholeheartedly subscribe, and I doubt whether my own views on particular prohibitions have any special

value in the context of this book. The facts of Irish censorship are themselves quite articulate and between these lines runs a thread of humour,
warm conviction, revulsion and dismay.

M.A.

I

Towards Censorship

1922-1928

It is perhaps trite to say that the Irish independence movement was little
more than a political affair—a movement for freedom and for the rejection
of British power in Ireland with no clearly defined ideology; there was
no 'blueprint for a free Ireland', no effective desire to dismantle the social
and economic and legal institutions of the country—although many of
the revolutionaries were passionately attached to the ill-defined ideal of
an 'Irish Ireland'.

The new State took over the whole body of British statute law—and the
English common law tradition—with a few minor exceptions consequent
on the terms of the Treaty; and in regard to the legislation controlling
obscene literature the establishment of the Irish Free State brought no
change at all. Consequently, Dicey's conservative assessment of contemporary English law relating to freedom of expression held true for
Ireland.

> 'When . . . the principles of the common law and the force
> of the enactments still contained in the statute-book are really
> appreciated, no one can maintain that the law of England recog-
> nises anything like that natural right to the free communication
> of thought and opinions which was proclaimed in France nearly
> a hundred years ago to be one of the most valuable Rights of
> Man. It is quite clear, further, that the effects of English law,
> whether as regards statements made about individuals or the
> expression of opinion about public affairs, or speculative
> matters, depends wholly upon the answer to the question who
> are to determine whether a given publication is or is not a libel.
> The reply (as we all know) is that in substance this matter is
> referred to the decision of a jury.

'Freedom of discussion is, then, in England little else than the right to write or say anything which a jury, consisting of twelve shopkeepers, think is expedient should be said or written. Such "liberty" may vary at different times and seasons from unrestricted license to very severe restraint, and the experience of English history during the last two centuries shows that under the law of libel the amount of latitude conceded to the expression of opinion has in fact differed greatly according to the condition of popular sentiment.'[1]

The statutes dealing with the subject were:

Obscene Publications Act 1857
Indecent Advertisements Act 1889
Dublin Police Act 1842, Section 14
Towns Improvement (Ireland) Act 1854, Section 72
Post Office Act 1908, Sections 16, 17 and 63
Customs Consolidation Act 1876, Section 42.

Of these, the Customs Consolidation Act (which is examined later in this chapter) and the Obscene Publications Act were the two main statutes being worked at the time. The latter, known as 'Lord Campbell's Act' ('for more effectually preventing the sale of Obscene Books, Pictures, Prints and other Articles') laid down the following procedure: a search warrant and power of seizure could be obtained by the police once a magistrate had received a complaint under oath that obscene articles had been purchased. The vendor would then be summoned to explain to a police stipendiary magistrate or to two justices in petty sessions why the seized goods should not be destroyed. If he were unable to justify the sale, a destruction order would be issued (appeal was available to the next general or quarter sessions); if the prosecution were unsuccessful, the defendant was unable to bring an action for wrongful procedure, etc. The Act itself contained no definition of obscenity, but since 1868 the British Courts had employed the definition given by Lord Justice Cockburn in *Regina v. Hicklin*: 'I think that the test of obscenity is this, whether the tendency of the matter charged as obscenity is to deprave and corrupt those whose minds are open to such immoral influences, and into whose hands a publication of this sort may fall.'

In addition to initiating proceedings under Lord Campbell's Act, it was also open to any individual to cause persons to be indicted for the common law misdemeanour of public selling or exposing for public sale or putting on public view any obscene book, print, picture or other indecent exhibition. The two proceedings were independent—indictment was initiated by a preliminary investigation before a magistrate, followed by a formal hearing before a jury and a judge if the magistrate was satisfied that a *prima facie* case existed; the procedure for seizure and destruction of the obscene matter consisted entirely of hearings before a magistrate. In practice, prosecutions in either case were usually initiated by the police and conducted at the expense of the State. If a private person set the law into motion the proceedings were conducted at his own risk and expense.

Although the legislation on obscenity was not changed in 1922, independence did mean that, whereas the English courts were in a position to reach the publisher of an obscene article, the Free State had to be content with penalising an individual middle-man—distributor, book-seller or newsagent. Most of the objectionable publications available were published outside the jurisdiction of the Irish courts, and retail outlets for books and periodicals were so numerous that it was virtually impossible to exercise control once sale and distribution had reached this stage.

2 THE MOVEMENT FOR REFORM

Even before 1922 various individuals and groups in Ireland were actively dissatisfied with the type of periodical and newspaper enjoying a wide readership in the country. Outstanding among these groups was the *Irish Vigilance Association* founded in 1911 to combat the spread of these publications. This Association brought pressure to bear on news-agents to sign a pledge against stocking or selling objectionable news-papers, and attempted to arouse public opinion by letters to the press, the distribution of handbills at opportune times, and so forth; an 'enrolment crusade' was also attempted and local Vigilance Committees were formed in different parts of the country. The Association was organised by members of the Dominican Order, and the *Irish Rosary* (edited by the Dominicans) was used as a vehicle for its ideas. An examination of the issues of that monthly for the years 1911-1914 gives a full impression of the Association's activities. The following editorial comment is typical:

> 'Vigilance Committees have been established, and are carrying on the fight with determination and perseverance. They have not, it is true, secured the total banishment of these papers that are condemned as bad, but they have materially lessened their circulation, and they have awakened a sound, healthy public opinion on this question. . . .

'The fight is not against the liberty of the Press, nor against Literature properly so called . . . it is a fight against a bad Press—against papers that fill their columns, issue after issue, with vile, filthy, immoral matter, unfit to be read by our Irish men and women—our boys and our girls—and which sully by their presence the sanctity and purity of our Irish homes. Happily the evil publications against which the fight is being waged are not the product of Irish brains, nor the output of Irish hands. They are foreign to every ideal and aspiration of the clean-minded Celt, and mostly inspired by hatred of the Catholic Faith and Christian morality' (February 1913).

This campaign was not particularly successful and the Association later came to the view that a 'voluntary organisation whose members, after their day's work was finished, tried to cope with such a vast work, could only be a palliative'.[2]

The very idea of a vigilance committee carries with it many unpleasant associations, but in all fairness it may be pointed out that this was the most effective of methods available at the time to private individuals who wished to hinder the distribution of certain types of reading matter, for the existing law was adequate only for the control of the importation, publication, sale or distribution of printed matter of an obviously or grossly obscene character: the Cockburn definition had come to be very narrowly interpreted, which meant that no court of law in England or in Ireland would have ordered the destruction of newspapers of the *News of the World* type, however objectionable such papers might have been. This was borne out by numerous witnesses who were to appear before the Committee on Evil Literature set up by the Government in 1926.

It does appear that the Vigilance Association and other persons and groups who sought stricter control over imported periodicals represented a large body of opinion within the country. Undoubtedly, nationalistic motives were involved—the idea of self-sufficiency, and dismay at the fact that most of the reading matter bought in the new State was written for an English public—but it is quite clear that these publications were objected to largely on moral grounds, and it is not difficult to accept these moral grounds as reasonable, given the state of Irish popular culture in the 1920's: a community predominantly Catholic and completely Christian but with a relatively low level of general education could not but look with dismay on the flood of products of the English gutter press which was finding its way into the country. And now that the country was self-governing it was in a position to control that flood by legislative action on its own account; the Irish public was no longer forced to rely on voluntary action as the only alternative to lobbying M.P.'s at Westminster.

The type of publication most severely attacked was the English Sunday newspaper and other popular daily, weekly and fortnightly periodicals. No strong plea was made for stricter control of books; reference was of course made to books, but in general the Vigilance Association's campaign was aimed at the protection of the mass mind and mass culture of the country, to which the main threat was the cheap press.

In 1923, under cover of night, a *Censorship of Films Act* was passed by the Oireachtas (the Irish Parliament), providing for the appointment of a full-time paid film censor to examine all films destined for public performance in the country whose decisions could be reversed by the majority decision of an Appeal Board of nine, whose decision is by majority vote. The Censor is obliged to grant a certificate permitting the showing of any film 'unless he is of opinion that such picture or some part thereof is unfit for general exhibition in public by reason of its being indecent, obscene or blasphemous; or because the exhibition thereof in public would tend to inculcate principles contrary to public morality or would be otherwise subversive of public morals' (Section 23); the Censorship of Films (Amendment) Act, 1925, extended the powers of the official censor under the principal Act to advertisements by extract. Probably the reason why it attracted so little attention was that the film had not by that time found its place as an artistic medium and the proposal to censor films would not then meet with much opposition from cultural and artistic quarters.

Although it is not possible to pinpoint the precise cause of the acceleration of the campaign for reform of the obscenity laws, the Lenten Pastorals of the Catholic Hierarchy, in the year 1924 particularly, were important. The bishops (particularly of Dublin, Galway, Tuam and Clogher) 'strove to stir the Catholic conscience and to awaken the people to a sense of duty by vigorous denunciation of the cross-Channel unclean press'.[3] However, the Hierarchy appeared to be well aware that no legislation could be brought in to strengthen the control on these publications until the general public was convinced that a serious state of affairs existed. The Pastorals were, then, an opening gambit, and they did succeed in inspiring some individuals and associations to action.

The first active response to the bishops' call was made by two Dublin priests, Fr R. S. Devane, sj[4] and Fr John Flanagan, members of the

Priests' Social Guild, who waited on Mr Kevin O'Higgins, Minister for Justice, in May 1925 to put before him their views in the matter. The Minister gave them a sympathetic hearing but indicated that he could not act without public opinion behind him; around the same time Mr O'Higgins received a deputation from the Irish Vigilance Association. Fr Devane proceeded to stir up public opinion, drawing support particularly from Catholic organisations. It would be impracticable to make a painstaking examination of Irish newspapers and periodicals of the time with a view to discovering in detail the sources of the campaign which now developed against the 'Imported Press'. Conducted by religious bodies in the main, through the *Irish Independent* and numerous right-wing political and Catholic journals, it was not a highly organised or centralised campaign, but consisted rather in a constant series of news-items, short articles, letters and so forth, spread over a period of about two years, which taken together indicated a general dissatisfaction with the existing situation. The interesting feature is that this was one campaign which created no controversy: for it was directed, as has been emphasised, at cheap newspapers; no impression was given of an attack on 'the modern novel' (this received only passing references)—which meant that writers in the country were not disturbed by the movement; indeed many of them would have approved of its general aims if they had considered it warranted their attention in the first place.

As an indication of the tone of the campaign in Ireland reference may be made to the part played by *The Leader,* a Dublin review of current affairs founded in 1900 and edited by D. P. Moran, one of the most forceful personalities in Irish journalism. *The Leader* had a markedly autarchic outlook and consequently argued for control of the imported press on nationalistic as well as on moral grounds (Moran's position suffered from the defects of an over-defensive Catholicism). It dealt with the subject at various times throughout 1925, and in one typical article pointed out that 'we commenced at the evil in No. 1, Vol. 1, and we have kept at it ever since'. It recalled the time 'when vigilance meetings were held in many parts of the country' and drew attention to 'the disorganisation and disillusionment of very recent years (which) has not only weakened the feeling against filthy papers, but like the fashion for objectionable dancing, the appetite for dirty papers, we fear, has grown' (9 May). Moran insisted on immediate Government action, a plea which he was to reiterate often in the following two or three years.

In a long article in the *Irish Ecclesiastical Record* (February 1925) Fr Devane outlined the need for legislative action and proposed (1) the revision of the definition of 'indecent' and 'obscene'; (2) the inclusion of 'Birth-Control or Race-Suicide literature' within the scope of such a definition; (3) the drawing up of an official black list of obscene books, magazines, etc.; and (4) the prohibition of newspapers which carried advertisements advocating birth-control. He called on Catholic organisations to send resolutions to the Minister for Justice based on his recommendations.

Parallel to Fr Devane's activities was the work of a special sub-committee set up in 1925 by the Catholic Truth Society of Ireland (the CTS), a body founded in 1899 under the patronage of the Archbishops and Bishops of Ireland whose principal objects are '(1) to disseminate among Catholics good cheap literature; (2) to assist uneducated or badly instructed Catholics to a better knowledge of their religion; and (3) to combat the pernicious influence of infidel and immoral publications by the circulation of good, cheap and popular Catholic literature'. This sub-committee for the investigation of the problem of evil literature with special reference to legislation on the subject held its first meeting on 1 May 1925, and was composed of nine legal members, three priests, Professor William Magennis, TD[5] and Professor Michael Tierney, TD, both of the National University of Ireland (Professor Tierney soon resigned). The Committee proceeded to gather all possible information about the control of printed matter, applying to the League of Nations and to various countries which had recently enacted laws to deal with this and allied subjects. It examined the definition of the words 'obscene' and 'indecent', and its general view was that it was impossible to fix their meaning in definite terms.[6] Some members favoured the establishment of a 'Censor Board' which would tax all imported publications considered by it to be 'silly' or dangerous. The Committee's most elaborate proposal took the form of a draft Bill drawn up by Mr James Geoghegan, KC 'to regulate the sale of . . . immoral or dangerous literature' by means of a system of licensing all booksellers and newsagents. Under the terms of the Bill 'any person who sells printed matter which, in the opinion of the District Justice or Circuit Judge on appeal, is immoral or dangerous shall be guilty of an offence'; the Minister for Justice would appoint a 'controller of printed matter . . . who shall keep and publish in such manner as the Minister shall direct a list of printed matter having a tendency to be dangerous or immoral, which list is hereinafter called "the cautionary list" '; any bookseller or newsagent selling publications which appeared on the Cautionary List would be liable to a fine and/or forfeiture of licence; a right of appeal to the District or Circuit Court was included. In the late summer of 1925 copies of this draft bill were circulated to members of the Hierarchy. In an (undated) letter to the bishops the Secretary of the CTS pointed out that 'if the Hierarchy in general approve of the legislation proposed by the Sub-Committee, an appeal will be made to the Catholics of Ireland at this final Conference meeting in the coming October to stand behind the CTS proposals, which will be submitted to the Government immediately' (RDP).

However, according to the Bishop of Galway not all the bishops were in favour of the proposals; the following letter to the Minister for Justice is of special interest in that it indicates his assessment of the Hierarchy's attitudes to the Bill:

> Mount St Mary's,
> Galway.
> 23 February 1926

Dear Mr O'Higgins,

When the Archbishop of Tuam and I interviewed you in January, you expressed a desire to see a copy of Mr Geoghegan's Draft Bill which was mentioned at the October meeting of the Catholic Truth Society. I intimated your desire to Fr Devane, SJ, but I have not heard whether he sent you a copy, so I have now got the enclosed from the CTS.

I may mention that the Draft has been rather severely handled by competent critics, including some of the Bishops. So much so, that Mr G. himself would not, I think, put it forward in its present shape.

The Bishops are anxious not so much for legislation or red-tape or any sort of puritanism, but for some real and effective check on the dreadful publications and circulars [a reference to birth control literature] which are being distributed and of which, I have no doubt, the Committee of Enquiry will be furnished with samples.

With all good wishes, I remain,

> Yours v. sincerely,
> (Signed)   T. O'DOHERTY.

This letter, which was forwarded by Mr O'Higgins to Professor R. Donovan, Chairman of the Committee of Enquiry, is the only letter from a member of the Hierarchy found in the papers of Professor Donovan. Its terms are noticeably calm and in particular it may be emphasised that Dr O'Doherty does not press for legislation specifically. It would appear that the meeting of the CTS in October 1925 did not result in a petition to the Government, but rather in the visit of the two bishops to the Minister in January 1926, some few weeks before the Committee was set up.

3 OBSCENITY A MATTER OF INTERNATIONAL CONCERN

At this juncture it is convenient to introduce some reference to the experience of other countries in connection with obscene publications. Opponents of this Irish censorship movement have made out that there was some peculiarly backward, even 'Catholic', inspiration behind it, but this was true only to a certain extent for, in fact, many other countries were at this time grappling with obscenity and allied problems. Various British dominions had in recent years tightened up their obscenity laws, both Canadian and Australian Customs operated a black list of prohibited books and periodicals, while in the United Kingdom efforts were being made to control the publication of detailed reports of divorce proceedings by the introduction of a Judicial Proceedings (Regulations of Reports) Bill. Inspired by a recommendation of the Royal Commission on Divorce and Matrimonial Causes (1912) this private member's bill was first introduced in the House of Commons in 1923 by Sir Evelyn Cecil, and referred to a Select Committee which in July of that year unanimously reported in favour of legislation. The Committee was of the opinion that 'the flaunting of immorality before readers of all ages and position must be injurious to public morals and making light of such conduct challenges the whole structure of family life on which society is founded'. When the bill was introduced in the House of Lords the Lord Chancellor agreed that 'some restriction on the present licence of publication is desirable in itself. . . . What is the real difficulty ? Why is it, although this publication (no specific publication was being referred to) is in itself a breach of the law, that it is so seldom brought with success to the notice of the Courts or, at all events, that it so seldom leads to a verdict against the person charged with that offence ? . . . But I believe the real difficulty is that the law, as it stands, makes indecent publication —that is, publication of a nature calculated to injure public morals, so much a matter of opinion. The law is really not quite definite enough. . . .'[7] The following year it was re-introduced in the Commons and had a speedy passage through both Houses. The only opposition it aroused inside Parliament came from two or three members who regarded the publication of full reports as an effective deterrent operating to reduce the number of divorces and who feared the advent of *in camera* trials;

outside it was ineffectively attacked by the National Union of Journalists. Sir William Joynson-Hicks, the Home Secretary at the time, expressed clearly the Government's attitude when he said: 'We are the only country in the world that has not already dealt with this question . . . I would like the House to understand that all those connected with public justice are in favour of the Bill . . . properly speaking, this Bill is not dealing with the liberty of the Press. The Bill is really endeavouring to promote public morals.'[8] It should be noted, however, that the Bill was given a minimum of parliamentary time and that therefore the debates were rather less exhaustive than the measure perhaps deserved.

Although this legislation was to prove effective, it referred only to a specific type of publication and it in no way modified the existing law on obscenity. But around this time in Britain, as in Ireland, there was a movement in favour of tightening control of 'obscene literature'; this concern centred round the markedly outspoken trend that current action was taking. Thus, in the debates referred to above, Viscount Burnham (a newspaper peer) could report: 'It is common knowledge—and the most reverend Primate will confirm me—that there have been protests, constant protests of late, rightly or wrongly, whether you take the moral or the artistic point of view, against many of the productions that are now being given on the London stage . . . it is exactly the same thing with the fiction of our time.'[9] Around the same time, the Home Secretary was in correspondence with the London Public Morality Council on this subject. In reply to a memorial sent him by the Council, he wrote to the Bishop of London (26 February 1926): '. . . I venture to suggest that . . . they [the Morality Council] can do far more by judicious propaganda than by the suggestions referred to above. [The most important of these was one that the Home Office should call a conference of publishers 'with a view to some control by the profession somewhat on the lines of the General Medical Council'.] Experience has shown that police action and censorship can only deal with the more gross offences against public taste. Plays and books which contain no indecencies in the narrow legal sense may, nevertheless, be unhealthy and demoralising . . . the cure for this state of things is a stronger public opinion, because it is the strength of public opinion against the production of plays and books of immoral tendency which ultimately determines the standard. . . .' (RDP).

The Home Secretary's active interest in this question soon made him the centre of considerable controversy when he hinted that he might strengthen the legal control of obscene publications. In October 1928

The Times reported an address of his to the London Diocesan Council of Youth: 'I am attacked on the one hand by all those people who put freedom of speech and thought and writing before everything else in the world, as if there was freedom in God's world to pollute the younger generation growing up. There must be some limit to the freedom of what a man may write or speak in this great country of ours. That freedom, in my view, must be determined by the question as to whether what is written or spoken makes one of these little ones offend . . . only if the Secretary of State has behind him the forces of the Christian Churches is he able to deal with his problems fearlessly and honestly.'[10] Two months later, speaking at a dinner of the Authors' Club, he appealed to British authors for support 'for the overwhelming majority of them desired to publish books which were uplifting and made for the welfare of the country (cheers)'.[11] In March of the following year he appealed to English authors 'to help themselves, their country and their trade by not forcing public opinion to such an extent that the demand for some amount of censorship will be impossible to prevent'[12] and went on to publish a pamphlet with the provocative title of 'Do we Need a Censor?'[13] Nothing came of all these efforts, partly because of the opposition he aroused and partly because he did not receive active support from his Cabinet colleagues. However, this episode does serve to illustrate that the Irish movement for legislative reform was paralleled by a similar movement in Britain.

At the international level, there was the 'International Convention for the suppression of the circulation and traffic in obscene publications' held at Geneva in August 1923, under the auspices of the League of Nations. This convention was to some extent a continuation of an earlier conference called by the French Government in 1910 and attended by representatives of sixteen countries. At the third Assembly of the League of Nations held in Geneva in 1922, the British Government had raised the question of international control, and it was agreed that the French Government should convene a new International Conference, under the auspices of the League, to be held at Geneva and be composed of plenipotentiaries empowered to draw up the text of a new convention and to sign such a convention. (There was little or no evidence that obscene matter was being manufactured in Great Britain but the report of the Children's Branch of the Home Office published in 1923, which contained a chapter on this subject, showed that the authorities were perturbed by the amount of indecent literature, photographs, etc., entering the country from abroad.)

The general feeling at the 1923 meeting was that there had been a noticeable increase in the traffic in obscene articles, an increase which was both consequent on and responsible for the general breakdown of moral standards and standards of reticence which marked the war period and its aftermath. The result was a new convention, unanimously supported by representatives of thirty-five States.[14] Under the terms of the Convention the contracting parties agreed to take measures to discover, prosecute and punish anyone engaged in trading in obscene articles; persons so discovered would be answerable to the Courts of the contracting party in whose territories the offence was committed. The agreement was important in its being but not in its effects. It attracted very little attention in Britain.

Reference is made elsewhere to other legislative measures dealing with obscenity, etc., taken by foreign countries around this time.[15]

4 THE COMMITTEE OF ENQUIRY ON EVIL LITERATURE—

The Committee of Enquiry set up by the Free State Minister for Justice in 1926 was composed of Professor Robert Donovan, BA (Chairman), Professor of English literature at University College, Dublin; Professor William Edward Thrift, MA, TD of Trinity College, Dublin;[16] the Reverend James Dempsey, MA, PP, Clontarf, Dublin; the Reverend T. Sinclair Stevenson, MA, BD, a Church of Ireland minister; and Mr Thomas J. O'Connell, TD,[17] of the Irish National Teacher's Organisation. Two of these members were Protestants and three Catholics. Mr T. C. Clare acted as Secretary. The Committee's terms of reference were 'To consider and report whether it is necessary or advisable in the interest of public morality to extend the existing powers of the State to prohibit or restrict the sale and circulation of printed matter'.

The Report of the Committee, published on 28 December 1926, examined the control of publications in the country at that time, and made a series of recommendations, many of which were later incorporated in a Government bill. Before discussing this Report it would appear useful to examine the evidence submitted to the Committee.[18] At its first meeting (17 February 1926) the Committee decided to invite various professional bodies, youth associations and other groups to submit evidence. These included most, if not all, the associations interested in one way or another in the problem on hand.[19] Evidence and recommendations were also submitted by Mr Charles Eason of Eason and Son Ltd. (the largest Irish wholesale firm dealing in newspapers and periodical publications); two representatives of the Irish Retail Newsagents, Booksellers' and Stationers' Association; an Assistant Secretary of the Department of Posts and Telegraphs; a superintending inspector of Customs and Excise; and a deputy commissioner of the Garda Siochana (the Saorstat police). A letter from Mr Clare to the members of the Committee (dated 12 March 1926) mentions that 'the Secretary, Catholic Truth Society, wishes to be informed for the information of his Committee whether the Irish Catholic Hierarchy will be invited by the Committee to give evidence and he is deferring a definite reply to my communication until he receives confirmation on this point'. There is no record of any such invitation being given later to the Hierarchy; it is likely that the Committee felt that Catholic opinion on the question could be adequately expressed by the various Catholic associations invited to submit evidence.

As might be expected, the views expressed and evidence submitted by these organisations and individuals varied appreciably from one to another as to their quality, nature, extent and objectivity.

The only evidence formally submitted to the Committee by a Protestant body was that of the Dublin Christian Citizenship Council. After appealing that the freedom of the press be safeguarded and that positive action be taken by 'the promotion of education, by better school attendance, by the establishment of town and village libraries, reading clubs, women's institutes, halls for music and drama, etc.' this body, in its statement and through its representative, the Very Rev. H. B. Kennedy (Dean of Christ Church, Dublin), who gave evidence, proposed legal control on the reporting of judicial proceedings; the appointment of a 'representative Advisory Council' of five members to assist the Minister for Justice in dealing with objectionable printed matter (members of the public should have the right to bring to the Committee's attention any publication which they considered objectionable, pointing out the passages considered to be injurious); that 'any person who for the purpose of profit sends, without a specific order, printed matter relating to birth control or sexual relations to any person under 21 years of age' should be liable to punishment; and that 'all publishers should be urged to take steps to prevent the insertion of advertisements apparently innocent, but intended to be followed up by the advertising of information relating to birth control and sexual relations'. Dean Kennedy gave the Committee to understand that the Protestant clergy were not unduly worried at the spread of objectionable periodicals for they did not seem to be read very extensively by members of the Protestant community; he felt too that much was being done by booksellers' organisations 'to exercise a certain amount of censorship. . . . Experience shows that they can do a great deal . . . a decent bookseller will often ask a publisher to withdraw an objectionable book to which his attention is drawn'. He spoke too of the effectiveness of 'an organisation called the White Cross (which in previous years) did a great deal by private representations, pointing out to shopkeepers, those who exhibited bad postcards in their windows, that the cards were injurious to morals'.

The most important part of the evidence of the Dublin Christian Citizenship Council dealt with the birth control issue. It is sufficient to emphasise here that both Dean Kennedy and Mr Stevenson—the Church of Ireland clergyman on the Committee—agreed that among Protestants there was a divergence of opinion which 'induced many people to withhold general condemnation'. *[20] They were also of the opinion that birth control was practised by the middle classes to a much greater extent than was recognised, and thought that the distribution of birth control literature could usefully be restricted by making the medical profession the main channel for it.

Taken as a whole, the case presented to the Committee by Catholic organisations was decidedly more formidable; this is not surprising, for Catholic public opinion had been responsible for the setting up of the Committee and these organisations could be expected to make a strong and coherent appeal for action.

Some of this evidence was of very indifferent value, taking the form of passionate diatribes against the cross Channel press. The following example illustrates what I mean :

> '(In immoral literature) we have the vulgar and the coarse, the suggestive, the unsavoury, the offensive, the smutty, the ill-smelling; we have gilded filth, unvarnished filth, gross animalism, sex-knowledge series, sexual science. . . . Is it any wonder that we should see a decadence of morals among the youth of our country ? Is it any wonder that we should have so many houses of infamy—the resorts of night birds and wild cats ?

* Dean Kennedy said that 'personally' he would like to go further than the Council's proposal regarding birth control. 'Nevertheless' he said 'there are and have been many eminently learned and earnest Christian people taking a different view. . . . The existence of that different opinion induces many people to withhold general condemnation.'

'In defining immoral literature, I would not at all recommend that the formula should cover only the worst type. The definition should embrace all grades from the vulgar and coarse down to the diabolical and blasphemous.

'Why, then, hesitate to draw up a definition to suit this country?

'Of what are we afraid?

'Are we not free to make our own laws, according to the desire of our own people?

'On what lines should the definition be framed?

'In reply to this question I answer that there is no necessity to addle our brains to seek a formula.

'We are not drawing up a definition to be accepted by all the countries of Europe. We are catering for the Free State and for the Free State alone. . . .

'The inhabitants of Bailieboro' signed a document with the simple heading: "We, the undersigned, strongly object to the sale in this town of publications insulting to modesty." This protest was signed by 67 of the principal inhabitants of the town—by priests, Protestant ministers, doctors, solicitors, members of learned societies, as well as by the two newsagents of the town. . . . The simple formula: "Publications insulting to modesty" was quite sufficient for the people of Bailieboro'.

'At present the spiritualised Irishman is quickly passing away, and all of the brute that is in him is being fed almost to the point of moral leprosy, to be followed by a tempest of fire from heaven.'[21]

The Irish Vigilance Association presented some twenty pages of written evidence devoted to the complete range of publications; books, daily and weekly papers and magazines and pamphlets. Its statement is an interesting document, emotionally charged but full of weighty evidence. Specifically it objected to the sale in Dublin shops of books by James Joyce, D. H. Lawrence and Warwick Deeping; the sale of books which advocated 'Race Suicide'; the publication of 'revolting details of sexual crimes and of divorce cases'; the 'whole tribe of little magazines for girls, devoted to stories of a highly sentimental character, which must be very injurious to young, unformed minds'; and sporting and betting papers (betting being described as 'one of the major evils of the day in Ireland'). The Association proposed the setting up of a censorship of publications analogous to the existing censorship of films and/or the imposition of a heavy tariff; it was convinced that the definition of 'indecent' used by the courts was inadequate; it disagreed with the terms of Mr Geoghegan's draft bill on the grounds that that bill proposed to proceed by the 'old vicious and abortive way of prosecutions', and that it was absurd to expect wholesalers and newsagents to censor each individual publication they sold.[22]

By far the most closely-argued case presented was made out by the Catholic Truth Society, which took the trouble of printing in pamphlet form an extremely useful account of the existing law, the current standards of all types of publications, and a series of recommendations. This pamphlet (*The Problem of Undesirable Printed Matter*) was prepared specially for the Committee and marked 'confidential until the issue of the Committee's Report'. In fact, it was never published and few copies are available today. It consisted of 99 pages in all, containing some 50 pages of appendices in 8-pt. type indicating foreign laws relating to obscene publications.

Its principal chapters dealt with '(i) The Existing Statutes, their Inadequacy; (ii) Neo-Malthusian Birth Control Propaganda; (iii) Newspapers open to Objection; (iv) Books of an Immoral, etc., Tendency; (v) Newspapers and Magazines which give Stories of Passion, etc.; and (vi) Photographic, etc., Prints of the Nude or Semi Nude'.

The pamphlet gave estimated circulation of the following seven English Sunday newspapers and five other periodicals to which it took particular exception:

News of the World	132,444
Empire News	76,698
Sunday Chronicle	46,188
The People	30,660
Reynold's News	28,772
Sunday News (formerly *Lloyd's News*)	22,198
Sunday Herald	15,842
TOTAL	352,802

and

Sporting Times (*Pink 'Un*)	42,709
John Bull	23,984
Thompson's Weekly News	7,308
Health and Efficiency (Monthly)	1,300
Health and Strength	1,307[23]

It then proceeded to give a summary of the general character of, and a list of the headlines of, each page of a 'typical issue' of each of these publications, thus:

> '*The News of the World*—2d. Sunday . . . the most widely read of the Sunday papers. Is devoted almost entirely to reports of murders, suicides, divorces, bigamy cases, indecent assault, incest, affiliation cases and crime in general, but particularly sexual crime. The papers gives the most revolting details in all such cases. . . .

> 'Page 13—S.C. Heads:—"Girl's Terrible Ordeal. Exemplary Sentence on Emigrant, Ten Years' Imprisonment and 21 Lashes" (case of rape). "Loveless Bride. Didn't know why she married. £500 for Husband who Spent Night in the Woods" (Divorce). "Indicted by Family. Grave allegations against Septuagenarian" (Incest, 12-year-old grand-daughter)' [taken from the issue for 14 February 1926].

Although the report did press for stricter control of books—as distinct from periodicals—and although it quoted, with implied approval, lists of books prohibited elsewhere, there is no doubt but that the CTS Committee was much more concerned with reading matter which had a mass circulation.

The pamphlet's recommendations, the distillate as it were of the vast body of its evidence, included: (1) That 'all printed matter advocating birth control or publishing birth control propaganda or sale of birth control appliances or drugs be banned absolutely under severe penalties;' (2) that with regard to newspapers a bill on the lines of the Cecil bill be introduced which would in general forbid the publication of any sexual immorality in any legal case; (3) that 'a large Censor Board[24] . . . be set up consisting of delegates nominated by (a) the heads of the various religious denominations in proportion to their relative membership, (b) representatives of the Universities and (c) the State. This body to be independent. . . . All members of the Board to be unpaid. The procedure to be: A citizen to have the right to submit a memorial asking that any book, picture, photograph, print, be considered by the Board. The memorial to be signed by ten other citizens, five of whom shall be members of the learned professions; . . . their (the Board's) decision on the matter would be final. . . . All articles blacklisted would appear in the *Iris Oifigiuil;* (4) as regards banned pictures and banned books required for professional or scientific purposes, these would be imported through specially approved booksellers, who would keep a register of all such sales, including the names and addresses of the persons to whom sold'.

The 'technical' evidence given before the Committee by customs and postal officials and members of different branches of the publishing trade was of the highest quality and furnished it with a full picture of the current situation.

Mr Charles Eason agreed with the various proposals for a Censorship Board, prohibition of birth control literature, etc., but remained convinced that voluntary action was 'the only effective remedy'. In the course of his evidence he indicated how censorship of books was practised in his firm: books were considered to be divided among four classes: Class A was allowed to sell quite freely; Class B was for 'limited sale'— these would not be displayed; Class C was not kept in stock and Class D books would not even be ordered for private customers. Unfortunately he gave no indication as to which books might belong to which class.

The statement received from the Revenue Commissioners indicated that few detections had been made in recent years of attempted importation into the Saorstat of indecent articles,* for such examination as was carried out was designed 'mainly to ensure the protection of the Revenue'; in those cases where indecent or obscene prints had been detained and had been deemed to come within the legal definition, action had been taken 'by way of seizure in respect of the goods, but legal proceedings were not taken against the offenders' (power to take such proceedings is vested in the Commissioners under Section 186 of the Customs Consolidation Act, 1876). The Customs Inspector examined by the Board stressed the difficulty that Customs officials had in deciding whether an

---

* '*Chairman*: You don't use your own powers under Section 42 of the Customs Consolidation Act 1876?

'*Mr Redmond*: No, in the case of postal packets it is left to the postal authorities who have rather wider powers.

'The powers conferred . . . by Section 42 . . . as regards indecent or obscene prints, books etc., are of a general character, and in practice are restricted to the prohibition of the importation of articles that are clearly indecent or obscene discovered in the ordinary course of examination.'

In borderline cases, a consignment might be detained and a sample sent by the Customs officers to the Revenue Commissioners, who determined what action should be taken.

In later years the Customs powers under Section 42 were to be much more widely used.

object was indecent, and agreed that a list of prohibited publications would be extremely helpful.†

An Assistant Secretary of the Department of Posts and Telegraphs, in evidence, stated that the Department was 'very strongly opposed to any powers to open packets beyond its present power to hold correspondence in special cases and only when authorised by a specific warrant',[25] and said that the Department would like to see legislation introduced to authorise the detention and destruction of all postal packets found to contain certain appliances for the prevention of conception or advertisements or lists of such appliances and giving power to prosecute senders.[26]

The other official agency involved in the control of obscene matter—the police—pointed out that, due to the narrowness of the legal definition of obscenity, the activity of the police had been extremely limited, while they had no power whatsoever to interfere with literature which advocated birth control. Their witness favoured the amendment of the existing law to permit the issue of a search warrant where the police had 'reason to suspect' that indecent articles were being kept for sale; and regarded a censorship board which would prohibit publications as precisely what was needed to enable the police to bring prosecutions with greater chance of success.[27]

Since it is desirable to convey an impression of the general tenor of the evidence submitted by the Committee, we indicate in the table on the next page the lines suggested by the various witnesses, and statements

† According to evidence given to the Committee by Mr P. de Burca of the Catholic Writers' Guild, 'the Department of Customs has a black list of publications, the importation of which is forbidden. The latest copy of it that I have seen contains the names of about one hundred periodicals and forty books.'

However, the Customs witness denied this:

'*Fr Dempsey*: "Have you any such thing as a list of names or firms, I mean a black list?"

'*Mr Redmond*: "No. Once an article has been condemned a record is kept and the officers are notified to be on the watch for that. (But) If the Commissioners of Revenue received official notice that an objectionable book prohibited by law was about to be imported, all officers would be notified".'

In other words, the Customs received no direction as to which books etc. they should detain. The initiative was always theirs and the responsibility also. In reply to enquiries made by the writer, the Revenue Commissioners state that they have 'now no record' of any black list (letter, 9 May 1963). On one book at least a Customs exclusion order operated at this time: James Joyce's *Ulysses*. This book was mentioned often in pleas for censorship at this time. The exclusion order was withdrawn in 1932, and the book was never banned by the Censorship Board—contrary to expectations.

TABLE I

PROPOSALS MADE TO THE EVIL LITERATURE COMMITTEE

NAME OF ASSOCIATION, ETC.	a	b	c	d	e	MISCELLANEOUS
Catholic Headmasters Association	X	X	X	X	X	
Catholic Truth Society	X		X	X	X	
Dublin Christian Citizenship Council		X	X		X	
Garda Síochána	X	X	X	X	X	Search warrant to be given on grounds of 'reasonable suspicion'
Irish Christian Brothers	X	X	X	X	X	
Irish National Teachers Associations	X	X	X	X	X	
Irish Retail Newsagents, Booksellers and Stationers Association	X	X	X	X	X	
*Irish Vigilance Association**	X	X	X	No	*	In favour of a heavy tariff
*Marian Sodalities of Ireland***	X	X	X		**	
Revenue Commissioners	X		X	X	X	
Mr Charles Eason	X	X	X	X	X	Voluntary action the only effective remedy
R. S. Devane, S.J.	X		X		X	In favour of a heavy tariff

a = prohibition of birth control literature
b = regulation of reports of judicial proceedings
c = improvement of the definition of 'indecent'
d = licensing of booksellers, etc.
e = censorship board (the majority favoured a small board with advisory functions only)
* = one censor   ** = one censor and an appeal board

for improvement of the legal means of controlling objectionable publications. It should be emphasised that the headings of the columns are necessarily general, and that it is not possible to indicate the different nuances which each witness gave to his suggestion.

In addition to this large body of evidence given by associations and persons within the Saorstat, the Committee also consulted the following statutes etc., then in force in other countries:

New Zealand:	Indecent Publications Act, 1910.
India:	Obscene Publications Act, 1925.
Tasmania:	Indecent Publications Act, 1917.
Western Australia:	Indecent Publications Act, 1902.
New South Wales:	Obscene and Indecent Publications Act, 1901.
Victoria:	Police Offences Act, 1915.
	Part V. Obscene and Indecent Publications.
South Australia:	Immoral Law Consolidation Act, 1876.
	Children's Protection Act, 1899.
	Police Act, 1916.
Great Britain:	Judicial Proceedings (Regulations of Reports) Act, 1926.
	Extract from the Report of the Joint Select Committee on Lotteries and Indecent Advertisements, 1908.
France:	Loi reprimant la provocation a l'avortement et a la propagande anti-conceptionnelle, 1920.
United States:	Federal Law passed in 1873;
	Penal Code, Section 211; and Penal Code, Section 245 State Laws.
	Twenty-three States made it a crime to publish or advertise contraceptive information, eleven made it a crime to have in one's possession any instructions for contraception. Seven States made exceptions in the case of medical colleges, medical books and physicians.
Great Britain:	Questions in the House of Commons in 1922 as to the legal position of printed matter relating to the prevention of conception.
Canada:	Memorandum received from the Office of the High Commissioner for Canada in London re laws and regulations governing sale, etc., of obscene matter or contraceptive information.

League of Nations: International Convention for the suppression
of the circulation of and traffic in obscene
publications (Geneva, 12 September 1923).

In comparison with the volume of evidence considered by the Committee the above account of it is undoubtedly sketchy; but it is nevertheless useful for it does indicate that the Committee conducted its enquiry
with an admirable seriousness and thoroughness and considered the
question of the control of printed matter from all its important angles.
In particular, in view of legal measures which were taken later by the
Government, and bearing in mind the manner in which they were
applied, it seems desirable to emphasise the almost universal dissatisfaction with the legal definition of words 'indecent' and 'obscene', the
unsuccessful effort made by the Committee to find a more applicable
formula, and its interest in protecting works of literary merit.

5 THE REPORT OF THE COMMITTEE

At the beginning of June 1926, four months after it began its enquiry,
the Committee reached agreement on the broad lines of its recommendations. On 20 November a draft report written by Professor
Donovan was circulated to the other members. Some modifications were
suggested by Father Dempsey[28] and Mr Stevenson, but it was the
Secretary of the Committee who suggested by far the largest number of
changes, all seventeen being accepted by the Committee. The more
substantial of these included: 'A *Statutory* . . . limitation of the
grounds on which a prohibition order should be based: the censorship
should not use political or economic criteria,' and the 'removal of a
defect in the Obscene Publications Act 1857 so as to allow the issue of a
search warrant to the police on the grounds of reasonable suspicion'.

The final and unanimous *Report* delivered to the Minister for Justice
on 28 December 1926 was a concise document which adequately conveyed the opinions of the witnesses examined by the Committee while
at the same time bearing a stamp of a balanced assessment of the situation
then prevailing.

Attention may be drawn in particular to those portions of the *Report*
which dealt with the definition of 'indecent' and the control of birth
control literature. With regard to the former the Committee shared the
general opinion that the Cockburn definition, however wide and far-
reaching, was difficult to translate into action in the Courts, and it
suggested that the scope of the term be extended to include not only

what was grossly 'indecent' and 'obscene', but what was generally demoralising and offensive in sexual matters to the moral ideas of the community generally. But even such an extension of the meaning would not in itself be sufficient to control undesirable literature: 'And while in the case of publications it is possible to distinguish between those which are written with an obviously obscene intent, and those into which the gross or indecent enter only incidentally as reflecting the reality of life, it cannot be always easy for a judge or magistrate in applying the criminal law with its penalties to draw a definite line. The tendency will always be in such cases to give the person indicted the benefit of the doubt, and hence there is likely to be always a gap between the standards that the moral sense of a community is endeavouring to uphold, and the standards maintained by the sanctions of the criminal law.'

Almost one quarter of the *Report* was devoted to consideration of the issues involved in the circulation of propaganda advocating the prevention of conception. After a lengthy argument of the pros and cons of permitting the indiscriminate distribution of these publications the Committee concurred in the opinion of 'the great majority of the witnesses (who) expressed the strongest repugnance to the toleration of such publications'.

The Committee recommended:

1 That the existing laws relating to indecent and obscene publications should be amended to give a wider interpretation to the terms "indecent" and "obscene" so as to make the law applicable to matter intended to excite sensual passion.

2 That legislative provision should be made on the lines of the measure recently passed by the British Parliament for the control of reports of judicial proceedings; but extended to apply the principles of that Act also to journalistic reports and writings other than reports of proceedings in the Courts.

3 That a Board or Committee consisting of from nine to twelve persons, representative of the religious, educational and literary or artistic interests of the Saorstat, would be constituted, with a permanent official as Secretary, to advise the Minister for Justice as to any books, newspapers or magazines circulated in the Saorstat that, in the opinion of the Board, are demoralising and corrupting; that the Minister should have power to prohibit by notice in *Iris Oifigiuil* the

circulation of such publications; that, after such notice, persons exposing for sale or circulating any prohibited book, newspaper or magazine should be punishable by fine or imprisonment or both; that the notice in *Iris Oifigiuil* should be sufficient evidence in the courts of summary jurisdiction as to the character of the publication, but that the ground of prohibition should be strictly limited and should not extend to questions of a political or economic kind.

4 That the sale and circulation, except to authorised persons, of books, magazines and pamphlets that advocate the unnatural prevention of conception should be made illegal, and be punishable by adequate penalties.

5 That the defect in the Obscene Publications Act 1857, which requires that before the police can obtain a warrant under that Act to search premises where indecent publications, books, etc., are known or suspected to be, they have to prove that a sale has been made from the premises, should be amended and provision made that the police may be granted a warrant by a district justice in any case where an officer of the Garda Siochana not below the rank of Superintendent applies for a warrant on the ground that he has reason to believe that the indecent articles are kept on the premises for the purpose of sale.

6 That, following on the lines of Australasian legislation, the Indecent Advertisements Act 1889 should be amended (a) to increase the maximum penalties, (b) to include within the definition of "indecent advertisement" any document or picture or printed or written matter which relates or refers, or may be reasonably supposed to relate or refer, to any disease affecting the generative organs of either sex, or to any complaint or infirmity arising from or relating to sexual intercourse, or to the prevention or removal of irregularities in menstruation, or to drugs, medicines, appliances, treatment or methods for procuring abortion or miscarriage, or preventing conception.

7 That supplemental to the power of prohibition recommended to be given to the Minister for Justice, the Customs authorities should be empowered to stop the importation of all books, papers, magazines and other publications included in the prohibited list referred to in our recommendation

No. 3, and unless they are consigned to authorised persons, the books, magazines and pamphlets referred to in our recommendation No. 4; and that the Post Office authorities should be empowered to refuse postal matter known to contain any such prohibited books, papers, magazines or pamphlets, and to detain such matter coming to notice in the post.

8 That the new definition of "indecent and obscene" matter should be made to apply to indecent prints, photographs and postcards.'

6 PREPARATION OF THE CENSORSHIP BILL

Although the Committee's *Report* was published in the Spring of 1927, the Bill eventually submitted to the Oireachtas did not receive its first reading until August of the following year.

This delay was by no means exceptionable—indeed the Irish experience has been that such Reports rarely result in legislation; in this case, however, there appears to have been an especial impatience on the part of certain groups with the Minister's slowness to make his mind known. *The Leader* for example wrote (26 March) that 'people are becoming restive under the inactivity of the Government with regard to imported printed dirt. The burnings of parcels has begun again'. (There were some few instances of trains carrying Sunday papers being held up by armed men and the papers summarily burned: a new outlet had been found for post-revolutionary passions.)[29] And in May it wrote again complaining that 'the Report on Evil Literature was handed to the Government on 5 January 1927 . . . and nothing has been done. . . . In the course of a sermon . . . Dr O'Doherty (Bishop of Galway) declared "that the Government had been dozing about it long enough" '.

Father R. S. Devane, SJ published at least two articles on the subject during this period of waiting. In one of these, a pamphlet,[30] he published the evidence he submitted to the Committee;[31] the second appeared in December 1927 in *Studies* under the title of 'Suggested Tariff on Imported Magazines and Newspapers'. This latter article was evidently written because Fr Devane was disappointed at the fact that the Committee had not recommended the imposition of a tariff; Fr Devane proposed a $33\frac{1}{3}\%$ or 50% tariff on magazines of the popular class, and of 100% on foreign dailies.[32] The main purpose of the article was to discover the attitude to be adopted 'by a young nation towards the dominating influence of an alien press', especially in view of the fact that Ireland was then 'engaged in an heroic effort to revive our national language, national customs, national values, national culture'. The article was followed by comment by Fr MacInerney, OP, of the Irish Vigilance Association; by Professor Michael Tierney, who objected to the English press more because of its anti-intellectualism than because of its indecency, and also criticised very forcefully the Dublin evening press; and by Senator Hooper, Editor of the *Freeman's Journal*, who wrote of the desirability of 'a censorship of culture'.

The Bill did not receive its first reading until 19 July of the following year. Two general elections in 1927 were partly responsible for this delay; and the murder of Mr O'Higgins in July 1927 must have been a set-back even to the running of the Department of Justice. Then again, the new Minister, Mr Fitzgerald-Kenney, found himself with a department which, from the legislative point of view, was perhaps the busiest in the Cosgrave Government. At all events, the Bill, at last, appeared.

II

The Censorship of Publications Bill
1928

1 ALIGNMENTS

In the summer of 1928 one campaign ended and another began. The long awaited Bill* received its first reading in the Dail on 19 July and on 13 August the text was published in the press. A deep sigh of relief was breathed by many who for years had been harrying the Government to maintain a stricter control on objectionable publications; but to other groups in the community the very idea of censorship, of restricting the freedom of the press, spelt heresy.

In its general lines the Bill was a fair reflection of the *Report* of the Committee on Evil Literature—although it differed radically from the latter in one or two aspects. It consisted of four Parts. Part I (Section 2) included a new definition of the term 'indecent' and distinguished between 'book' and 'periodical' for the purposes of the Bill. Part II dealt with 'Censorship of Publications' and contained a provision (Section 3) for the establishment of a Censorship of Publications Board consisting of five members (including a Chairman), to be appointed by the Minister for Justice for a period of three years—not the twelve-man board recommended. Members would be eligible for reappointment (and, as was made clear in the Dail debates, their work would be unpaid and part-time).

Section 6 clearly contained the seeds of controversy: it empowered the Minister for Justice to 'recognise for the purpose of this Act any group or association of persons' to be the source or sifting-ground of complaints about specific publications (ss. 1); this device was not

---

* The preamble to the Censorship of Publications Bill read: 'A Bill to make provision for the prohibition of the sale and distribution of unwholesome literature and for that purpose to provide for the establishment of a censorship of books and periodicals, and to restrict the publication of reports of certain classes of judicial proceedings and for other purposes incidental to the matters aforesaid.'

traceable to the Committee of Enquiry. The Minister was permitted to refer such complaints to the Board (Section 7, ss. 1) and was further empowered (on the recommendation of the Censorship Board) to prohibit the sale or distribution of a book which 'is indecent or obscene or tends to inculcate principles contrary to public morality or is otherwise of such a character that the sale or distribution thereof is or tends to be injurious or detrimental to or subversive of public morality' (Section 7, ss. 3). The grounds for banning a periodical were similar, but the Board was required to examine a number of recent issues of a periodical before sending a recommendation to the Minister (Section 8). Any prohibition order made by the Minister might be revoked or amended by him after consultation with the Board (Section 9) and members of the public could, if the Minister thought fit, be granted permits to sell or distribute prohibited publications (Section 11). The third part of the Bill was virtually a copy of the recent Westminster Statute—the Judicial Proceedings (Regulations of Reports) Act 1926 to which reference has been made above.

The last part of the Bill discreetly entitled 'Miscellaneous and General' contained important clauses which would have the effect of making it unlawful to print, publish, sell or distribute any publication which advocated 'or might reasonably be supposed to advocate the unnatural prevention of conception or miscarriage or any method, treatment, or appliance to be used for such prevention or such procurement' (Section 17).* Of the concluding sections the most important was Section 19, which gave the Gardai power to obtain search warrants on the grounds of reasonable suspicion (not of proof, as had until then been the case).

Critics of the proposed law became vocal immediately, using in particular the correspondence columns of the *Irish Times,* although several other papers offered a considerable amount of criticism: notably among these were the *Irish Statesman, The Irishman, An Poblacht* and *The Nation.*

The *Irish Times* was the only daily paper to publish the text of the Bill in full and its first reaction set the tone for the criticism which it maintained throughout the whole period of its passage through the Oireachtas. While admitting, in its first leading article, that there was a need for 'some form of censorship in the case of indecent newspapers and of certain quack advertisements' it feared that the proposed censor-

* In the course of this study this prohibition is often for brevity's sake described as the 'birth control' prohibition.

ship would saddle Ireland ('a land where opinions are so numerous, so diverse and so stubborn') with an *index expurgatorius*' and it regarded 'with suspicion and uneasiness' the Bill's 'looseness of . . . terminology'.[1] Correspondence on the subject in this newspaper's columns continued unabated until the month of November, every so often receiving a fillip in the form of a severe leading article against the Bill. Readers wrote of their fear that the works on the Roman *Index* would be included *en bloc* in the new Irish list of prohibited publications; some objected to the banning of birth control literature; others suspected that the real objection was not that the literature being imported was immoral but that it was English; others again, with greater subtlety, pointed out the danger of gratuitous advertisement which inclusion in an official list would give to objectionable books.[2] Now and again, it is true, a feeble voice was raised in favour of the Bill—such as that of the Protestant canon who pointed to the *practical problem* which the importation of objectionable publications was presenting; or that of Dr W. F. Trench of Trinity College, Dublin, who suggested that 'what is required of us is the courage to believe that, when this law comes into force it will be administered in such wise as to operate for the general good'. But these supporters were ignored in the editorial columns of the paper, in which, it should be mentioned, a distinctly sectarian approach became evident —a view of the Bill as a Catholic plot against Protestant freedom of thought. A leading article on 29 September referring to the Bill as 'a grave menace to moral and intellectual liberty', agreed to the prohibition of certain newspapers, but feared that such works as *Origin of Species* might be banned as being contrary to that 'public morality' mentioned in the Bill, and sought to rally the support of Trinity College in its fight against the Bill:

> 'Above all Dublin University and her representatives in Parliament cannot afford to be silent. . . . If she (Trinity College) fails to speak now on behalf of that great body of citizens that has been bred in her culture and ideals, we fear that for ever after she may hold her peace.'

The following month in a leading article on 'Censorship and Liberty' it defended the criticism offered to the Bill by the 'minority', an emotive word which it used to excellent effect. The attitude of the minority it justified by reference to Buffon's description of a certain animal as 'very wicked; it defends itself when attacked'. But the same leading article contained a strong complaint that Trinity College and the Protestant Churches had not attacked the Bill enough.[3]

The Standard, a Dublin Catholic weekly which described the Bill as a 'sound measure of moral sanitation' (18 August), took issue with *The Times* pointing out in an editorial on 'Schund-und-Schmutz' how Germany had recently adopted a severe attitude to obscenity, thus giving the lie to those who criticised censorship as being against the Protestant tradition: 'even in the Land of Luther' censorship obtained. It then spread itself in another article entitled 'The *Irish Times* plunges': 'After much hesitation it at last plunged into opposition to the Censorship Bill. Not since it rallied its forces behind Sir Edward Carson has it been so decided as now, when it hoists the flag of the decadents and Marie Stopes.'

Since little notice will be taken of it elsewhere in this chapter, it may be said here that the other Dublin morning paper, the *Irish Independent*, adopted a spineless attitude to the Bill—as it did to almost all important issues at the time, being content to avoid controversy at any cost. Thus, for example, on the day following its publication it concentrated its attention on the bread and circuses of the *Aonach Tailteann*, an attempted revival of an ancient Gaelic sporting event, and gave the Bill only the second leading article; in this it spoke of the *Report* of the Evil Literature Committee as 'a model of moderation, good sense and brevity' and of the new Bill as 'a fair and reasonable scheme for checking a grave menace to public and private morality, without unduly interfering either with the liberty of the Press or the liberty of the subject'. In the following weeks and months there was no sustained correspondence on the subject in its columns—simply a haphazard series of letters, mostly unsigned. Editorial policy changed slightly, when the Dail debates began, from one of uncritical support to the view that 'there must be no compromise . . . (re) birth control and the broad framework of the Bill'— but that there was plenty of room for amendment of its details. At least one newspaper questioned the *Irish Independent's* support of the Bill: *The Irishman* suggested (2 February 1929)[4] that if certain English newspapers were prohibited under the Act 'the *Irish Independent* and *Sunday Independent* will do very nicely. No wonder they support the Bill'.

In all this the *Irish Independent* was merely echoing the opinions of most members of the Oireachtas, for the Censorship of Publications Bill proved to be in one way at least a unique measure in that the attitudes adopted by members of both the Dail and the Seanad were not based on Party alignments. This community of outlook is particularly remarkable when one recalls the acute Party strife which characterised Irish politics at this time. For more than a year now the position of the Cumann na nGaedheal Government had been constantly attacked from inside as well as outside Parliament. In the second election of 1927 Mr de Valera's Fianna Fail party—founded in April 1926 and now the official Opposition—won 57 seats to Cumann na nGaedheal's 61, and the Cosgrave administration was forced to rely on the smaller parties for support (these were: Labour, 13 seats; Farmers, 6; National League, 2; Independent Labour, 1; Independents, 12).

Mr de Valera had announced* early in the course of the Bill that his Party would facilitate its passage, but despite this, several members of that Party criticised it severely.[5] However, within the Oireachtas the most critical members were backbenchers of Mr Fitzgerald-Kenney's own party, Cumann na nGaedheal;[6] these in effect acted on the suggestion made by the leader of the Labour Party (Mr T. J. O'Connell) that 'while it had been the growing custom that a Government measure . . . is and must be deemed to be the last word so far as members of a certain side of the House are concerned . . . a measure of this kind is one to which all Parties should be encouraged to put amendments. . . . It is essentially one in which all Parties should join their efforts, so that when it emerges from this House it will be satisfactory to all concerned, and in that way give expression to the opinion which is generally held throughout the country by people of all shades of political and religious opinion'.[7] Prominent among the Cumann na nGaedheal critics were Professor Michael Tierney and Mr Hugh Law, two backbenchers, and Mr Patrick Hogan, the Minister for Agriculture.

The casual reader of the Dail and Seanad debates on the Bill cannot fail to be impressed by the fact that the speeches contain extremely few references of a Party nature. However, a closer examination of the divisions on amendments shows that although the Party Whips were off† there was by no means complete fluidity in the voting: there was cer-

---

* Cf. *Irish Times*, 13 August 1928. One of Mr de Valera's biographers, Mary Bromage, relates his attitude here to his views on other social matters: 'His strictures extended beyond the evils of drink to the evil of jazz, the evils of betting on the races, the dangers from indecent books, and he concurred in the Government's Bill to censor publications' (*De Valera and the March of a Nation*, London 1956, p. 229).

† A fact attributed to Deputies Law and Tierney. Two years later, on the eve of a general election the *Catholic Mind* made a bitter attack on both of them arising out of their attitude to this Bill: 'We will say the final word: *Professor Tierney and Mr Law forced the Government to take off the Party Whips and this engendered rebellion against the Bill*. That was their chief offence' (their italics): June 1931.

tainly sufficient to ensure that when the Bill was passed it was substantially different from the original measure, but by and large the Cumann na nGaedheal deputies were uncritical[8]—this is particularly true of the members of the Executive Council, with the notable exception of the Minister for Agriculture.

Although the extreme supporters of the original Bill were annoyed by the Government's leniency in this matter, in general the non-Party nature of the debates and voting was praised. Thus, for the *Irish Statesman* 'the number of Deputies, Fianna Fail, Cumann na nGaedheal, Labour and Independent who resisted [certain proposals] and defeated them was a pleasant surprise' (2 March)'. When the Bill had passed all its stages the same paper summed up the behaviour of the Oireachtas in the following glowing terms:

> 'Many members of the Dail . . . for once displayed keener insight and sounder political judgement than the Government front bench. . . .
>
> 'The Bill, as it stands today, is in the main the creation of the Oireachtas, and is remarkable as one of the very few examples in Parliamentary history where a botched and haphazard job has been reshaped into a decent piece of work by the constructive criticism of private members.
>
> 'On the whole, we have managed things much better than at one time seemed possible ' (13 July).

The Irish correspondent of the *Round Table* wrote in March in a similar vein: 'The debates on this measure in the Dail have been more courageous than was to be expected'; and in a later article praised 'the courageous criticism' which had borne fruit: 'Deputies of all Parties have combined to resist and defeat the worst features of this dangerous Bill.'

Since in some ways, separate consideration of the Dail and Seanad debates could confuse the account of how the Bill fared in the Oireachtas, it seems practical first to isolate the treatment given there and in the press to three of the most controversial provisions of the Bill, and then to concentrate attention on its passage through each house. These concerned (1) the institution of 'recognised associations', (2) the grounds of prohibition, and (3) the censorship of books as distinct from periodicals.

2 THE 'RECOGNISED ASSOCIATIONS'

The one main point on which the Bill and the *Report* of the Evil Literature Committee parted company was the section of the Bill which put
the initiation of proceedings against obscene publications in the hands
of recognised associations, the procedure being, in the Minister's words,
that—

> 'a body of men will come together and examine books and
> periodicals which they think are likely to be dangerous. If they
> see that there is a *prima facie* case, because final responsibility
> does not rest on them, they will send it (the publication) to the
> Department of Justice and there, when it is seen that the charge
> is not entirely frivolous, it will be sent on to the Censorship
> Board. . . . Their duty ceases when they have placed before
> other persons the books and periodicals which they consider
> to be censorable. They will probably contain amongst them a
> considerable number of social workers who will get down to the
> backstreets and slums of our big cities and see there in small
> stationers' shops, and shops of that class, the kind of literature
> that is being sold. They will be in a position to send forward for
> consideration especially baneful and harmful periodicals and
> magazines. On the other hand, if this matter were left entirely
> to unorganised effort, if it were simply to be left to here and
> there a casual individual being spurred up for a moment or two
> to a little exertion . . . I do not think the work would be
> properly or efficiently done.'[9]

Despite Mr Fitzgerald-Kenney's passionate belief in the need for
these associations the provisions came in for some sharp criticism during
the Dail second reading, particularly from Professor Ernest Alton,
Deputy for Dublin University, and Deputies Law and Tierney, and when
the Committee stage was reached some months later these three members, who had expected to find themselves in a tiny minority on this
point, instead discovered that a large section of opinion in the House
was inclined to suppress the provisions referred to and to adopt the
position of Sir James Craig who was in favour of making private complaint the first rung of the censorship ladder. Professor Tierney asked
for the total rejection of these provisions which were, he suggested,
largely the products of the Minister's mind. The 'recognised associations'
section of the Bill introduced, he said, 'an element which goes far to
vitiate the whole Bill and which has done a great deal to cause the

criticism of the Bill about which so much has been made. . . .'[10] The Minister for Justice tried to wean the House by saying that twelve to fifteen such associations would be sufficient to work the whole country without overlapping; but he could not deny that another sub-section stating that if the Minister revoked a ban on a publication which a recognised association had 'indicted' the association would cease to be recognised, implied that the associations were assumed to have a power to censor. The Minister's principal worry was that without the associations the Act's functioning would be seriously impaired due to lack of complainants; but he did not explain why the associations had to be 'recognised': could not groups in the community help the implementation of the Act in a voluntary way, thus leaving the door open for private individuals to complain if they wished? The House, at any rate, remained unconvinced of the need for intermediary censors and by a vote of 74 to 54 it removed from the Bill all mention of these bodies.

This substantial and unexpected modification of a Government Bill was very well received in certain quarters and encouraged pressure for further re-modelling. But the Minister was surprisingly tenacious on the point, and in his opening speech at the second reading in the Seanad he pleaded for the re-installation of the associations—'associations which would work for the spiritual benefit of the population, very much as big charitable associations like the Saint Vincent de Paul . . . work for the material benefit of the poorer classes of the population.' However, he found the Seanad as unsympathetic as the Dail and more ready to listen to a future victim of the censorship, Oliver St John Gogarty who, (debating an amendment to reintroduce the associations) described the section as 'the most monstrous proposal that has ever been made in this country. The proposal is that we should make use of our recently won liberty to fill every village and hamlet with little literary pimps who will be "recognised",'[11] (a remark which, it should be pointed out, did not concur with the Minister's estimate that there would probably not be more than fifteen associations in the country, all told). The amendment was rejected by 23 votes to 15.

It may be noted that in the course of debate on this point Deputy O'Connell emphasised that disagreement as to these clauses of the Bill did not mean disagreement over principles, considering it necessary to do so in view of the 'many resolutions that Deputies have received from various parts of the country . . . resolutions which seem to condemn any and every amendment to the original Bill'.[12]

Considering the matter in the light of forty years' experience of censorship it is difficult now to understand the Minister's insistence on the need for these recognised associations. He was proved right in his view that individual members of the public could not be depended upon to forward to the Censorship Board a sufficient number of objectionable publications, and he was probably impressed by the work done already by voluntary associations such as the Irish Vigilance Association and the Catholic Truth Society, and felt that such bodies could be depended upon to play the part of recognised associations. These bodies might well have been, through pressure put on the Minister, themselves responsible for this provision.[13] At all events it seems clear that the Minister in no way foresaw the extent to which the Customs Authorities would help in the channelling of suspect publications to the Censorship Board: a procedure which, as it turned out, was far more efficient than the setting up of special voluntary groups. It should also be mentioned, in the Minister's favour, that he envisaged the associations as dealing more with harmful periodicals and magazines than with books, whereas the opponents of the provision were concerned more with the associations' possible treatment of books in respect of which artistic and literary considerations were of very great importance.

3 THE GROUNDS OF PROHIBITION

Whatever may have been the mind of the Minister as to the scope of the proposed censorship, there is no gainsaying that the grounds of prohibition indicated in the Bill* were so phrased as to cause grave apprehension. The relevant portions of the Bill read as follows:

> 'The Minister may prohibit the sale or distribution of a book that is 'indecent or obscene or tends to inculcate principles contrary to public morality, or is otherwise of such a character that the sale or distribution thereof is or tends to be injurious or detrimental to, or subversive of public morality' (Section 7, ss. 3).

and:

> 'The word "indecent" shall be construed as including calculated to excite sexual passion, or to suggest or incite to sexual immorality, or in any other way to corrupt or deprave' (Section 2).

* In the following paragraphs the 'birth control' grounds are not referred to unless that is specifically stated.

Although it is true that the very title of the Bill was sufficient to provoke immediate criticism from any complete liberal there can be no doubt that for those who took the trouble to examine the measure in detail it was these particular clauses which spelt real danger—while they provided excellent material for criticism for those who regarded themselves as custodians of freedom of opinion and expression. Indeed, anyone who concerned himself with the Bill would have been prepared to admit, however reluctantly, that a mere change in the *method* of controlling objectionable literature was a matter of relative importance. Bernard Shaw, George Russell, William Butler Yeats, Oliver St John Gogarty— Irish literary figures who were extremely outspoken in their criticism[14]— did acknowledge that there was such a thing as pornography, that there were and always had been cheapjack writers prepared to earn a living by pandering to sexual instincts without reference to other values, that control of the sale and distribution of such writings was a social good, whether that control be exercised by the existing method of prosecution for obscene libel and by means of Lord Campbell's Act, or by the proposed method of censorship carried out by a Board of five reasonable men. The original Bill however contained no precise indication that the censorship would confine itself to the field of pornographic publications. This fact explains the vigour, extent and quality of the criticism it received. *

As an indication of this criticism, mention should be made of a few noteworthy comments which appeared in newspapers and journals at the time. Æ's article on 'The Censorship in Ireland' in the *Nation and Athenaeum* in December 1928 was typical. 'The Irish Free State' he wrote 'through the publicity given to its Censorship Bill . . . has become . . . a butt for the wits of the world. . . . To what must we attribute the Bill ? It is, I think, a consequence of arrested growth; or, in other words, moral infantilism.' The proposed definition of 'indecent' amounted to 'reviving an ancient Manichean heresy' and 'sciences, philosophy, political theory' ran the risk of being regarded as 'detrimental to public morality'. He hurled invective at the prudery he saw in Irish social attitudes, concluding his article in a lyrical strain, more calculated perhaps to win support for his view than any other part of his remarks :

> 'The fanatics . . . do not denounce these things (dances, short skirts, books etc.) because they are vulgar or unbeautiful.

* The Censorship of Films Act, however, contained references to 'principles contrary to public morality', which provoked no similar criticism (cf. above p. 17).

They do not try to create a superior beauty, which is the only way to overcome bad literature. They create nothing . . . I believe in no prophet of the Lord unless his words, even in anger, break in a foam of beauty on the ear.'

At home, Æ was strongly upbraided by *The Nation* for thus pouring 'vulgar abuse on his fellow-countrymen'. 'It is uphill work indeed' it complained 'growing public spirit and welding together an Irish nation' (22 December). But in fairness to Russell it should be emphasised that he spoke out as fearlessly against the Bill at home as he did in England; he made quite clear his opposition to the 'public morality' clauses, and most important literary figures who contributed to the *Irish Statesman* shared his point of view.[15]

Other outbursts which are traceable to apprehension regarding these clauses were those of Bernard Shaw ('Ireland—that is to say the Free State—has apparently decided not to be a cultured country. . . . Ireland is going to relapse into the dark ages'),[16] W. B. Yeats ('Every educated man in Ireland hates the Bill . . . Medieval legislation. . . . There is that taint of hypocrisy about the whole proceeding')[17] and Ezra Pound, who wrote letters from Rapallo to the *Irish Times*:

> 'the idiocy of humanity obviously knows no limits but the text of your proposed Censorship Bill adds yet another clause to the axiom. If any nation produces a debased imbecility in thought or legislation, some other nation will follow it. . . . A few of your voters might reflect on the effects of the American Censorship Law before sinking to the level of their perpetrators. . . .'[18]

Numerous other small journals criticised the Bill even before the Dail second reading, as the Minister for Justice acknowledged when, introducing the Bill, he claimed that he was 'heartened, emboldened and encouraged by the widespread criticism the Bill has received since it was published'[19] and suggested that the 'attacks from extremists . . . coming from the right and coming from the left' ('in the form of carefully thought out and closely reasoned articles and letters to the press') were due to misinterpretation of the Bill's provisions. He then allayed fears to a considerable extent in the second reading debate by stating that he was prepared to consider modifying the definition of 'indecent' and that the 'public morality' clauses should be interpreted applying the *ejusdem genera* rule: 'This Bill deals solely with questions of sexual morality or sexual perversion.' As an indication of this limitation he gave the example of *The Shropshire Lad*, which by advocating suicide was in some sense contrary to public morality, but which could not come within the scope of the 'public morality' clauses in the Bill. However, although Mr Fitzgerald-Kenney may have been correct on this matter of the legal interpretation of the working of the Bill, there is no doubt that to the average educated member of the public the meaning of these provisions was decidedly ambiguous; even those members of the Dail who had a legal training were critical at the Bill's looseness of terminology. By the time the Committee Stage was reached (20 February 1928) seven amendments to the definition of 'indecent' had been tabled; these were withdrawn to make way for the Minister's own amendment:

'(The word "indecent" shall be) construed as including calculated to suggest or incite to sexual immorality or unnatural vice or in any other like way to corrupt and deprave.' But Professor Alton (Dublin University) objected to the words 'like' and 'calculated', and the rendering eventually agreed upon was:

> 'the word indecent shall be construed as suggestive of, or inciting to sexual immorality or unnatural vice or likely in any other similar way to corrupt or deprave.'[20]

This is the definition which has reigned right through the history of the Irish Censorship Board.[21] The least that can be said in its favour is that it was the end product of serious debate.

4 A CENSORSHIP OF BOOKS?

However some Deputies were reluctant to place books (other than birth control books) within the scope of the Act at all. Patrick Hogan spoke very clearly on this point:

> 'Deputy Tierney made the point that if there was to be a censorship of books at all that censorship should be limited in the most stringent and specific way. I entirely agree for two reasons. One, I believe, that any censorship of books will only mean a double circulation for these books in this country. I believe, having regard to our circumstances, our proximity to a neighbouring country, that is certain to happen, and I think it will be extremely difficult to get anyone in this country fit to censor books. For these two reasons I agree that if there is to be a censorship of books . . . it should be a censorship which is limited in the most stringent and most specific way.'[22]

These views were shared by Professor Thrift who, drawing a sharp distinction between books and periodicals (regarding the actual extent to which these publications were read in the country and by whom), asked that the powers of the censors be very restricted regarding books, and much wider in dealing with the fugitive periodicals which he considered to be having in fact, a most depraving influence on the public at large. The other side of the coin was shown by Domhnall Ua Buachalla who maintained that in the country districts it was precisely the cheap novels, i.e. books, which were doing the most harm.

The Minister for his part disagreed that there was anything necessarily dangerous in setting up a book censorship. It may well be that his apparent carelessness concerning the parts of the Bill dealing with this censorship was due to his tendency to conceive the Bill as mainly concerned with periodicals. Indeed, he is on record as suggesting at the Dail second reading that 'the most useful function the Bill will perform will be to prohibit the sale in this country of objectionable newspapers.' The Deputies—and the public—were, however, considering the Bill in itself and not through Mr Fitzgerald-Kenney's spectacles: a fact which must have been responsible in some measure for their failure to allow the Bill to pass by them unnoticed.

Turning now to the 'public morality' clauses, the most interesting feature of the criticism was that offered by Patrick Hogan, whose main speech on this point was described as 'by far the most caustic and sensational' of all by the Irish correspondent of *The Round Table*.*[23] Speaking during the second reading in the Dail Hogan said: 'On this Bill there seems to be a general consensus of opinion in the Dail that as far as possible the operation of the Bill should be limited to offences against public morality of a sexual kind, but it is not at all clear, I submit, that the Bill contains any such limitation. We must remember that in this regard it is not the intentions of anybody that counts but the words of the Bill. . . . The Minister has expressed his readiness, in deference to suggestions made by Deputies of all Parties, to meet that point (that the scope for prohibition was too great) in Committee by accepting amendments specifically designed to limit the scope of the Bill to offences against public morality of a sexual kind.'[24]

Despite these revisions, and the Minister's assurance that 'a book can be fairly condemned only when in its whole course it makes for evil, when its tenor is bad, when in some important part of it is indecent, when . . . I might put it in this way . . . it is systematically indecent . . .

* This is the only instance I am aware of of a Cumann na nGaedeal Minister opposing a Bill introduced by one of his colleagues.

a book to be condemned must be *ex professo* immoral; it cannot be condemned if it is immoral merely *obitur*,'[25] the deputies felt that the measure needed some type of built-in safeguard to restrict the scope of the censorship to pornography only[26] and the House accepted an amendment moved by Professor Thrift, a member of the Evil Literature Committee, that books should be banned only if they were *in their general tendency* indecent or obscene. It also favoured amendments moved by Professor Alton and by Professor Tierney and Mr Law which would draw the Censorship Board's attention to the literary or artistic merit, etc. of books which come within their purview; these were finally embodied in a Ministerial amendment to the following effect:

> 'When considering a complaint referred to them . . . the Board may* have regard to all or any of the following matters, that is to say:
>
> (a) the literary, artistic, scientific or historic merit or importance [and the general tenor†] of a book. . . .
>
> (b) the language in which such book or edition is printed or produced,
>
> (c) the nature and extent of the circulation which, in the opinion of the Board, such book or edition is intended to have,
>
> (d) the class of reader in Saorstat Eireann which, in the opinion of the Board, may reasonably be expected to read such book. . . .
>
> (e) any other matter relating to such book . . . which appears to the Board to be relevant.'[27]

On this score, as on most other parts of the Bill, the Dail left the Seanad little to do. Many senators went out of their way to congratulate the lower House on the improvements it had made. One senator, for instance, was quite confident that 'there is not the slightest chance under this Bill as it stands at present that any book, except a book that is outrageously objectionable, will be interfered with in any way'.[28] The Minister himself drew the House's attention to the Dail amendments in order to emphasise the limited range of the Bill. However, some of his remarks on this subject were ambiguous:

> 'The object of this Bill is, of course, that books which are likely to do harm to the morality of the country should be kept out of the country. It must be recognised, of course, that a book may

---

* 'May' changed to 'shall' by the Seanad.
† These words were inserted by the Seanad.

be harmful to one person and not harmful to another. A book which a man of forty, fifty or sixty can read without any harm might be very injurious to a boy of eighteen or nineteen, or to a girl of the same age, and in consequence, it is only books which are likely to get amongst persons who would be injured by the reading of them, the circulation of which we believe should be prohibited. . . . To be condemned it must be really intrinsically, *ex professo*, immoral, not merely immoral *obitur*, that is, immoral because there is, possibly, here and there an objectionable expression in it.'[29]

He appeared to indicate here that a *virginibus puerisque* test would be applied, while he was emphatic that only *ex professo* obscene books would be banned. Senator Sir John Keane, for one, was dissatisfied with the Minister's assurances: 'He [the Minister] drew a totally imaginary pictures of what the censors would do. As far as I can understand it, when the censors are set up they will be in the position of a quasi juridical body. They will form their opinion on their own judgement and they will in no way be bound by what the Minister said here . . . or in the Dail as to what he thinks they should do.'[30]

Remarks such as this encouraged the House to reinforce certain provisions of the Bill including the addition of an explicit instruction to the Board to regard the 'general tenor' of the book. Mr Fitzgerald-Kenney considered this unnecessary but did not press his point of view. However, Senator Johnson, who moved the amendment, explained that 'the Board would probably not be a Board of lawyers, and that particular legal definitions on fine points as to what is allowable and what is not, and legal interpretations, may not be apparent to a non-lawyer. I think it is desirable that the intention of the Oireachtas should be conveyed as clearly as possible to the Board.'

In the course of the Seanad debate mention was made at various times of particular books: works by Balzac and Zola, Joyce and Yeats and other established or classical authors.[31] In almost all these cases the Minister pooh-poohed the idea that they could possibly be banned under the Act. At least one of these books is noteworthy in the light of subsequent events—*The Midnight Court*, an eighteenth century bacchanalian poem in Irish by Bryan Merriman. Sir John Keane[32] avowed that if the Censorship Board were in existence this book would come under its ban very quickly whereas Comyn (who was of the view that the Bill was 'very reasonable and . . . very moderate. . . . A necessary measure . . .') thought the *Midnight Court* was 'a very good poem' and would not be censorable. As it turned out an English translation of this poem, made by Frank O'Connor, was banned sixteen years later (see page 249).

Summing up, it may be said that these provisions defining the grounds of prohibition of books were the core of the Bill, and that the attention which the Oireachtas and the public gave to them was absolutely necessary. This is not to say that all this effort, discussion and controversy bore fruit. A cynic could readily make out that it was wasted, for as future events were to show, the Censorship Boards came to many decisions which would have surprised even quite conservative deputies and senators, and which in the opinion of many, amounted to disregarding the terms of the Act.[33] This is true at least in the sense that some Boards tended to give little weight to the literary qualities of books which they reported to be in their general tendency indecent and obscene; it would, however, be difficult to prove that they blatantly used religious, political or other such criteria in coming to their decisions.

5   THE DEBATES IN GENERAL

In the course of the above examination of the two most important aspects of the Bill, considerable attention has been paid to how the measure fared at the hands of the Oireachtas. It remains to refer to the minutiae of the Bill, for which purposes it is enough to survey generally the debates in the Dail and the Seanad.

The Second Reading debate in the Dail, which began on 18 October 1928, clearly indicated that although deputies from all Parties criticised it, this criticism was never aimed at the broad principle of the Bill, understanding this as the need to devise a stricter control of objectionable publications. Introducing the measure Mr Fitzgerald-Kenney was almost jaunty in his self-confidence—as if he expected to have little trouble in hurrying it through the House. He was not blind to the opposition which it had already engendered, but he tried to play down the intrinsic importance of the Bill by suggesting that in the last analysis it was the Board and not the Bill which mattered; he scarcely envisaged that this House would devote more than eighteen hours of Parliamentary time to it.

One of the dangers which the Bill implied was that it might become a sectarian issue. In fairness to the Dail it must be said that this potential danger never became an actual one, and this was due in large measure to vigorous remarks such as the following by Mr Hugh Law:

'I regard it as absolutely the right and the duty of the State to

have a care for the moral as well as the physical well-being of its
people. . . . I make these remarks for a special reason. It is
because I have observed that some of those with whose detailed
criticism of certain portions of this Bill I agree, have allowed
themselves to take up what I regard as an entirely indefensible
position.'

and:

'A friend of mine said to me the other day that he did not want
to have his literature dictated to him by the Catholic bishops.
I replied to him that for my part I was not in the least afraid
of the bishops; that what I was afraid of was busybodies.'[34]

Mr Law was supported by Mr T. J. O'Connell and by Professor
Thrift[35] who were both anxious to see that the non-sectarian character
of the Evil Literature Committee (on which both had served) be imitated
during these debates. De Valera also spoke in this vein. The insistence by
so many deputies on this point does suggest that they were trying to
forestall accusations in the Dail that the Bill was of Catholic inspiration—
as well they might have in view of the direction which criticism of the
Bill was tending to take in the newspapers, especially in the *Irish Times*.
Unfortunately the Seanad was not quite so successful in this matter.

If religious issues were avoided nationalist issues were not, and remarks
such as that of Deputy P. S. Doyle that:

'The Bill seems to me to need no defence. It is but a step in
the realisation of the intellectual autonomy which has already
had its counterpart in other domains of national expansion
(*sic*)'[36]

were calculated to provoke some deputies and to remind others of how
the Act, when in operation, could tend to reinforce the very definite
tendency towards autarchy which was to be found in the country at large.

Turning to the details of the Bill one finds that the points on which the
Minister for Justice was most adamant was that of the prohibition of
birth control publications (Section 17): he refused to accept that this
matter should be treated as a 'social question' and that its merits and
demerits should be argued out:

'That is a proposition to which we cannot and will not assent.
. . . We will not allow, as far as it lies with us to prevent it . . .
the free discussion of this question which entails on the one side
its advocacy. . . . We have decided, call it dogmatically if you
like . . . and I believe almost all persons in this country are

in agreement with us . . . that that question shall not be freely and openly discussed.[37]

He received general support in this view.[38]

On the grounds that birth control books were easily recognisable as such to booksellers the Minister refused an amendment of Professor Thrift which provided 'that no prosecution for an offence against this Act shall take place unless the book or periodical publication in question shall have been referred to the Board for report, and that the Board shall have reported that its indiscriminate circulation should be prohibited. The Section remained untouched and this made it an offence to sell books or periodicals of this particular class, whether they had or had not appeared in the list of censored publications. If a bookseller showed that he had exercised all reasonable care and could not have known of the contents of the particular book he was selling, he would not be liable for prosecution under this section.

There was a lengthy debate on the question of the size of the Board. The Bill provided for a five-man Board—not the Board of 9 to 12 members recommended by the Evil Literature Committee—and the Minister was particularly anxious to keep this size. However, by one vote (66 to 65) the House approved a Committee Stage amendment for a nine-man Board.

Of interest in view of subsequent censorship controversies was a short discussion centred on the question of whether the proposed Censorship Board should be required to 'examine' or 'read and examine' the publications which came before it. The deputies of a not very practical turn of mind insisted that the only safe and just course would be to read each publication as a whole; but the other view predominated: that the Board should not be committed to reading the whole of a book, that some books could be recognised as indecent after a cursory examination.

The desire to prohibit the spread of birth control publicity led the House to reject one amendment which would have excluded the distribution (as distinct from the sale) of prohibited books from being a punishable offence. It was pointed out that to allow this would vitiate against the whole idea of banning 'birth-control' books and propaganda since these were often distributed free. Another reason for the prohibition of 'distribution' was, of course, that the censorship would be ineffective if it did not apply to library distribution. And the suggestion that individuals should be able to get prohibited books by post was rejected on the basis of impressive figures reported by the Minister, who referred to the case of *A Manual of Birth Control, with a preface by H. G. Wells*, which was selling at the rate of 500 copies a week by direct mail as compared with only 100 through booksellers.

Another important amendment proposed that when the Board had reported unfavourably on a book the Minister 'shall forthwith' (not: 'may') by order, prohibit the sale and distribution of the book. The Minister commented:

> 'This amendment provides that this Board of Censors should be set up, that they should be final, that they should do administrative acts in condemning books and that they should be subject to no control at all. That is an amount of bureaucracy which I am opposed to. In my opinion the final judgment in condemning a book should be the judgment of the Minister responsible to this House.'

While admitting that the Board and the Minister would probably disagree only on an infinitesimal number of cases he insisted: 'It may not be in practice a very important departure, but in constitutional and democratic theory it is a very big departure.' On this point the Minister followed strictly the advice of the Evil Literature Committee. The amendment was quietly and unenthusiastically withdrawn: but almost twenty years later, a new Censorship Bill was introduced to some extent because the Minister wanted the Board to ban directly. Later on in the Debate an amendment wanted revocation orders to be *with the consent of the majority of the Board*; this was refused, again because of 'constitutional' reasons.

The partnership of Deputies Law and Tierney was responsible for another notable amendment to the Bill involving the introduction of a ban on periodicals which devoted 'an unduly large proportion of space to the publication of sensational matter relating to crime.'[39] This was one of the few amendments with which the hard-pressed Minister was pleased, and the one which enabled him to show the Seanad that the Dail had enlarged the scope of the Bill.

Before turning to the treatment which the Bill received in the Seanad a few remarks on the structure of that house seem appropriate.

The 1922 Constitutional arrangements made provision for a Seanad consisting of sixty members—thirty elected by the Dail and thirty nominated by the President of the Executive Council with special regard to the need of representation for groups or parties not adequately represented in the Dail; one third retired every three years. The best study of the Seanad under this Constitution is that made by Mr Donal O'Sullivan, who has written:

'Taking the Senate as a whole, and apart from the absence of adequate legal representation (in the early years of its existence), we see it as a body admirably qualified for the task of expert revision. It was much more truly a microcosm of the country as a whole than was the Dail, comprising as it did representatives of the professions, commerce, agriculture, letters, organized labour, banking and the landlord interest. . . . Throughout the thirteen years' history of the Senate, allegations were dishonestly made by some, and ignorantly repeated by others, to the effect that it was predominantly a Protestant and Freemason body . . . the largest number of non-Catholics ever present in the Senate was twenty-four out of a total of sixty. . . .'

Commenting on the activity of the Senate in legislation at this time, Mr O'Sullivan notes the reduced number of mendments (17) which it made to the Censorship of Publications Bill:

'(This figure is lower than usual compared) with those of the previous three years, and this is probably attributable to three causes. In the first place the number of Bills that were not susceptible of amendment was larger than previously. Secondly the presence of Fianna Fail as the official Opposition in the Dail must have ensured, in some degree at least, a more careful scrutiny of Bills before they left that House. Thirdly, the new Senators, with the important exceptions of Senators Johnson and Wilson, were hardly as competent for the work of revision as those whom they had succeeded.'[40]

A comparison of the Dail and Seanad debates on the Censorship Bill shows clearly that the Dail effected the most important changes, and that the character of the Seanad debates was somewhat diffuse and impractical.

The Minister arrived in the Upper House somewhat peeved at the treatment he had received in the Dail and hoping that the House which he now addressed would go as far as to restore to the Bill the recognised associations and five-man board, two provisions which he regarded as essential to an effective censorship. He tried, however, to forestall vehement criticism from the more intransigent senators by pointing out that the amendments introduced during the Dail debates affected the machinery but not the principle of the Bill. The general tenor of his remarks differed little from that of his Second Reading speech in the Dail.

He was followed in the debate by Sir John Keane whose speech constituted the first full-blooded attack that the measure had undergone or was to undergo in Parliament. A long speech, it was a classic example of the liberal approach—at once passionate and reasonable, marked by a strong tendency to see the question in terms of black and white. It makes interesting reading, especially that part of it which gave Sir John's general attitude to the Bill:

> 'It has been said by some people of consequence that so popular is this measure in the country, and so influential are the forces behind it, that anybody who has the temerity to oppose it in principle will no longer be acceptable in public life. . . . I claim to speak on behalf of a minority who contribute in no small measure to the amenities of this State, to its literature and to its art . . . I would even go so far as to say that the intelligent section of the community, those who are capable of appreciating the arguments for and against, are about equally divided.'[41]

Sir John then went on to theorise on methods of disciplining the mind and character:

> 'There is the method of repression and control and the method of selection and liberty. We know the method of prohibition and control. I do not wish to say anything ungracious, but I may say that it is generally the method of the majority church in this country. It is a method which tries closely to control reading, which fosters good and discourages bad, which sublimates some things and conceals others, and which calls upon the will to surrender its ordained power. There is nobody but has great respect for those methods. They have been tried all down the ages . . . but there is another method. I do not say it is a better alternative. There is liberty of thought and the freedom of choice. Speaking generally, it is the Protestant method. . . . It is a way where there is no forbidden territory. . . . The State has no right to interfere between those two schools . . . I go so far as to say that in the spirit of this Bill there is almost a breach of the Constitution.'

This outburst was not well received. Some Protestant senators, notably the McGillycuddy, and Colonel Maurice Moore, dissociated themselves from Sir John's remarks. Senator Dowdall, for his part, offered Sir John the opinion of Sir William Joynson-Hicks—also a Protestant—on the subject of control of modern fiction; and the Minister refused to accept that Sir John had spoken for the minority because indecency was banned by all religions and both Catholic and Protestant say 'And lead us not into temptation'. The debate, which included speeches by Senators Bagwell, Dowdall, Gogarty, Johnson, Comyn, Farren, Hooper and others, did little more than delineate the attitude of the Senators to the Bill, but the Third Reading which took place later was a closely argued and well-worked session.

The first important amendment to be carried dealt with the size of the Censorship Board. Senator Dowdall, in proposing a five-man Board, laid much emphasis on the fact that there was a majority in the Dail of only one in favour of the larger Board. In the debate on this subject much was made of the fact that the Committee on Evil Literature had recommended a 9—12 man Board,* but the Minister's remarks were probably what swayed the House eventually: he pointed out that if they tried to make the Censorship Board representative of all shades of opinion 'it simply will not work—it will fight. It is a Bill upon which there is no room for difference of opinion, except on one ground: "Is this book decent or indecent?" . . . Everybody knows when a book is indecent' (probably the most naive remark made by the Minister in debate).

This amendment was approved by 17, and Mr Fitzgerald-Kenney was not to be deprived of his smaller Board again because the Dail accepted all the Seanad amendments without demur. Also on the subject of the Board, Senator Sir John Keane tried to debar persons in Holy Orders from being members of the Board, but the Chairman considered this unconstitutional, and some senators found it in bad taste.[42]

When the debate reached Section 10 some senators questioned the purpose of forbidding the *distribution* of prohibited publications, on the grounds that it might make mere lending a criminal offence: and indeed the Minister's own interpretation of 'distribution' was, in fact, 'handing round': so that if people were to lend a book indiscriminately they would undoubtedly be distributing it for reading purposes. However, Senator Comyn was of the opinion that 'distribute' in the context of the Bill simply meant distributing for reward, so that lending to a friend was not included in the term, and he advised Senator Keane not to press an amendment to this provision. On the same subject the Minister pointed out that there would be no question of prohibition on the keeping of any banned book.

The House added a new sub-section to Section 16 which provided that:

* For Gogarty 'the ideal (number) would be zero'.

'a book or periodical publication containing an advertisement relating to a book or periodical publication which advocates or might reasonably be expected to advocate . . . (the unnatural prevention of conception, etc.) . . . shall not, by reason of its containing such advertisement, be deemed itself to advocate any of such matters, provided such advertisement is inserted for reward and is not and could not reasonably by supposed to be itself an advocacy of any such matter.'[43]

Among amendments rejected was one that authors resident in the Saorstat should have the right to appear before the Board to defend their writing. As Senator Comyn put it 'that would mean a State trial . . . it would place the Board in a most difficult position and would seriously hamper them'.

The final readings in both Dail and Seanad were rushed affairs—mere formalities, which rendered it impossible to learn in detail the members' opinions on the Bill in its final form. Not that it is difficult to gauge the general attitude to it: all were glad that it was over and done with, even if many suspended judgement as to its worth until they had seen in operation the censorship which they had created. For the Government it had been an unpleasant experience but one fruitful in lessons for the future, while members of all parties must have breathed a sigh of relief and felt in some way happy that a Bill of this nature had been taken on its merits and not debated on Party lines. The *Irish Statesman*, though reasonably pleased with the Bill in its final form, in its leading article maintained some of its critical spirit, not content to let sleeping dogs lie:

'The members of the Executive Council . . . knew better than anyone else that the whole affair from their point of view was deplorably handled. . . . As a matter of fact, the question rightly approached need not have been controversial at all. . . . In an evil moment Ministers permitted themselves to be influenced by the din of a strident minority who had convinced themselves this was a golden opportunity not only to suppress pornographic stuff, but to enforce prohibition on any and every kind of book that ran contrary to their prejudices or soared above their intelligences. . . . The only explanation we can advance for the surrender to this imprudent crusade was that our rulers came to the conclusion that it would be simpler to give the fanatics what they asked on the very cynical ground that the mass of the Irish people did not care two straws one way or the other' (13 July).

The legislators in 1929 did attempt to steer a middle course between the extremists of either side. No one, approaching the matter calmly, could rightly have said that the Act of 1929 was a plot against freedom of expression—or a charter for pornography, for that matter. Looking back on the controversy surrounding the Bill, one could hardly have expected the measure to receive any rougher treatment than it did. A similar controversy in the sixties might well produce a very different result but viewed in the context of the twenties (the British as well as the Irish context) the passing of the Act was very much in keeping with the prevalent attitude to the limits of artistic freedom of expression.

6 STATUTORY REGULATIONS

Before proceeding to examine the conduct of the censorship in the years from 1930 onward, it is at this point suitable to mention the statutory rules made for the operation of the Act.

When the first regulation was published—on 3 March 1930—the press quoted an official of the Department of Justice as emphasising (1) that it was the Minister who was the censoring authority; (2) that the Censorship Board had an advisory function; and (3) the limits of the grounds for prohibition:

> 'It (the Censorship of Publications Act) does not purport to vest in the Minister power to create a high standard of taste among the reading public . . . it aims at suppressing that which the vast bulk of responsible people would desire to be suppressed on grounds of ordinary decency. While the Minister is at liberty to reject the advice of the Board, it may be assumed in practice he will not.'[44]

The regulation referred to[45] fixed the number of copies of a book or periodical which were required to accompany a complaint made by members of the public: this ranged from one to three depending on price.[46] The phrasing of the complaint forms, etc., was also given, the only notable feature of these being a paragraph to the effect that:

> 'I refer particularly to the passages marked on pages . . . in support of my view and I have the following comments to make on the general tendency of the book as regards indecency or obscenity . . .':

a provision which suggested that the Board's attention could be drawn to isolated passages of the book with the result that it might neglect to take into account the general tendency: that it would run the risk of advising the prohibition of books which were indecent only *obitur*.

With regard to periodicals the following notes on the model complaint form may be quoted:

> '(1) Copies of not less than three different issues of the periodical must be furnished by the complainant; (2) in the case of Dailies, the issues should have been published within 14 days of the date of the complaint; in the case of Weekly Periodicals, within six weeks; in the case of Monthly Periodicals, within six months; (3) when the complaint relates to a periodical published at a price not exceeding sixpence, six copies of each issue must be furnished with the complaint; (4) when the complaint relates to a periodical published at a price exceeding sixpence, three copies of each issue must be furnished.'

The fact that the Regulations did impose a certain financial inconvenience on members of the public who might wish to make complaints was objected to very strongly in certain quarters. For once this criticism bore fruit, for five months later the Minister made a new regulation[47] which simplified the complaint procedure considerably. Thus, it was required that only one copy of a book (whatever its price) need accompany a complaint, and only one copy of each of three different issues of a periodical. In fact, it is rather surprising that this was not decided on in the first place, because Mr Fitzgerald-Kenney had more than often expressed his fear that few members of the public would put themselves to the inconvenience of lodging a formal complaint to the Board.

Despite this modification, these regulations were still criticised—one popular journal, the *Catholic Mind*, later accused Mr Fitzgerald-Kenney of 'gross betrayal of the popular will' by frustrating in this way 'the reasonable administration of the Censorship Act', and called on Mayo voters to reject him at the forthcoming general election (3 January 1932).

Nevertheless, as for the Act so for the statutory rules: their importance was completely bound up with the conduct of the censorship as exercised by the Board.

III

The Beginning of an Experiment

For the greater part of the period between the passing of the first Act and the appearance of the second Bill in 1945, comment and controversy on the subject of censorship were somewhat meagre. This is true both of the Oireachtas itself and of public opinion as expressed in newspapers, professional journals, magazines and so forth. In the Dail in the nineteen-thirties a few parliamentary questions are all that is to be found; while in the Seanad the only debate on the subject of books dealt more with the Customs' activities in their regard than with the Censorship of Publications Board itself. Reference is made to these debates later in this chapter.

A detailed examination of the files of Irish newspapers and magazines for this period does show that the censorship was exposed to a considerable deal of criticism, but for the most part this criticism was concentrated on precise issues—the appointment of the first Censorship Board, the banning of specific books, the resignation on one occasion of a member of the Board.

1 THE FIRST CENSORSHIP BOARD

Six months after the passing of the Act the appointment of the first Censorship Board was announced (13 February 1930). Naturally the Minister's choice was a matter of great importance, for these five men were going to set the standard of censorship and their interpretation of the Act was, from the practical viewpoint, of much more significance than the terms of the Act itself.

The *Irish Statesman*, which was moderately pleased with the Bill in its finished form, received the news of the appointments with dismay and anxiety. 'After prolonged delay,' it wrote, 'incidental to finding people so exalted in mind that they could be trusted to supervise the reading of the Irish people, the composition of our Board of Censors has been announced. Two of these are entities, the other three are nonentities. . . . We shall await with interest the first list of books which we are to be prohibited from reading. The nonentities can outvote the entities.'[1]

The 'two entities' in question were, presumably, Canon Patrick Boylan, the Chairman (a distinguished scriptural scholar and professor of Eastern languages of University College, Dublin), and Professor W. E. Thrift (a member of the Evil Literature Committee, a Dail deputy for Dublin University, and later Provost of Trinity College); the 'nonentities', Mr W. J. O'Reilly, Mr W. B. Joyce and Mr Patrick J. Keawell, MA. This rather unmannerly article drew a sharp letter from Fr Stephen Brown, SJ, who hastened to give the credentials of the three last-mentioned members.[2] Æ, however, refused to be won over: their qualifications were not quite good enough—he wanted 'literary experts' on the Board and anyway, he wrote, 'they (the people appointed) are also suspect in our eyes because they are appointed by the Minister whose first dreadful Bill was torn to pieces in the Dail, whose definition of indecency was as foolish a definition as ever was made' (1 March 1930).

Of the five men appointed to the Board, two had already interested themselves in the obscenity question. Professor Thrift had expressed his views clearly during the Dail debates. The Minister also knew—or should have known—Mr Joyce's attitude towards the new censorship, for, as the representative of the Dublin branch of the I.N.T.O., he said in evidence before the Evil Literature Committee that he considered the following 'immoral novels' should be banned: all the works of Paul de Kock, Guy de Maupassant, Rabelais, Elinor Glyn and Victoria Cross and 'one or two' books by Balzac. It is a pity that the *Irish Statesman* was not aware of this fact. One would have liked, too, to know its reaction to the first list of banned books, but unfortunately financial pressures killed this energetic journal just before the list appeared. Its viewpoint was maintained in a somewhat modified form by the *Irish Times*.

2 THE CATHOLIC MIND AND THE CATHOLIC BULLETIN

On the other side of the fence were the *Catholic Mind* (began publication in 1930) and the *Catholic Bulletin*; two cheap monthly magazines which at times were little less than scurrilous. They had an unlimited capacity for argument and when they were not fulminating against Trinity College or the Ascendancy, they wrote violent editorials against each other. The *Catholic Mind* in particular was of the 'more Catholic than the Pope' variety and indeed, for the first two years of its existence carried a *Permissu* which it paraded as evidence of its superiority.

In its issue for May 1930 the *Catholic Mind* gave considerable coverage to arrangements made by the Catholic Truth Society for the 'systematic examination of books and periodicals for the purposes of the Censorship of Publications Act. About 500 selected persons of steady judgement have been circularised with a view to enlisting their co-operation in the heavy work the Society has undertaken'. The article went on to point out how the Minister's regulations had put an additional financial burden on the CTS co-operators: 'These vexatious regulations cannot be regarded otherwise than as well designed to kill the Act. We protest against them; we interpret them as an attempt to make a bad Act worse.' Then followed the full text of a CTS circular, which included a call on the public to send marked copies of objectionable periodicals. This attempt by the CTS to organise voluntary 'recognised associations' was not successful. The main reason for this was that the Secretary of the Society (at the time), Mr Frank O'Reilly, held that it was not proper for the Society, whose function it was to spread good literature, to expend money on objectionable books (even if only for the purpose of examination).

In the following issue the same journal attacked *The Star* (the organ of Cumann na nGaedheal) for expressing the hope that few books would be banned under the Act, *The Star's* view being that banning was likely to create a demand for books which otherwise might not have been bought. It had also protested against the banning (*inter alia*) of various books by Dr Marie Stopes on the ground that it would be far better if the suppression of birth control books were in the hands of the police. In October 1930 the *Catholic Mind* directed its criticism at Mr Fitzgerald-Kenney for his handling of the Bill and protested that 'many' objectionable birth control publications were circulating in the country.[3] The quality of this criticism may be judged from the fact that one of these publications was a magazine in which a certain 'rising young novelist' was 'advocating divorce and birth control'. The following month the paper expressed its grave misgivings at the news that the same young novelist (Mr Evelyn Waugh) had become a Catholic.[4]

The *Catholic Mind* continued its pro-censorship campaign by indulging in severe criticism of Professor Michael Tierney and Mr Hugh Law as well as of Mr Fitzgerald-Kenney and Mr Ruttledge in an attempt to dissuade voters from supporting them in the next general election.[5]

In November 1930 it wrote: 'The Censorship Act is today but the emaciated remnant of the original Bill. Why? Professor Michael Tierney.' And the following month it painted such a picture that the uninformed reader would surely have thought Professor Tierney had positively advocated birth control during the Dail debates. Shortly after this it attacked the *Irish Times* and the *Cork Examiner* for printing in full the lists of banned books published in the *Iris Oifigiuil*—recommending its readers that they boycott advertising in these papers; the *Examiner* discontinued this practice some years later, leaving the *Irish Times* to keep the public informed of the Board's latest decisions.[6]

As for the sale of British periodical publications in Ireland the *Catholic Mind* was for their wholesale prohibition. In its view 'the British popular press is morally, nationally and economically an evil' (for Ireland). Thus, when a tax of $\frac{2}{3}$d. was imposed on English daily papers in the 1933 Budget it argued for a higher tariff and pointed out that 'moral harmfulness, however, was not the prime cause of the new tax, but the fact that the papers entering the Saorstat were for the most part anti-Government'.[7]

These references to the *Catholic Mind* should not suggest that it was an influential organ of public opinion; it deserves less than a niche in the history of the Irish press, but it was a colourful publication, even if an embarrassing one.

The *Catholic Bulletin* was a horse of the same stable. Founded and edited by Senator Patrick J. Keohane it was extremely right-wing in character and immoderate in expression; many of its caustic editorials were written by Fr Timothy Corcoran, sj, Professor of Education at UCD—a remarkable individual in his own right. Its editorial comment on censorship included an attack on the *Irish Times* (June 1930) on the censorship; severe criticism of Mr St John Ervine for his article, 'Behind the Irish Censorship' in the *Week-End Review* (21 June 1930)[8] and of a lecture by Dr Newport White of Trinity College, Dublin, to the Associated Booksellers of England (at whose week-end meeting in Dublin censorship seems to have come under heavy fire); and an attack on Professor Michael Tierney for his part in the Censorship debates. It also commented favourably on the 1934 Lenten Pastoral of the Archbishop of Tuam on the proper functions and dangers of the lending libraries and agreed with the Archbishop in his description of the censorship as 'altogether inadequate'. In the second half of the decade, however, it commented very rarely on the subject.

In the 'thirties it was still quite common for the British press to treat Irish affairs as provincial news and to give them considerable coverage. However, as far as can be seen, the censorship question, especially after the Act had been passed, was not considered as warranting attention—except possibly at the beginning of the period. Thus, *The Tablet* reported the appointment of the first Board and around the same time (22 February 1930) gave an interesting news-item entitled, 'The Holy Father and Censorship' from which it seems appropriate to give the following extract:

> 'In the course of an address at Dundalk last week . . . Cardinal MacRory stated that, during his interview in Rome with the Sovereign Pontiff (Pius XI), His Holiness said, referring to the Free State Censorship, that he was very glad that legislation had been passed for the censorship of publications, and he hoped that such legislation would be pressed and made effective, adding "I hope you will make known my desires on the matter".'[9]

The *Round Table*—whose trenchant articles on Irish politics by John J. Horgan have already been referred to—reported on the first list of prohibited publications. Of these it considered 'only three' as of any importance: Aldous Huxley's *Point Counter Point*, Radclyffe Hall's *The Well of Loneliness* (already the subject of a successful prosecution in England) and Bertrand Russell's *Marriage and Morals*; and it reported the Minister's complaint that the public were not sending books to the Board for examination, explaining that 'the fact is that very few people in Ireland read any modern books at all, and those who do are not likely to take the trouble of acting as literary informers to the Censorship Board' (September 1930). 'Informer' was an extremely meaningful word in Ireland at this time.

Having referred to these articles on censorship in the Irish and British press, I should stress again that censorship was never an issue of transcendental importance; the actual practice of censorship, the activity of the Board, was naturally for some a source of irritation, but for many more it spelt security. True, even in its early years the Board banned books by A. J. Cronin, Austin Clarke, William Faulkner and Sean O'Faolain (to mention only a few), but it should be remembered that many of these were not at that time writers of indisputable quality: and that if the *Catholic Mind* had had its way the toll of well-known writers would have been much greater.

3 PARLIAMENTARY DEBATES IN THE 'THIRTIES

The suggestion that censorship was not an important public issue is borne out by the fact that very little parliamentary time was given to the subject in the first decade of the Act's operation.

Dail activity was limited to some three or four questions. The first of these, which was put by Professor Patrick McGilligan (Cumann na nGaedheal) was ostensibly aimed at testing the meaning of one section of the Act, although it is likely that its real purpose was to discredit the *Irish Press*, a newspaper founded in September 1931 by the Fianna Fail Party, which Party had now been in power since 1932. Professor McGilligan tried to prove that by reviewing a banned book and giving the publisher's name and the price, the *Irish Press* had in effect advertised the book and thereby contravened the Act (Section 10, 1(b)). The Minister refused to accept this interpretation of the Act, stating that 'the power vested in the Minister for Justice under the Act is to make an order forbidding the sale and distribution in Saorstat Eireann of a banned book', implying that a review did not constitute an advertisement.[10]

In a question put to the Minister on 11 March 1936,[11] a deputy asked why a member of the public had been refused a permit to import a book subsequently serialised in full in a paper selling in the country. In reply a Minister excused the anomaly on the grounds that, although the *book* was banned, the Minister for Justice had received no complaint about the periodical which serialised the story, and reminded the House that 'permits are issued only to responsible people who have good reasons for requiring to have possession of the publication'. It seems clear that the anomalous situation referred to did, in fact, arise and the Minister's excuse was not really adequate.

Another question put on the same day concerned the case of another person who was permitted to import six copies of a banned book: but this Ministerial largesse was suitably explained by the fact that the individual in question was the author of the book.

The Seanad in the 'thirties devoted a short debate to the subject on 20 June 1934 when Senator Sir John Keane (who, it will be remembered, was one of the most vigorous opponents of the original Bill) proposed a motion 'that in the opinion of the Seanad closer co-ordination is desirable with regard to the detention of books on importation under Section 42 of the Customs Consolidation Act . . . and the Censorship of Publications 1929. . . .' The first-mentioned Act had been the main means of control over the importation of obscene articles up to 1929 and it was not repealed at that time. Sir John pointed out that from time to time books were being held up under this Act and he requested the Government to declare the policy under which that Act was being administered. In particular he objected to the Customs' inconsistent and arbitrary use of their power, alleging that the importation of each book seemed to depend on *where* (at which port) it was being imported, and not so much on the content of the book in question.

He questioned the Revenue officers' action of withholding copies of a novel by Norah James called *Straphangers* (ordered by private persons) citing a favourable review in *The Times Literary Supplement* as evidence of the book's harmlessness. Sir John went on:

> 'If there is to be this hidden censorship we surely ought to have the right to be told by what method it is to be regulated. Is there some central authority studying these books, and are certain instructions sent out to the Customs officers as to the books that are to be stopped . . .? The matter is really very aggravating. This is one of the minor aggravations that make life in this country very annoying to sensitive people, perhaps of leisure and of taste, who do not want to carry on a perpetual wrangle with the authorities.'

The Minister for Lands, replying, showed that during the previous four years a practice had grown up where customs officers who held up books under the terms of the 1876 Act forwarded them to the Censorship Board; and when they did so they acted on their own judgement. He took the opportunity of insisting that there was very little tendency among people in the country to remove the Censorship Board or to abolish the censorship; and stated that he considered that the co-ordination the Senator had requested had, in fact, been achieved: that the two bodies worked well hand in hand. He was, however, prepared to admit that the period of time between the detention of a book by the Customs and the decision of the Censorship Board should be made shorter (i.e. less than the period of two months or more mentioned in the debate): but he was not prepared to consider that the powers of the individual Customs officers were unduly wide. The motion was withdrawn once the House's attention had been drawn to the matter.

The interesting thing about this debate was that it showed that the Act was coming to be operated in a manner which was not anticipated during the Dail or Seanad debates in 1928–29. Although it was not explicitly mentioned in the debate under review, the Customs officials had, in fact, come to play a part analogous to that envisaged in the 1928 Bill for the 'recognised associations'. When that Bill was going through the Oireachtas the Minister for Justice had tried in vain to retain those clauses which would have created a dozen or so committees throughout the country to sort out the books to be fed into the machinery of censorship. His main reason for insisting on these associations was his fear that if the 'indictment' of books and periodicals were left to private individuals, the working of the Act would be seriously hampered by lack of complaints. The members of the Censorship Board, being part-time, unpaid officials, could not be expected themselves to forage for objectionable publications in addition to censoring them (itself a time-consuming occupation), and so it was essential to the success of the Act that others should do this work. As it turned out, private individuals and societies did not lodge a number of complaints at all proportionate to the volume of undesirable literature entering the country, and so it came to pass that the Customs began to play the role of complainant *par excellence*. Their activity in this regard is indicated by the fact that criticism of the treatment of books over the years was often directed at them rather than at the members of the Censorship Board. Statistics are not available of the proportion of complaints attributable to the Customs during the period 1929–1946; but on the basis of the figures given for the post-1946 years (when Annual Reports of the Board were published which included these details; see page 135) it may be supposed that the Customs were responsible for the vast majority of the complaints which reached the Board.

4 PUBLIC OPINION IN THE THIRTIES

Turning to the country at large one finds the censorship scene reasonably calm. The censorship operated efficiently and, for the most part, discreetly. Few readers consciously felt that their reading was being controlled, and of those who did the more resourceful took the trouble of applying for a permit,† chanced importing prohibited books by post (liable to confiscation) or smuggled them into the country on their person or in their luggage. The classics were still available—contrary to the prognostications of many in 1929—and the less passionate modern novelists.

The Censors worked with considerable industry (in the years 1930–1939 they banned some 1,200 books and some 140 periodicals) and

† Figures are not available of the number of permits issued. See pp. 173f.

although in general they attracted little attention, at least once in the decade their work, or better, working methods, were exposed to public view by one of their former members.

On 5 January 1937, Lynn Doyle (Mr Leslie A. Montgomery), an Ulster writer living in the Saorstat, was appointed a member of the Board in place of Mr William B. Joyce. His colleagues at the time were Canon Boylan, Mr W. O'Reilly, Professor Magennis (of University College, Dublin) and Professor Fearon (of Trinity College, Dublin). A little over a month later he resigned and announced his reasons for doing so in a letter to the Minister published in the *Irish Press*.

The very appointment of Lynn Doyle was remarkable. The Minister for Justice, Mr Ruttledge, described it as 'something of an experiment'[12] and indeed it caused considerable surprise among both opponents and supporters of the censorship idea and must have raised the hopes of many who had come to regard the Board as being a reactionary institution.

Lynn Doyle was an opponent of the Irish censorship, for less than two years before, in his book *The Spirit of Ireland*,[13] he had criticised the censorship vehemently. 'Irish literature,' he had written, 'has in the Board of Censors to face another attempt to impose on Ireland a Victorian prudery. . . . The appointment of such a Board is a retrograde step in a country that has but recently regained freedom. The Board is a secret tribunal. There is no appeal from its decrees. . . . Public offence should have public trial.' He also made the point that while an Irish writer whose chief circulation was in England could snap his fingers at the ban of the Censors and would even gain by the notoriety a sincere and courageous author writing in Irish 'may be compelled to emasculate a work of genius, or starve. It is an adroit way of bringing back a lost sheep . . . The empty ass keeps his kicking end down'.* In addition to this, only a few months before his appointment Lynn Doyle had protested in the correspondence columns of the *Irish Times* (22 September 1936) against the banning of Sean O'Faolain's *Bird Alone*. But to return to his resignation:

> 'After examining books under the system for some five weeks,' he stated,[14] 'I have come to the conclusion that I could not with fairness to the State or myself go on acting on the Board. . . . The books are sent to the Minister by private objectors in

---

* 'Well, empty asses with warm imaginations have a friend among the Censors now' was how the *Catholic Bulletin* greeted the 'highly perplexing' appointment (January 1937). The *Bulletin* did not comment on Lynn Doyle's resignation. In fact, no book written in the Irish language has ever been banned.

different parts of the country. A permanent official marks, by writing folio numbers on a card, passages that he thinks come under the Act. The marked books are then sent to the members of the Board in turn. Now the Board is required to make recommendations according to the general tendency of the book. It is nearly impossible to report on general tendency after reading the marked passages. Even when one reads the book through afterwards one is under the influence of the markings.'

He also felt that the marked passages procedure constituted a grave temptation to the lazy censor; he criticised the element of chance involved in banning, showing how the justice meted by the Board was hardly even-handed: because some books happened to be caught in the first month of their publication while others remained scot free for a number of years. 'Moreover, to ban a book of eight or even three years age is to revive a harmful thing that was become happily moribund.' Mr Doyle was evidently no enemy of banning in itself. He went on to underline the danger to authors who had not been fairly treated (i.e. those whose books had been wrongfully banned) and their understand-able temptation either 'to emasculate to the damage of their art or, in indignation and revolt, to set out deliberately to shock'; and suggested further that the punishment involved in banning weighed more heavily on Irish writers, reckoning that 30–40% of their circulation might be in Ireland as compared with perhaps 5% for non-Irish writers.

Lynn Doyle concluded his letter to the Minister by remarking that in practice the Irish censorship worked wonderfully well in that 'between a book's issue and its banning the more cultured and the more hardened readers have read it. The unsophisticated have not in general got to know about it. But I do not think it is worthy of our State to trade on an Act whose excellence consists in its bad drafting'.

One relevant fact about this resignation which did not appear in the press at the time—or since—was that when the other four members of the Censorship Board learned of Lynn Doyle's appointment they refused to sit on the Board with him until he publicly withdrew the charges which he had earlier made about the Board; they contended that Lynn Doyle was not a 'fit and proper person' to sit on the Board (accord-ing to the Act, this was entirely the Minister's concern). It is not clear, however, whether Lynn Doyle was aware of their objection to him or whether his resignation was based solely on his own objection to the 'marked passages' system.[15] At this time, little controversy was aroused by this resignation[16] although the affair re-echoed often in subsequent years—notably in an important Censorship debate in the Seanad in 1942, and in numerous newspaper controversies in which his disclosures were used as ammunition against the Board and its methods.

By far the greatest amount of hostile criticism of the Censorship was expressed in the editorial and correspondence columns of the *Irish Times*. In the beginning of December 1935 a correspondent, 'This Freedom', wrote a general anti-censorship letter to the *Irish Times* depicting the prevailing position in rather dramatic terms: 'I can picture standing over our island a terrible gargoyle figure. He is the demon of censorship, and he censors our books, our films, our plays. . . .'[17] About a month later another reader discussed rumours that a press censorship would be established by the Government and expressed the fear that with the Seanad abolished (as it soon would be)[18] opposition to such an idea would diminish. Two months later, on the day after a question had been asked in the Dail on the subject of censorship, the paper devoted a leading article[19] to attacking the Board; it insinuated that the value of the question lay entirely in the fact that it elicited from the Minister a reply 'so evasive in its generality as to suggest that he was thoroughly ashamed of the Censorship Act'.

> 'So indeed,' it continued, 'is every decent person in the Free State. The Act has been in operation now for the best part of seven years. It has done nothing to improve the general standard of behaviour . . . it has made our country a laughing stock in the eyes of liberal peoples; and its administration is ridiculous in the extreme. We would not be taken as rejecting out of hand any and every form of censorship. Some measure of control over undesirable literature is necessary, and every civilised country forbids the unfettered purveying of reading matter which is nothing more than pornography. . . . It (the Censorship Board) has paid no regard whatever to that section of the Act which provides that a book, in order to come under the ban, must be "in its general tendency indecent or obscene" . . . [For the time being the *Irish Times*] would laugh at the whole censorship affair, hoping that the time would not come when it would have to take it seriously.'

Some months later, however, the *Irish Times* did think it necessary to take the subject seriously. On 21 September a letter from Mr Frank O'Connor was published protesting against the recent banning of a book by Mr Sean O'Faolain called *Bird Alone*. O'Connor insisted: 'There is not an indecent line in it. Yet O'Faolain is paraded before the public view as a common pornographer in company with the authors of *Women Had to Do It* and *A Lover Would be Nice*. His property is confiscated and the law allows him no defence or appeal. . . . By adopting the profession of literature O'Faolain has put himself outside the pale of decent society and shown himself unworthy of our great Gaelic heritage of intolerance and indecency.' An 'Ordinary Citizen' wrote to accuse the Board of blunder after blunder and urged that the country needed to cultivate a more interested and robust form of public opinion on the subject. The Secretary of Irish PEN called it 'legalised slander' for the Board to describe O'Faolain's book (his second to be banned) as in its general tendency indecent. 'Surely,' he insisted, 'the time has come for the institution of an appeal board.' This 'appeal board' theme ran through all the correspondence of this period, adding a constructive note to all the comment and criticism at the time.

The correspondence on *Bird Alone* lasted for another three weeks or so and included an allegation that the real reason for the banning was that the fact that the protagonist who loses his faith does not return to it in the end. Professor W. F. Trench (of Trinity College) agreed, and called the banning 'irresponsible': 'I say that to tolerate it is to be a party to an assault upon the soul of Ireland.'[20] *Bird Alone* was the one book that was the subject of an appeal to the Minister under the 1929 Act (banned periodicals, as distinct from books, were frequently the subject of amendment orders made by the Minister after consultation with the Board). The ban remained in force until it was revoked in 1947.

The *Bird Alone* episode was, however, an isolated case, and in the 'thirties the more liberal quarters by and large held their peace on the censorship question. It was from them that criticism could most naturally be expected: they had been the losers in the 1928–29 battle and were thus discontented at the outcome. The conservatives (supposedly interested more in nationalist and moral rather than artistic values) were for their part inclined to rest on their laurels: they would be provoked into action only if the Censorship Board was not sufficiently vigilant. Reference has been made earlier to the *Catholic Mind* and the *Catholic Bulletin*, but there are other journals of higher standing which should be mentioned at this point.

Broadly speaking, *The Leader* would have been quite happy with a 'When in doubt, ban' instruction for the censors. Its reasons for supporting censorship were primarily nationalistic in character—the preservation of the Irish heritage, the suspicion of things foreign, especially

English—although it was in agreement too with the censorship on the moral aspect of the question. After the Bill became law, *The Leader* kept its eye on the activity of the Board. Thus, it complained (7 June 1930) that no newspapers had so far been banned when there was every reason that they should be since they advertised banned books. A month or more later it prophesied a 'dismal future' for the Board, and complained that only five periodicals and 'a lot of unheard-of books' had been prohibited (the implication seems to be that the books worth banning are those which have a certain fame or notoriety). From this time onwards, however, right through the decade the review ignored the Censorship Board completely: which suggests that it became less exacting in its demands, or satisfied with the Board's behaviour.[21]

Another interesting journal is *An Leabharlann*, an official publication of the Library Association of Ireland. As a professional journal *An Leabharlann* (revived in 1930) could be termed as either pro- or anticensorship. However, since librarians are much concerned with the selection of reading matter for a large section of the public, and their choice or rejection of titles is in effect similar to the work of the Censorship Board, the internal politics of the libraries and the social repercussions of their activity would offer material for a special study. I should refer to one case which occurred around this time and which reached national proportions: that of Miss Laetitia Dunbar-Harrison. This lady, a Protestant graduate of Trinity College, Dublin, had been appointed County Librarian for Mayo, but some county councillors and priests considered her unsuitable for a position which involved book selection for Irish Catholics.[22]

From the point of view of formal censorship it is sufficient to mention that librarians' book selection problems were not solved[23] by the advent of the new legislation. This suggests three possibilities: that the Board was less rigorous in its banning than the libraries desired; that the influx of objectionable books was greater than the Board realised or was able to deal with; or that the public taste for the sort of reading matter which the libraries considered objectionable was increasing in the country at large. The second of these is the most likely, for though the Censorship Board was strict, it did not cope with the whole range of fiction available in the British Isles; and the libraries' criteria for acceptable books appears to have been stricter than that of the Board—this being due to some extent to the fact that the libraries are in direct contact with the public and are inclined to take into account complaints made by their members.

5 THE CTS REPORT

The only contemporary survey of the first decade of the Irish censorship appeared in the *Catholic Truth Quarterly*. Like *An Leabharlann*, this
was a magazine of limited circulation, but linked to an influential
organisation, being an official publication of the Catholic Truth Society
of Ireland. The Society had played an important part in the pre-1928
campaign and took the whole subject of censorship most seriously, in a
spirit of vigilance.

In the issue for January–March 1940 the *Quarterly* published what
may be called a major article, editorial in form, entitled 'Ineffective
Censorship: Why the Act is not doing its work: Official Remissness.' A
lengthy treatment seems appropriate because the article gives a useful
view of the attitude of supporters of censorship and at the same time
contains some interesting statistics.

'The Society' it began '. . . . has taken an intimate interest in the
promotion and working of the Act. Its experience in working the Act
over a period of about eight years led it, in 1937, to appoint a Committee
to draw up proposals for its amendment. This Committee was composed
of Mgr Lyons [later Bishop of Kilmore], Dr Michael Browne [the present
Bishop of Galway], Mr C. J. Joyce, MA [later a member of the Censorship
Board], and Dr F. O'Reilly, KCSG. The Committee reported that the Act
as it stands at present fails in its purpose; for it does not ban the highest
possible percentage of the worst books within the shortest possible time
after their publication; and it does not provide for sufficiently close
supervision of periodical publications.'

This Report, together with proposals for remedying 'the faults in the
existing Act', was submitted to the President of the Executive Council,
Mr Eamon de Valera, on 1 October 1937. The President notified the
Society that he had put the matter in the hands of the Minister for Justice
and on 8 December 1938 the Minister wrote stating that on the whole he
did not think it necessary or advisable to introduce an Amending Bill or
to alter the regulations or practice. The Society's reply (11 February
1939) stated that it could not accept the Minister's view that the Act had
achieved its object to a very large extent. To remedy the faults in the Act
it proposed:

> '(a) to provide the Censorship Office with adequate funds* for
> the purchase of books and periodicals . . . and an adequate
> staff; and to increase the number of members of the Board to

*On the financing of the Censorship cf. pp. 176-7.

ten panels of three members each, so that the present cumbersome system of examination may be abolished and be replaced
by a simple, expeditious system;

'(b) to make such changes in the Minister's Regulations
regarding the submission of complaints against newspapers
and periodicals as are necessary to prevent evasion of the Act.'

Pointing out that the Board received only one copy of each book from
the complainant, the Committee reckoned that since the censors must
wait one on the other there was a delay of at least six weeks before a book
came before the Board as such. 'In fact, however, the Board seldom acts
within the minimum period: there might be a delay of months, during
which time the objectionable book would be freely sold by booksellers
and stocked by libraries throughout the country. Even if the Board were
to be given or to get five copies of the book, the problem would still not
be solved because there might be ten complaints on the go at the same
time—which would cause a delay all the same.'

The Committee had also complained of the delays involved in banning.
The table below indicates the relationship between bannings (listed in
the *Iris Oifigiuil* at the time of the Report) and the period of time (since
publication) for which the book had been on sale before being banned:[24]

	within 3 mths.	3–6 mths.	6–12 mths.	0–10 mths.	12–24 mths.	24–30 mths.	after 36 mths.
percentage of total no. of banned books	6	14	21	41	28	20	11

In regard to proposal (b) the following statistics were given. As the
Committee put it, 'newspapers can, under the [1930] Regulations
advocate, say, contraception, without danger of legal consequences in:

daily newspapers   : approximately 90 out of 312 issues per year
weekly newspapers: ,,   26 ,, ,, 52 ,,   ,,   ,,
monthlies   :   ,,   6 ,, ,, 12 ,,   ,,   ,,

'and this simply because the Minister's Regulations permit them to
do so. . . . In co-operating in the working of the Act we have repeatedly

found ourselves rendered powerless against offenders, by these regulations. . . . The fact that newspapers of the high standing of the *Daily
Telegraph* habitually publish advertisements of books advocating
artificial birth control (which advertisements are permitted by the Act,
though certainly they should not be) and less frequently, recommend
these books in reviews, should give the Minister assurance that the less
reputable newspaper takes full advantage of his Regulations to evade
the Act.'

The Committee felt that annuals should be treated as books, not as
periodicals, and in particular mentioned the fact that it was difficult to
get consecutive issues of American magazines, so that by the time a
banning order was made back numbers of these magazines were circulating freely in the country. It went on to remind the Minister of the wording
in the original Bill—'indecent or obscene or tending to inculcate principles contrary to public morality' pointing out that at the time of the
debates 'fears were expressed that the clause might be used to hamper
political action'. But since then, the words 'public morality have been
enshrined in the Constitution'[25] and, the Report complained, 'our
definition includes only "suggestive of, or inciting to sexual immorality
or unnatural vice or likely in any other similar way to corrupt or deprave"
and is governed by many restrictive clauses, e.g. those relating to literary
and artistic merit, the general tenor of a book, language, to mention
some of them only. . . . It is surely right that our Constitution should
be implemented by legislation as soon as possible. It cannot be held
that public morality is served in this country by a law which specifically
permits advertisements of books which advocate practices contrary to
the Constitutional pledge that the State shall protect the family and
shall guard with special care the institution of marriage.'

Another matter of interest raised was the *notification* of banning: the
prevailing method of publishing lists of banned books in the *Iris Oifigiuil*,
in the *Register* of Prohibited Publications, and in the *Irish Times*. This
the Committee considered unsatisfactory and they suggested that in
addition to publishing notice of the bannings in the *Iris Oifigiuil* and in
the *Register*, the local police should inform traders of bannings, and in
addition the trade papers for booksellers should be asked to publish
details. They recalled the recent cases (at Roscrea in February 1938 and
at Sligo in May 1938) where district justices 'commented on the futility
of the present method, and refused to impose fines in fully proved cases.
This, of course, has naturally had an effect on the Gardai.'

The Report concluded with a tribute to the work of the 'Censor Board' and a re-statement of the Committee's conviction that whatever faults there were were due to the Act and the Minister's Regulations. In subsequent issues the *Catholic Truth Quarterly* still complained of government inaction but in 1941 its Committee gave up its campaign: 'This Committee, recognising that the adequate amendment of the Censorship of Publications Act could not be demanded of the Government at this juncture with due regard to national interests, has not pursued the matter further with the Minister. The question has been put back for post-war consideration. In the meantime the restrictions imposed upon cross-Channel publishers as a result of the War have made the problem less pressing.'[26]

The *Catholic Truth Quarterly* report represents the one serious attempt[27] made during the period to strengthen and modify the machinery of censorship so as to maintain a stricter control over the importation of books. As such it was deserving of attention, but there is no evidence of its having had an immediate effect; it created no stir of the same proportions as say such incidents as the resignation of Lynn Doyle or the banning of Halliday Sutherland's *Laws of Life* in 1942.

Invigilation of the type carried out by the CTS was not necessarily undesirable. It was simply one more expression of public opinion, and as such was as worthy of attention as was the criticism offered to the Board by those other sections of the community which considered the censorship to be unduly strict or even essentially objectionable. Its report shows clearly that the Board was subjected to criticism from both the conservative and liberal sections of opinion, each of which was in its own way working for a revision of the Act.

IV

A Purpose of Amendment

1 SEAN O'FAOLAIN AND *THE BELL*

The early forties ushered in a period of heightened controversy when criticism of the Board's 'backwardness' grew increasingly more vocal and more vigorous. A very definite trend towards reform can be ascertained which, beginning around 1940 in the columns of journals and newspapers, developed to the level of parliamentary debate, proceeded to the introduction of a Private Member's Bill in 1944 and culminated in a Government Bill in 1945. During all this time the liberal view predominated, while the defenders of the Board and its behaviour seemed to attract little attention.

The acknowledged leader of the opposition to the Board and the Act was *The Bell*, a review founded by Sean O'Faolain. Throughout its short lifetime (1940–48, 50–54) this magazine gave unremitting attention to the censorship problem. In an editorial on 'Standards and Taste' in one of the first issues of the magazine O'Faolain criticised the censorship on the grounds that it was out of touch with the literary and moral atmosphere of the country.

> 'That (the literary censorship) was an attempt to codify certain alleged native instincts about literature, and what has been the result: Time has proved that these alleged instincts are not native [for the simple reason that a large number of Irish writers have written books which have been banned . . .]; it is the instinct of these writers against that of five censors, none of whom has ever written a piece of fiction, a play or a poem*.
> . . . I am not concerned (here) with which is right or which is wrong, but with the fact that our tastes and standards are in a most debatable state of flux. . . . There are certain guiding first principles, universally accepted. To state them is useless.

---

* The truth of this is borne out by the fact that the only literary creation by a Board member was Senator Fearon's play *Parnell of Avondale*.

It is only by repeated experiment that we establish the convention which relates these universal principles to native practice.'[1]

It is clear that the line taken in this article is not that of the old-style opponents of censorship who, in Ireland, were liable to be suspected of free-thinking and of moral relativism. By accepting certain unspecified 'universally accepted guiding first principles' O'Faolain was able to forestall criticism from those who might accuse him of being careless of the morality of the country; and by suggesting that the problem of censorship was not one of distinguishing immorality from morality, but rather of deciding what was merely unconventional and what immoral, he could argue against the Censorship Board's doings with greater freedom and with better chance of success and support. (O'Faolain realised that it was not good politics in Ireland to espouse an opinion such as that expressed by Lennox Robinson, who in an earlier issue stated he was 'ethically opposed to censorship of any kind'.) In this editorial he also drew the public's attention to one banning which was later to attract attention in the Seanad: that of *Land of Spices* by Kate O'Brien: and remarked that to describe that book as "in its general tendency indecent" clearly . . . is a lie.'

In September 1940 the magazine gave prominence to an article entitled 'Sex, Censorship and the Church'. The writer took a liberal-orthodox view similar to O'Faolain's own attacking in particular the 'reading aloud in the home' test which, he suggested, was used by the Board. If anyone wanted that, the writer warned, 'we are now in the presence of a definite conflict between the Roman Catholic standard of literary decency, and an obscure puritanical instinct which can formulate absurdities like the "family circle" test for literature, in all its ill-formed opposition to the sane, humane, civilised outlook of Roman Catholicism on life and literature'. He cited and commended the example of Padraig O Conaire, a well known modern writer in Irish (died 1928), who refused to delete a few passages in a manuscript now lost, because 'he evidently believed that the thing called Art required greater outspokenness than the publishers thought safe to print in Ireland, and he had the moral courage to sacrifice the interests of his pocket to his belief'. Why, Mr Murphy asked, had the Irish habit of evading sex not only continued but got worse and more aggressive? Because: 'The average Irish mind has not, and perhaps never had, a properly balanced outlook on sex. Either it runs away from sex or it runs after it: it never seems to stand and look at it objectively.'

The calm tone of this article was very similar to that of the editorial already quoted: it tried to prove its case, not to fulminate against the Board; it suggested that the Board was to be criticised, not because it banned indecent books but because it did not distinguish between indecent literature and writing which, though strong, was suitable for adult readers; it sought to prevent a clash between churchmen and the opponents of the Board's actions and instead win clerical support for the campaign. In a later article ('Censorship: Principle and Practice') in which the same tone is retained, the writer reiterated his approval of censorship and agreed that the censors must be expected to make mistakes but, he concluded, 'surely there is a limit, and our censorship is well beyond it' (January 1942).

Some months later *The Bell* returned to the attack with an article on 'Censorship, Law and Conscience',[2] in which Mr Henry Bellew pointed out that, whereas under the British system of controlling indecent literature (by a prosecution for obscene libel or by a case for a destruction order) the author or publisher was given the benefit of the doubt, in the case of an appeal under the Censorship of Publications Act, the Minister, not the author, was the one who would be given the benefit of any doubt as to the meaning or application of the word 'indecent'. Mr Bellew found that in practice the only real appeal left for an author was 'to the court of public opinion': and this he naturally considered inadequate. Without articulating any proposal for reform what in effect he wanted was an Appeal Board which would take the sting of 'finality' out of the decisions of the Board. His article went on to accuse public opinion of having been for too long indifferent to the question of censorship . . . 'by silence and indifference it has allowed the cranks . . . to harness the principle of censorship to their own notions', and reminded the reader of the words of the *Report of the Committee on Evil Literature* which insisted that 'the State could not accept the former (*virginibus puerisque*) test for what is permissible without destroying a liberty that authors have always enjoyed': and yet this test seemed to be that which the Board was applying.[3]

These references to *The Bell* (and earlier ones to the *Catholic Truth Quarterly*) are, I think, sufficient to indicate the existence and character of criticism of the censorship, but if one single event had to be chosen it would be the Seanad censorship debate in 1942 during which the Seanad became a court of enquiry on the actions of the Board, for of itself it contained sufficient evidence to warrant the introduction of an amending Bill.

2 THE 1942 DEBATE

In the beginning of October 1942 a letter to the *Irish Times* from Frank O'Connor began a new censorship controversy. O'Connor complained against the banning of *The Tailor and Anstey*,[4] an account of the lives of two County Cork peasants, written by an Englishman, Mr Eric Cross. Sean O'Faolain wrote a few days later to remind the public that this was not an isolated case, and instanced the banning by the Minister of *Laws of Life* by Halliday Sutherland, a book which, he stated, carried the *imprimatur* of the Cardinal Archbishop of Westminster (and therefore could hardly be supposed to contain unacceptable doctrine); he went on to launch a bitter attack on the 'five addle-pates' who composed the Censorship Board; spoke of their 'slovenly methods' and 'sheer incompetency' and considered that the Board was 'an embarrassment to the Government and a humiliation to the people'. There followed more letters about *Laws of Life* and another from 'The Irish Society for Intellectual Freedom', on the same lines, objecting in addition to two other bans: Bernard Shaw's *Adventures of the Black Girl in Her Search for God*, and Ernest Hemingway's *For Whom the Bell Tolls*. The direct result of this controversy was the Seanad debate which began on 18 November.

The motion before the House was tabled by Senator Sir John Keane and read as follows:

> 'That, in the opinion of Seanad Eireann, the Censorship of Publications Board appointed by the Minister for Justice under the Censorship of Publications Act, 1929, has ceased to retain public confidence and that steps should be taken by the Minister to reconstitute the Board.'[5]

The debate, which was resumed on four different days before the motion was finally put to the vote on 9 December, constituted the first really serious examination by either House of the functioning of the Board since its inception. In 1942, with practically all Europe at war, the neutralist position of Eire is typified by the fact that her Parliament was able to find a considerable amount of time in which to discuss a matter of this kind.

Sir John Keane made it clear that he was not challenging the principle of censorship: that battle had been fought and lost thirteen years earlier; he had contested the 1929 Bill 'resolutely in its entirety', considering that the methods employed in the United Kingdom were quite adequate to safeguard the country's morals as regards reading. He was now 'striving for the legal safeguards' embodied in the 1929 Act; and he chose to remind the House of some of the then Minister for Justice's remarks during the 1928–29 debates, recalling in particular the *ex professo/obitur* [immoral] distinction made by him: 'A book can be fairly condemned only when in its whole course it makes for evil, when its tenor is bad, when in some important part of it it is indecent, when—I might put it this way—it is systematically indecent.' For his case against the Board he chose the bannings of *The Tailor and Anstey, Land of Spices* and *Laws of Life*. Amid protests from parts of the House he read out passages from the first two books mentioned, justifying his doing so on the basis that the Minister was responsible for the banning and that for this reason the matter was being raised in the Oireachtas. Senator Professor Magennis, Chairman of the Censorship Board and one of the protagonists in the debate, insisted that an instruction be given to the official reporters not to record the quotations: 'Otherwise we shall have some of the vilest obscenity in our records, and the Official Reports can be bought for a few pence.'[6]

The Tailor and Anstey Sir John passed off as being Rabelesian in character but not obscene;[7] in *Land of Spices* he pointed to one passage on page 157 dealing with homosexuality ('For that phrase and that phrase alone that book was banned');[8] and he claimed that the Sutherland book was banned because it dealt with the 'safe period', which, to his mind was not an unnatural method of birth control; and that it would not have been banned if the Board had realised that it had received the *imprimatur* of Westminster.

Sir John did not confine himself to the terms of his motion but ranged wide over the whole subject of censorship—suggesting that it was physically impossible for the censors to censor properly because since 1930 an average of three books had been banned per week (about 1600 altogether); 'that the Board was too Victorian in outlook: too academic and detached from the stream of life and the outlook of youth'; that there was an undue time-lag between the publication of a book and its banning: 'incidentally it defeats the object of the Act if this poisonous matter, as the censors consider it, is in circulation for two or three years before being banned'; and that 'if anybody wants to get a censored book there is no trouble in getting it; I do not mean any ordinary plain person, but anybody who knows their way about'. There was 'hardly an author of repute who is not represented on the banned list . . . Shaw, Linklater, Morgan, Hugh Walpole, Maugham, Hemingway, O'Brien, Frank O'Connor, Sean O'Faolain, Liam O'Flaherty, and—would you believe it ?—Austin Clarke, who I believe is recognised by the Church as one of the outstanding poets'. He spoke of a 'literary Gestapo' and claimed that if the *virginibus puerisque* test being applied then 'we are turning the whole country into a national seminary'. He went so far as to say that he had legal opinion which suggested that one could have a 'very good shot' at proving *mala fides* in the *Land of Spices*[9] case 'but in general all that you could prove would be ridiculous narrowness . . . (and) in any case as far as I can see, if you do upset the legal end of censorship, there is another Act under which it (censorship) can be done . . . the Customs Consolidation Act. Without right or reason, and acting under an Act originally intended to deal with obscene publications, the Government can stop any book, without censorship, coming through the post . . . I want clean, fresh air on the facts of life'. It will be evident from these references to Sir John's remarks that he did not restrict himself to the area of his motion, but ranged far and wide over the whole subject of censorship.

Senators sprang to the defence of the Board. Senator Sean Goulding, for example, was utterly shocked by the excerpts he heard from *The Tailor and Anstey*: 'Apart from the moral censorship I think there should be a censorship of books that portray us Irish people in the way I have indicated [as a nation of drunkards, etc.]. . . . I hold that the Censorship Board is quite justified in banning a book if it contains one passage subversive of Christianity or morality.'[10] Senator Liam O'Buachalla of University College, Galway (the present Chairman of the Seanad), also suffering from disgust, pressed the Minister to do all he could to increase the power of the Board (he had, he said, been a member of a small, unofficial committee of Senators which had met a short time before to investigate the effectiveness of the censorship and found that very much 'evil literature' was getting through despite it). Senator Desmond Fitzgerald (a former Cumann na nGaedheal Minister) made a conservative but reasonable speech and some of his remarks may be worth recalling: 'I am afraid that if I were on a censoring board, and if I could read all that mass of print (16,000 books were published annually in Britain at that time) I would have felt called upon, and according to the Act, to censor most of them, because not merely are these books a waste of time, but the reading of them has a corrosive effect upon the mind. . . . So far as this country is concerned, our whole standard is that of a flunkey. We accept what has been acclaimed as a great book in England. Every Irish writer who is acclaimed by completely unimportant English critics immediately establishes himself in this country as an outstanding pundit on all matters of literature, philosophy, politics and the ordering of society. That is our weakness. We have no critical standards.' He referred to 'hyper-sensitiveness' about the way Irish writers depicted Irish characters as undesirable. And, he concluded: 'I do not think Sir John could establish what he states in the motion. I am quite prepared to believe, and quite prepared not to believe, if the proofs came forward, that the Censorship Board has not acted strictly within the terms of the Act. That is the only thing that could be established. I do not see how we can propose that censorship in this country be abolished.'[11]

In fact, Sir John Keane's motion had really only two supporters—the McGillycuddy, a reluctant seconder, and Senator Professor Joseph Johnston (Trinity College) who did accept Sir John's case as convincing and conceded that the books under discussion might be in some way indecent (though they certainly did not incite the reader to irregular sexual indulgence), but considered that 'in matters of art and literature we have to recognise different standards of decency and indecency from those we are accustomed to give attention to in the ordinary affairs of life', instancing the Bible's 'brutal realism'.

The speech of the Minister for Justice, Mr Gerald Boland, is notable for one prominent blunder of which he was to be reminded more than once in the course of the debate. After paying tribute to the work of the Board ('very onerous task . . . great credit . . . untold benefit'), he reminded the House of the 'eminent ecclesiastic' [Mgr Patrick Boylan] who had been on the Board at the time of the banning of *Laws of Life*, and went on: 'whether the Board was technically and legally right, whether the book in its general tendency was indecent or obscene, may be open to question, but on the grounds that it was calculated to do untold harm, I was perfectly satisfied that it should be banned',[12] thus justifying the ban on the basis of his own opinion (or somebody else's) of what was detrimental to public morality . . . not necessarily on whether the book came within the scope of the Act.[13] Or, as *The Bell* later put it, it was an attempt 'to make the word "indecent" a mere technicality capable of interpretation at will, an endlessly expanding portmanteau-word'.

The main speech of the whole debate was that of Professor Magennis[14] who spoke for four and a half hours on two consecutive days (newspaper comment called it a record speech for the Seanad). Calmly, academically, with a certain ponderousness, Professor Magennis made a closely argued defence[15] of the three bannings which were under attack.[16] In many parts of his speech Professor Magennis spoke in as scathing a manner as had Sir John Keane in his opening speech; for each blow that Sir John had dealt the Board or himself personally, he returned another—even to the point of quoting, Keane-wise, from the blurb of *The Tailor and Anstey* and complaining when the Chairman instructed that his readings as well as Sir John's be erased from the Official Report. Even the phrasing of the motion he abused: its 'ceased to retain public confidence' he told the House reminded him of 'the story of the three Tailors of Tooley Street who wrote a petition to the King of England and it began: "We, the people of England . . .".'

On the question of *The Tailor and Anstey*, Professor Magennis suggested that Sir John had borrowed his ideas from the correspondence columns of the *Irish Times*, and complained bitterly that the persons who so vigorously attacked the Board seemed simply to have never read the Act: they seemed to forget that it was the Act which had made the Board and the definition of obscenity and not vice versa. Regarding the definition of 'indecent', he emphasised that the definition contained in the 1929 Act was not a formal one, 'for the genius of the English mind is to avoid putting itself into a straight-jacket. It leaves itself elbowroom for the play of commonsense and prudence. . . . Observe the word "likely" . . . it implies probability. Probability is estimated by a human mind'. But while all this is quite true, and while any statute is open to different interpretations, this is not the same as to say that it may mean simply anything or, that in the case in question, the Act virtually allowed the Board to define 'indecent' in whatever way it wished. Professor Magennis would have given the Board (of which he was the most forceful member) a *carte blanche*; this had never been the intention of the legislators in 1929.

Before the debate was resumed on 2 December the senators had the opportunity of reading the *Irish Times'* comment on the proceedings of the first day, in which it spoke of 'that immoral body' [the Censorship Board] . . . [the censors] 'all of them good, honourable and educated men who have made themselves objects of laughter' . . . 'thirteen years of oppression'; and other remarks in similar vein. As a practical suggestion it slyly proposed that the members of the Board should be paid out of public funds: so that the public would not feel embarrassed at criticising a body of men who had so generously dedicated some of their time to this disagreeable task of censorship.

On the second day of debate Professor Magennis made a detailed defence of the banning of *Laws of Life*. This was a curious case, rendered more obscure than necessary by the attempts of Professor

Magennis and others to justify a prohibition order which was plainly unjustifiable.

Laws of Life was the subject of a prohibition order published in the *Iris Oifigiuil* on 8 October 1941. Written by Dr Halliday Sutherland, a distinguished gynaecologist and a Catholic, and published by Sheed and Ward of London, the book was the subject of a complaint made to the Board in the appropriate manner by 'a Protestant father'[17] who considered that the information which it so clearly gave on the 'safe period' method of birth control would be liable to abuse by young people (yet the book was banned as being 'in its general tendency indecent and obscene'—not for advocating the unnatural prevention of conception). Professor Magennis—who once went as far as to describe the book as 'the fornicator's *vademecum*'—was at his most characteristic when speaking of this ban during the debate:

> 'Let me now come to the book, the banning of which involves this terrible thing that shocked the heart and conscience of Frank O'Connor and Sean O'Faolain and their associates. The monstrous enormity of banning a book that had the *imprimatur* of an Archbishop! When they first made that they thought they could get away with it. They had eventually to add . . . a little diluting matter and then it became a book that had the sanction of a board under the Archbishop of Westminster. . . . They find that there was a second edition —and even the second edition did not bear an *imprimatur*; it had, as I said already, the words *permissu superiorum*—and then they proceeded to slang us with renewed vigour.

> 'They never thought of going into the second edition and comparing it with the first, but I did, and this is where, in the popular phrase, they lose their horse. The very points in the original book on which I fastened when we were examining it are the very points that, in order to get the *permissu superiorum*, have had to be omitted or removed.'[18]

At this juncture I should point out: (1) the edition of the book examined by the Board did not carry an *imprimatur* or *permissu* of any kind; (2) the prohibition order covered 'all editions' and thus Professor Magennis's examination of the textual differences between one edition and another was from the practical point of view irrelevant; (3) no edition of the book carried an *imprimatur*; (4) the first edition of *Laws of Life* was published in November 1935; this edition carried no indication of ecclesiastical permission. The second edition was published in

November 1936 and carried the formula *permissu superiorum* (dated '28 julii 1936') on the back of the title page. A detailed examination of the two editions reveals only marginal differences. No important deletions were made for the second edition and the only interesting new matter was an expansion of the paragraph dealing with Catholic teaching on the 'safe period'. Whereas in the first edition (p. 48) Dr Sutherland wrote:

> 'Moreover, for those who object to contraceptives on ethical and religious grounds, the safe period offers a solution to a most difficult problem. The Catholic Church prohibits the use of contraceptives, but permits the use of the safe period. The safe period does not represent heroic virtue, but it does call for the exercise of a reasonable amount of self-discipline. If, then, the safe period be permitted, an accurate knowledge of what it is should be available for all engaged or married couples.'

This was modified in the second edition (p. 48) to:

> 'For those who object to contraceptives on ethical or religious grounds, the safe period solves a most difficult problem.
>
> 'The Catholic Church forbids contraceptives, but explicitly teaches that the safe period may be suggested to those who would otherwise use contraceptives. Since the primary aim of marriage is procreation, only grave reasons entitle married people to avoid this obligation even by legitimate means. Thus it would be wrong for people to marry with the intention of avoiding children by means of the safe period. Indeed, if people marry with the intention of avoiding a family, such an intention might render the contract invalid in Canon Law. It would be equally wrong to use the safe period to maintain a motor car in place of another child. Only when grave reasons exist, such as the ill-health of the wife, or financial embarrassment threatening the necessities, as distinct from the luxuries, of life, is the use of the safe period permitted to Catholics. That said, and the grave moral obligation is individual, an accurate knowledge of the safe period should be available to those entitled to make use of it.'

This was the only important change made for the second edition; consequently Professor Magennis misled the House; unfortunately, it seems that no other senator had examined the two editions side by side and certainly few had even read one edition.

It would appear that Dr Sutherland did not submit the first edition of the book to ecclesiastical censorship, probably because it was a medical book written from the point of view of a doctor, not from that of a moral theologian (Catholic laymen are required by Canon Law to submit for ecclesiastical examination—before publication—only writings dealing with theological or moral matters). However, since most of Sheed and Ward's customers were Catholic booksellers and since Dr Sutherland did comment on the Catholic teaching on the safe period, it is likely that Dr Sutherland or his publishers thought that the inclusion of an ecclesiastical approval would have the desired effect of leaving the reader in no doubt as to Dr Sutherland's orthodoxy. Therefore, the competent Board of the Archdiocese was approached and the Board gave the *permissu superiorum* (which was in effect the equivalent of an *imprimatur*) on condition that the Catholic teaching was more explicitly and unequivocally dealt with.[19] Assuming that the requirements of the English ecclesiastical censorship are no less stringent than those of the Irish State censorship, one might have expected that the second edition would have been exempted from the ban. But no exemption was made. Mr Boland explained in debate: 'I read that book before it was banned. . . . The *permissu superiorum* to which reference has been made may exist in England because conditions there are different from conditions here. Birth control is, I believe, freely advocated there. . . . The free advocacy of birth control is not allowed here, and I think the Censorship Board were bound to recommend the banning of the book. I have no apology to make for the Board.'[20]

These remarks did not explain why the book had been banned on the grounds of obscenity, not of advocacy of birth control. Professor Magennis's explanation appears to have been that when assessing the indecency of a book the 'circumstances of publication' must be taken into consideration. The Board considered that the indiscriminate spreading of knowledge about the 'safe period' could lead to indecent conduct and public immorality. 'We saw also the risk there was of its falling into improper hands. He himself [the author] in express words points out that the circulation, without safeguards or without precautions, of knowledge about methods of birth control, is one of the causes of the displacement of the professional by the amateur. [In banning this book the Board] acted exactly according not merely to the spirit of the 1929 Act but to the very words of it.' The Professor also suggested that engaged couples would find knowledge of the safe-period an incentive to sexual immorality.

Quite apart from the inaccuracy of these prognostications, it is scarcely possible that Dr Sutherland's work could come under the definition of 'indecent' as given in the Act. Professor Magennis was clearly using the 'public immorality' definition of indecent, a definition on which the legislators in 1929 had firmly turned their back.

One indication of just how confusing the *Laws of Life* affair was is the fact that a later Chairman of the Censorship Board, Professor J. J. Pigott, 'lost' a very long argument in the correspondence columns of the *Irish Times* on the subject years afterwards, simply because he made an error of *fact* as to the editions of the book which were banned.[21]

With reference to the motion itself, Professor Magennis tried to make out that since the current Board did not take office until February 1942 there was no point of accusing it of unjustifiably banning books which had been banned before that date (of the three books mentioned only *The Tailor and Anstey* had been banned by this Board). Technically this was a valid point but if the Senator really thought it important he should have logically refused to comment on the banning of the two other books in question. And he omitted to acknowledge that the composition of the Board had scarcely altered in the period since 'the sodomy book' as he called it had been banned (the only change being the appointment of one ecclesiastic for another in February 1942).

Other points in Senator Magennis's speech included: (1) a complaint about the Board's financial handicap: it had only an allocation of about £15 per annum for the purchase of books; (2) a complaint about the terms on which the private circulating libraries were bound to buy their books (they had no choice but to take the selections of titles which the wholesalers made for them); (3) an expression of his extreme dislike of Lynn Doyle's 'foul contribution to the attack on the institution of censorship, our State censorship . . . Lynn Doyle is the original source of this accusation of being a secret body'[22]; and (4) his conviction that really the attacks being made were against the principle of censorship, not just against the Board . . . 'I have no doubt he (the Minister) will have little difficulty in getting five fit and proper persons (to constitute a new Board), but the same campaign will be conducted against them because the persistent effort is to destroy censorship under this pretence of having no quarrel with censorship, that is an institution necessary to a civilised State'.[23]

The debate dragged on. Senator Rowlette attacked censorship as such. Senator the McGillycuddy disagreed with him, but asked for a little more latitude in its operation. The *Irish Independent* in its only comment on the debate 'preferred to err on the side of stringency rather than of laxity' and in every way supported the Board. The *Irish Press* also came out in favour of the Board, suggesting that while occasionally it had suppressed a work of some literary value, it had 'in no case . . . taken action arbitrarily or through caprice'. In the Seanad again, Professor Tierney reminisced about the first Bill ('a fairly unreasonable and, to a certain extent, a rather wild measure') and stressed that the Act 'should not be interpreted in a watertight way . . . (but) fairly widely and a certain amount of discretion must be exercised under it'. The general tenor of his remarks was critical of the operation of the Act. Senator O'Donovan asked for a revision of the Act to make it applicable to more than the written word; 'to the spoken word and what is shown on the screen', asking for extended powers to enable the Board to stop vulgarity as well as indecency. Senator Douglas was unhappy with the whole system: 'I am still unconvinced that you are reducing the amount of rubbishy reading by the present method as against a more open but definitely State-controlled method'; he favoured the English method of dealing with obscene literature (earlier in the debate Professor Magennis had compared this to the Irish method; 'But the idea is the same; the machinery alone . . . is different'). He also suggested to the House that to attack the Board was a mistake. He remarked on the growing minority which was dissatisfied and which was becoming more vocal ('If I read it aright, it is an objection to the general principle of censorship and not an attack on a particular Board . . .') and tried to channel this criticism into a plea for an appeal board for Irish authors, who, he thought, suffered more than others if their books were banned.

The debate was brought to a conclusion by Sir John Keane, who spoke with nostalgia of the demise of Lord Campbell's Act in 1929. He felt that the two Acts could have been enforced concurrently, giving authors or publishers a choice of submitting to the Board or of facing prosecution in the person of their book: 'I am not at all certain that Irish authors would not have preferred prosecution . . . where the case would be made and they could defend themselves . . . than to be treated by their books being banned entirely without appeal'. With regard to censoring as distinct from appeal, Sir John suggested that instead of having individual censors, there should be a number of societies on a panel (he mentioned in particular the Universities, the Royal Dublin Society, the Catholic Truth Society and PEN) which would tell the Minister whether in their opinion a book came within the meaning of the Act: shades of the 'recognised associations'?

Sir John announced that he was ready to withdraw the motion; but this was not permitted him. On a show of hands it was declared lost; but various Senators pressed for a division, because they felt that the public should know exactly what was the state of feeling in the House on the subject. The motion was lost by 34 votes to 2 (those of Sir John Keane and Professor Johnston), but this result belies the effect which the debate had. Had the motion been more reasonably worded, and had Sir John and Professor Magennis abstained from the rather disagreeable personal remarks which they had made in the course of the debate, probably the vote might have indicated that there were many in the House who were unhappy about the current position of censorship. And if we regard public opinion at large, the very fact that the Senate had debated for four days on the subject must have introduced into the minds of many others a certain doubt as to the effectiveness and the justice of the existing practice.

Following immediately on the debate came a severe article by Fr Patrick Gannon in the review *Studies* on the subject of 'Art, Morality and Censorship'. This contained a vehement apologia for the Censorship Board, and a violent attack on the Editor of the *Irish Times* and the 'literati'.

> 'Everyone remembers,' he wrote, 'what a storm of protest the very notion of it (censorship) aroused. You would fancy that all the liberties of the land were in danger. Characteristically enough, the campaign was led by a newspaper which, throughout its history, fought with all its influence against political liberty and had no word of protest against the suppression of such organs of opinion as voiced the aspirations of the Irish nation for political emancipation.'

Father Gannon did more than defend the Board: he criticised the 1929 Act as being a 'weak and halting compromise, too limited in scope to exclude the most dangerous of all works—namely those which preach and propagate false philosophies subversive to society. Neither did it deal with those subtly subversive books in which—if the proprieties were not enraged—the ethics of naturalism were substituted for Christian asceticism'.[24]

This article is notable mainly for vehemence; impassioned and vigorous, it lacked the academic tone which is characteristic of *Studies*. It was as if the supporters of the Censorship, realising that its opponents were monopolising the limelight, saw the need to re-convince public opinion that censorship was necessary and that conditions had not changed appreciably since the 1920's.

The end of 1942 was, then, a period of activity on both sides and the criticism which the Board and the Act received at this time was rather more sustained than on other occasions. Responsibility for this follow-up is due in large measure to a 'Council of Action' formed in November 1942. In the following pages the story of this body is examined in some detail, firstly because the Council did play a part in the campaign for revision of the Act, and secondly because of the Council's interesting examination of the incidence of censorship in the years 1930–1943.

3 THE COUNCIL OF ACTION

At a meeting[25] held in Jury's Hotel, Dublin, on 6 November 1942 representatives of nine organisations concerned with literary affairs and civil liberties[26] formed a 'Council of Action to secure the administration of the Censorship of Publications Act in accordance with the provisions of the Act', and discussed a statement prepared by the representatives of PEN. A sub-committee of six[27] was instructed to write to the Censorship Board to secure an interview, or failing this, to go to the Minister for Justice and to put before him concrete proposals for securing the proper administration of the Act.

The next meeting of the Council of Action took place on 11 March 1943. In the meantime the sub-committee met the Minister, who had promised 'to consult the Council in the event of a vacancy occurring on the Board'.[28] As regards further action it was decided that: (1) each censor be written to individually and the views of the Council made clear to him; (2) a further letter be written to the Minister, putting the Council's case in writing and submitting a list of all the banned books by Irish authors, and (3) that 'the use of the *Times* Library should if possible be denied to the Secretary of the Board'.

It would appear that the third meeting, held on 21 November 1944, was the last of the series. It was reported that the members of the Board, and the Minister, had been written to, as also had the *Times* Library:

> 'The *Times* Library had been informed that the Secretary to the Minister (*sic*) was misusing the library, but the library was unwilling to take action in the matter'.

Since the time of the last meeting a vacancy had occurred on the Censorship Board: 'The Minister had been reminded of his promise to consult the Council in the event of a vacancy. . . . He evaded this application by suggesting that the appointment (in the place of Senator Fearon) had always been a Trinity man and must be so in future. Dr Wigham was appointed without consultation with the Provost.[29] Dr Wigham was written to and the case for the Council was put to him. He had replied helpfully and hopefully. Then the announcement of the new Censorship Bill was made. In the belief that the old Act would not be inoperative, pressure on Dr Wigham ceased.'

The most interesting feature of the work of this Council of Action was the Memorandum drawn up for submission to the Minister towards the end of 1944. The Council stated that 'it is recognised that in theory the existing Censorship is not designed to prevent liberty of thought or discussion, but reasons will be given . . . to show that consciously or unconsciously it is operated to achieve this result'.

As regards the grounds for prohibition, it agreed that advocacy of abortion should not be tolerated; it felt that advocacy of artificial birth control was not so obviously objectionable, but it made no concrete proposals as to what type of birth control discussion it thought should be available in the country. On the grounds of 'in general tendency indecent and obscene' the Memorandum made a more detailed examination, distinguishing (1) 'books which are frankly pornographic, such as the works of de Sade, Cleland, etc., but which have definite historical or literary merit' (these should not be banned provided their sale is confined to expensive editions); (2) 'ephemeral publications, pornographic in intent, cheap in price, and of no literary merit' (these should be banned); (3) 'scientific treatment and study of sex problems by authors such as Freud, Havelock Ellis, Kraft, Ebbing, etc.' (are usually expensive; it might be legitimate to prohibit their exposure in a shop window or their advertisement); (4) 'the novels which deal incidentally with sex both in theory and action' (prohibition of these is objectionable and ineffective). As regards 'Particular Defects and Unfortunate Results of our Censhorship' the Memorandum pointed to: the banning of books published by religious or semi-religious publishing firms such as the Mothers' Union, Student Christian Movement Press and the Society for Promotion of Christian Knowledge; the banning of books by a large number of Irish authors (77 books by 44 authors)[30] . . . 'Irish writers would seem on this showing to be the object almost of persecution; a large number of reputable English authors had books on the banned list;[31] among continental books banned were titled by Marcel Proust, Thomas Mann, Mikhail Sholokhov, Anatole France and others . . . 'once again it will be seen that the list includes the greatest contemporary writers'; a number of eminent American writers including Ernest Hemingway, John Dos Passos, Sinclair Lewis, Thomas Wolfe, John Steinbeck and William Faulkner: 'the result of such indiscriminate, and may we say, unintelligent banning has been to hold this country up to ridicule and to gain for the Register of Prohibited Publications the alternative title of "Everyman's Guide to the Modern Classics".'[32] The Memorandum also suggested that some books had been banned on religious and political grounds: 'It is difficult to convince anyone that such books as Bernard Shaw's *The Adventures of the Black Girl in her Search for God* [this could not possibly have come within the meaning of the Act], *The Grand Design* by David Pilgrim, the *Green Lion* by Francis Hackett, *The Gadfly* by E. L. Voyrich or *Stephen Hero* by James Joyce were banned on any ground other than the religious, or that an objection to left-wing politics were not the motive in banning *Wide is the Gate* by Upton Sinclair and *Pemberton* by David Footman.'

The last third, and most satisfactory part of the Memorandum was concerned with improvements to the Censorship machinery. The Council proposed: (1) that there should be only one Censor, a full-time official; (2) that when a book was banned the name of the person who lodged the complaint should be published ('People who seek to affect the reputation and living of an author[33] should have the courage to stand over their own beliefs and accusations and not be allowed to take refuge in anonymity'); (3) that the Censor in advising the Minister to ban any book should sign a form stating that he had *read* [my italics] the book, that in reading it he had had regard to its literary, artistic merit, etc. (Section 6, ss. 3 (a-e)), and his conclusions; (4) that an appeal board should be set up composed of five members, one each appointed by the Senate of the National University, the Senate of Dublin University, the Royal Irish Academy, the Irish Academy of Letters and the Association of Irish Publishers; (5) that there should be room for appeal to the courts in matters of law (presumably against the Appeal Board); and (6) that the system of 'marking passages' should be absolutely eliminated.

Much of this criticism and many of the proposed changes in the system are to be found at other times during the period under consideration, voiced by different people and groups. The Council of Action, however, does appear to have investigated fully the extent of the Censorship's operation and to have taken at least some action to improve matters. For all that, it did not represent a very high-powered force, and never made any real impression on public opinion (or tried to do so, for that matter). But it did influence the Minister for Justice of the time and was to some extent responsible for the amendment Bill which appeared in 1945: or so Senator Magennis complained in the Seanad (28 November 1945).

4 LAST THINGS

The high-water mark of criticism of the Board was 1942–43. In April of the following year Sir John Keane, realising that it was necessary to 'consolidate the gains' made in the 1942 debate, introduced in the Seanad a 'Censorship of Publications (Amendment) Bill, 1944' providing for the setting up of three-man appeal tribunal nominated by the Government and the Universities; the appeal to the Minister (Section 8 of the 1929 Act) was retained.[34] Appeals would take place before the prohibition order was promulgated.

The first reading attracted little attention in the press, and the new Bill was further eclipsed when some three weeks later the *Irish Times* reported (in a leading article on 'Book Censorship')[35] that it was Mr de Valera's intention to propose a modification of the censorship system if he was returned after the summer election; this modification would consist of the appointment of a single book censor (on the lines of the film censorship) and the introduction of an appeal board.

In June 1944 Sir John withdrew his Bill when the Minister for Justice confirmed these reports: 'I do intend to bring in a Bill dealing with this matter. As a matter of courtesy I informed the Censorship Board that I intend to oppose the Bill and that, when I got an opportunity, I intended to bring in an amending Bill. The position, so far as I have seen it since I became Minister for Justice, has been most unsatisfactory.'[36]

V

The Act of 1946

On 10 October 1945 a Bill 'to make further and better provision for the censorship of books and periodical publications' received its first reading in Dáil Éireann. It came as no surprise, but its appearance provoked little criticism and no excitement. Indeed, outside the Oireachtas, the new Bill received no reception at all. The papers, reviews, and journals maintained an uncanny silence about the whole affair.[1] The main newspapers certainly reported the Dáil and Seanad debates but one might almost say that their comment on the Bill and the debates is expressed only in their selection of headlines: the *Irish Times* choosing to express its views by headlining its report 'ALL CENSORSHIP IS EVIL' while the *Irish Independent* in its usual non-committal way figured 'SEANAD VIEWS ON BOOKS CENSORSHIP DIFFER'. There was an almost absolute lack of editorial comment or of correspondence on the subject.

The only plausible reason that can be put forward for this behaviour is that the Bill pleased all the interested parties and contained no ground for controversy: and that when there is agreement of this nature there is little to be said or discussed. It is also true that the attention of the press was distracted by other events. The Nuremberg Trials and that of Pierre Laval, the Bank of England Bill brought in by the new British Government, the death of Cardinal MacRory: all these coincided with days on which the Bill was being debated. And yet the main newspapers could find precious space in those days of paper rationing, to include mention after mention of parish hall bazaars and ordinations of priests and marriages of clergymen. This lack of interest in the Bill is all the more surprising when compared with the storms of controversy which greeted the appearance and progress of the first Bill in 1928.

If sparsity of comment was a feature of the secular press, the religious press gave no coverage at all. An examination of the relevant files of the *Standard*, the *Irish Catholic*, *Hibernia*, the *Irish Monthly*, the *Irish*

Rosary and the *Irish Ecclesiastical Record* shows that there was absolutely no editorial comment, and no sign either of special articles or even news reports. The two first mentioned, being weekly, are the most likely sources of comment; however, in these months—from October 1945 to February 1946—their attention appears to have been attracted for the most part by the deaths and creations of Cardinals, the Spanish political scene, the recommendations of the Committee on Vocational Organisation (which had recently reported) and a controversial Health Bill brought in by the Fianna Fáil Government.

The *Leader* did mention the censorship question once when, on the publication of the Bill, it remarked that 'it would be hard to discover either [freedom or philosophy] in the actions of our dying Censorship of Publications Board. A new body, or bodies, is to be set up to operate in this Department of Journalism. It is to be hoped that it will not operate in such a way that nuns in their convents in other countries can read and even recommend publications that our Censorship Board would not allow into the hands of our Democracy'.[2]

The British press, needless to say, did not mention this amending Bill.[3] This dearth of material in the press generally means that the student of the 1945 Censorship Bill must largely depend on the Oireachtas debates themselves to assess the public reaction to the measure.

To his disappointment, the treatment which the Bill received in the Lower House was itself comparable to that given it by the organs of public opinion. There the Second Reading took some twenty minutes, the Committee Stage one hour, the Report and Fifth Stages about forty-five minutes.[4] Admittedly it was an amending Bill: but it was amending an Act which had caused a considerable amount of trouble during its fifteen years' operation. The fact that the Dáil was very busy at the time is hardly sufficient justification of the summary treatment the measure received; the House devoted much more generous amount of time to the Rent Restrictions Bill 1945 (which was subjected to an unexpected amount of proposed amendment and for which the Minister for Justice was also responsible), the Local Government Bill 1945 and the Lough Corrib Navigation Bill 1945: three other items which were passing through its hands during this period. The Government or, more particularly, the Minister for Justice, Mr Gerald Boland, did nothing to impress on the House the importance of the measure: which could easily have been done in view of the fact that the subject was definitely non-Party in character.

The new Bill was consolidated in form: it consisted of a 'writing-in' of amendments into the 1929 Act, a praiseworthy method of legislation which meant that the greater part of Censorship law would be still contained within the boundaries of one single Act. In effect the new Bill embodied almost all the censorship law: leaving in force only that part of the 1929 Act which related to restrictions on the publication of reports of juridical proceedings (Censorship of Publications Act 1929, Part III). The main amendments provided for two important changes in the procedure of censorship: empowering the Censorship Board itself to make prohibition orders; and establishing an Appeal Board.[5]

1 THE DAIL DEBATES

In his introductory speech on 17 October Mr Boland pointed out that there was no provision for appeal in the 1929 Act although that Act did provide that the Minister, after consultation with the Board, might vary or revoke a prohibition order. But this procedure was, to his mind, unsatisfactory because it meant making the Minister a Court of Appeal from his own orders.[6] Surveying the story of the censorship since 1929, Mr Boland reported 'complete success and no complaints' with regard to the censorship of periodicals,[7] and while he admitted that there had been some complaints about the treatment of books, he pointed out that these were in fact very few, in comparison with the total of nearly 2,000 prohibited in the period: few—but sufficient to warrant the establishment of some form of appeal so that 'however rarely the right of appeal may be exercised, the mere existence of that right will provide an answer to such criticisms as have been made'.[8]

A Fine Gael deputy welcomed the Bill but expressed concern lest the establishment of an Appeal Board might increase the cost of the censorship (his mind was later put at ease when the Minister informed him that the current annual cost of censorship was about £1,000 and that no appreciable increase was expected); he did criticise one Section of the Bill (Section 5) which empowered customs officers to detain on importation any book which, in their opinion, ought to be examined by the Censorship Board, asking that this power be extended to cover periodicals. Mr Boland indicated that this could seriously affect the circulation of periodicals (since their sale cannot be held up for an indefinite period while the Board are examining one issue)[9] : thus the Bill provided that periodicals could be prohibited only on complaints being made by members of the public.

Mr James Larkin (Junior), speaking for the Labour Party, welcomed the Bill, while referring on the general distaste for the principle of censorship in itself, and complaining that the Bill was 'merely a remedial Bill, confined to keeping down the abuses instead of getting at the root causes of these abuses'. He asked that it be made clear that the proposed Appeal Board would be enabled to consider bannings made under the first Act.

The Bill, then, was favourably received in the Dail; and in fact the debates to follow were as free from party politics as were those of 1928. Without enthusiasm or disapproval, the House in general was prepared to take the calm attitude of the Minister as expressed in his speech at the close of the Second Reading: 'I hope that the new scheme will work. Like everything else done by human beings, it is only by trial and experiment that we can arrive at anything like an approach to a perfect system'.[10]

The Committee stage in the Dail one week later was quite uninspiring; the phrase 'an amending Bill' seemed to have hypnotised the House and perhaps the meagreness of the debate may be attributed to an unconscious awareness that 'this was really a Seanad affair, anyway'.

Five amendments were tabled and two of these were ministerial; vast areas of the Bill were simply put and agreed to with no discussion at all. The House did stop to consider more seriously the powers of the customs officials, and was assured by the Minister that the Section did not constitute a *change* in the censorship procedure; ever since 1929 books had been banned as a result of being held up by the customs authorities who then sent them to the Board for examination[12]; he was unable to give precise figures but he understood that 'almost half the books that were censored [since 1929] came from that source'.[13] The purpose of the new Section in the Act was simply to make known explicitly this procedure.

According to the terms of the Bill right of appeal belonged to 'the author or the publisher, or any five persons (each of whom is a member of Dail Eireann or Seanad Eireann) acting jointly': the two first of these being required to make a deposit of five pounds as a safeguard against frivolous appeals. Many deputies of all parties objected to the involvement of senators and deputies in the affairs of censorship. They foresaw themselves being plagued by authors and others to appeal against banning after banning, and disliked the prospect of having to yield to pressure to read banned books in addition to their other heavy duties; they invented 'theoretical' excuses for not keeping the clause: saying that it meant that they would be interfering in administration when, in fact, their task was essentially legislative in character. The Minister explained that this provision would be one way of avoiding motions on censorship in the Oireachtas (or at least of postponing them or of immunising Parliament to some extent); he had introduced it because his experience of deputies' complaints had led him to the belief that they should be given this power of appeal 'inasmuch as I shall be out of the picture in the future in so far as banning of books is concerned' (no longer would it be the Minister who banned; and consequently the Oireachtas could not with the same ease as previously deal with the subject of censorship in debate).[14] The deputies were not readily convinced on this point but during the Report Stage they were won over by the Minister (and by Mr James Dillon, then an Independent who rarely supported the Fianna Fail Government. There was no further discussion of note during the Dail debates. The Fifth Stage was characterised by careless, unprepared speeches by Deputies Larkin, Cogan and Dillon.[15]

2   THE SECOND READING IN THE SEANAD

On 7 November the Bill was introduced in the Seanad by the Minister for Posts and Telegraphs, Mr Little, in words almost identical to those used by Mr Boland in the Dail. At the very beginning of the debate the Senators asked for time to give the matter serious consideration, and the Minister, for his part, promised that he would make no attempt to rush the measure through the House.

Senator James Douglas, who spoke on behalf of the Opposition,[16] congratulated the Minister on the structure of the Bill, but expressed dissatisfaction with the form of appeal embodied in the measure: 'insofar as it purports to remove responsibility from the Minister for Justice I am not quite satisfied with it. There is a great danger that Parliament may lose any possible control over that committee'. He objected also to the 'new' provision that customs officers might detail books which formed part of a traveller's personal baggage on the grounds that 'the general attitude adopted hitherto . . . was that the main object of censorship was not to interfere with the liberty of the individual but to prevent the sale and distribution of undesirable literature'.[17]

Again, on the ground that it would cause unnecessary trouble to members of the Oireachtas, the Senator criticised the provision which gave to any five members acting jointly the right of appeal; he suggested that certain recognised bodies (such as the Royal Dublin Society and PEN) should play this role.

The debate on this stage and on all subsequent stages was dominated by Professor Magennis, the chairman of the Censorship Board and a member of that body for over eleven years. It gave him his first opportunity to speak in public of the internal workings of the Censorship and of the relations between the Board and the Minister. Up to then the Professor had always been on the defensive, in public controversies and parliamentary debates, and thus had been in a situation which demanded that both Minister and Board present a united front.

Senator Magennis reviewed the Board's experience of the working of the Act and the House was probably surprised to hear that 'one of the first things that the Board of Censorship did after it began to function . . . was to approach the then Minister . . . to ask for an amending Act';[18] the Minister asked them to defer their representations until they had gained practical experience on the working of the Act. Contrary to what had been supposed, there had been considerable friction between the Minister and the Board,[19] one of the most frequent causes of which lay in the fact that the former regarded himself as both censor and as appellate tribunal.

This divergence of views was caused by differing interpretations of one section of the 1929 Act. Section 6 stated that whenever the Board reported that in their opinion a book should be prohibited, 'the Minister *may* [my italics] by order prohibit its sale and distribution'. The Minister interpreted this 'may' as 'can if he wishes', while the Board, according to Professor Magennis, understood it to mean 'ought to'. 'He [the Minister] had legal aid. I do not know from what source he received it.' The Professor went on to quote in support the Board's interpretation of a judgement given in the case *Julius v. Bishop of Oxford* which stated that 'may' will be ordinarily taken to be a permissive word, but if the power conferred by the word 'may' is one which, as in this case, is to be exercised on behalf of someone who has a special interest . . . the complainant and the people of the Twenty-Six Counties . . . thereupon the 'may' which confers the power also imposes the duty of exercising that power. . . . They [the Prohibition Orders] should have been his [the Minister's] only technically. Thus the Minister should have felt in no way uneasy about being the Appeal authority.[20] (This was a far-fetched interpretation of a legal point.) At this stage Professor Magennis reminded the House that there was in fact provision for appeal in the 1929 Act.[21] He cited one such case[22] (in the event unsuccessful) which was the subject of appeal to the Minister; and concluded that it was the public's fault that they had not made use of this provision. However true this may in fact have been, one would have thought that had the Professor valued this provision he should have brought it to the attention of the public at some other time than the very eve of the death of the 1929 Act.

Referring to the Board's 'lack of success'[23] Professor Magennis mentioned representations which it had made from time to time to the Department of Justice: 'The Minister has been informed that the Act has been, to a great extent, a failure, for the following reasons: inadequacy of funds and inadequacy of staff, resulting in inability to deal with the maximum number of new novels with the minimum time after their publication.'[24]

Commenting on various other aspects of the Bill the Senator said that he and Professor Fearon, TCD, (a former member of the Board) would have liked the Board to deal with the cheaper circulating libraries. He also made a mild suggestion that bookshops should be required to have licences; but no more was heard of this.[25] He criticised the attitude of the Gardai Siochana who, from the time that the Act began to function had 'folded their arms' and laid the whole problem of obscene literature on the shoulders of the Censorship Board. Nor had the District Justices been of any assistance; one, for example, had refused to convict because 'in his opinion "a notice in *Iris Oifigiuil* was not sufficient a notice";[26] another because "lending library distribution was not distribution within the meaning of the Act".'[27]

As to appeal, the Senator went on, every member of the Board was in favour of it.

> 'The philosophy of which I was a professor for half a century holds that it is contrary to natural justice for such a thing to happen as that a body of men pronounce an author's book offensive to morality . . . and to leave the author and his publisher financially no opportunity of appeal . . . we who are operating the Act of 1929 are not callous to the sense of grievance which banned authors and publishers may have.'[28]

However, he objected to the actual appeal provisions of the Bill: particularly to the fact that the proposed Appeal Board was composed of three persons to the Censorship Board's five (as though the Appeal Board consisted of 'experts' whose opinion should hold more weight); he wanted the Censorship Board to be the smaller. In addition, he wanted a provision which would give one member of the Censorship Board a position on the Appeal Board.[29]

Other points made by the Senator were that the phrase *in its general tendency* (indecent or obscene) taken from the 1929 Act, was superfluous, had no meaning and had been the 'bugbear of the press, of authors, of members of the Board and of the Department of Justice', and should be deleted;[30] that the Bill should make some reference to Article 40 of the 1937 Constitution; and the very accurate observation that the 'Dublin press had lulled the public into apathy . . . all quite confident that this is a fine measure'. In Professor Magennis' opinion it was not.

Mr Kingsmill-Moore, a noted opponent of censorship who followed Professor Magennis in the Second Reading debate,[31] gave the Bill a 'very hearty welcome' and found it to be a 'careful, conscientious and *bona fide* attempt to make workable or partially workable' the system of censorship which, in his opinion, had up to then provided nothing but irritation for the people of Ireland and amusement for cultured people outside the country. Assuming that it would not be possible for him to persuade the House that a more drastic measure would be desirable, the Senator confirmed his remarks to the question of appeal. He began by demonstrating the need for appeal machinery. The *Register of Prohibited Publications* he described as 'Everyman's Guide to Modern Classics', containing 170 books by 44 Irish authors; publications of the Student Christian Movement, the APCK and the Mothers' Union; and works by seven American authors who were chosen by the *Saturday Review of Literature* as being among the ten best American authors in the previous twenty years. And, only recently, the Board had banned several volumes of Proust's *The Remembrance of Things Past*. In the Senator's mind there was no doubt that appeal was vitally necessary; but he suggested that the new Board include a High Court, Supreme Court or Circuit Court Judge, one member nominated by a body such as the Irish Academy of Letters; a third chosen from the ordinary reading public; two other members: a Catholic and a Protestant minister of religion. As a final rallying-cry Senator Kingsmill-Moore told the House that he would resist with his last breath the right of Senator Magennis to tell him what he might read or might not read.[32]

Senator Campbell (Labour Panel) was not interested in the niceties of the censorship, in the delicate problem of freedom and responsibility; he bluntly reminded the House of the position in the country before censorship was introduced and felt that the Bill was quite unnecessary: 'the working class do not want it but the pseudo-intellectuals tell us that we must let up on the censorship. They are making a mistake if they think that the plain people are going to stand for a reintroduction of the vicious type of literature which the original Act was largely successful in keeping out'. To his mind the Ten Commandments provided an adequate definition of indecency; he asked that the Board be given powers to ban books which were 'subversive of public morals'; he supported Professor Magennis' plea for more funds and was ready to permit the Board to have to examine only one issue of a periodical before coming to a decision.[33]

Among other comments and suggestions made by speakers in the debate were: a tribute to the Censorship Board on behalf of the women of Ireland for what it had done (Senator Mrs Helena Concannon);[34] a suggestion that the new Board be given powers to ban books which were blasphemous or which condoned divorce; a doubt as to whether Customs officials were suitably qualified to detain books on importation;[35] a repetition of the old fear that the public sale of the *Register of Prohibited Publications* would encourage the purchase of the publications themselves.

In his speech at the end of the debate Mr Little made various points in reply to the senators. The Customs, he insisted, were the only persons in a position appreciably to control objectionable publications at the point of entry; although it was true that the Board had a small allowance for the purchase of books it had never in fact exhausted this allowance;[36] in answer to Senator Douglas (who was disturbed at the fact that Parliament would not wield control over the Board, as had formerly been the case) he pointed out that there was a germ of parliamentary control in that the Bill empowered the Minister to remove a member of the Board if he was unfit, or had failed, to act. He concluded by dismissing as 'baloney' Senator Kingsmill-Moore's opinion that all censorship was 'rooted in evil', and asked him to have a sense of proportion; 'While the whole world is trying to destroy a whole set of ideas, here we are trying to do something mild in censorship.'

The Seanad Second Reading demonstrated that the House was obviously more critical of the Bill than was the Dail. On the whole, it was the conservative body as of old: a few lone liberals; many others who were prepared to accept the broad lines of the Bill; and some who preferred to retain the 1929 Act, but who could readily be persuaded to support the measure. With regard to the Government's attitude (which became more noticeable in the succeeding debates) it may be observed that the Minister has a very clear idea of what he wanted, of the points on which he was ready to give ground and on which not. While it is true that there were no recognisable party 'lines' regarding the Bill, the Minister personally (Mr Little in this case, and more so Mr Boland) was determined to tolerate 'no nonsense'; no matter which side it came from. He was aware of the past experience of the Censorship Board: he was convinced that censorship was necessary. It is true that he had consulted Professor Magennis regarding the drafting of the Bill but he had by no means accepted all the Professor's views. The Bill was Mr Boland's and the Act also would be his.

3 THE LATER STAGES IN THE SEANAD

During the Committees[37] and Report[38] stages a total of 95 amendments were tabled; 18 of these belong to the Fourth Stage. For clarity's sake these two stages are here taken together, rather than in order of time.

The first amendment of interest dealt with the definition of 'indecent' provided in the Bill (and taken from the 1929 Act). As it stood, the definition read as follows: 'The word "indecent" includes suggestive of, or inciting to, sexual immorality or unnatural vice or likely in any other similar way to corrupt or deprave.'[39] Professor Magennis proposed a broader definition: 'The word "indecent" means any matter the publication of which and general distribution thereof would be likely to affect public morals injuriously': an amendment which aimed at implementing Article 40 (Section 6, ss. 1 (i)) of the Constitution in a Bill[40] which was 'the appropriate place' for matters relating to the right of utterance and publication.[41] The greater part of the discussion on this amendment hinged on the distinction between the 'means' of Professor Magennis' amendment and the 'includes' of the original definition. The Professor, with the tone of one who had authority, reviewed the past experience of the Act and discovered that 'those who attacked the former Censorship Board for breaking the law, disregarding the law, and other enormities', based their criticism on their interpretation of 'includes' as equivalent to 'means',[42] and held the erroneous view that what followed in the 1929 Act after the word 'includes' confined the Board to a consideration of just those things, 'so that a book which was frankly obscene was excluded from the purview of the censorship unless it incited'.[43] At first sight one is inclined to dismiss this point of the Senator's as being somewhat forced: and possibly it is. It is a pity it was not aired some years earlier . . . at the time of the *Tailor and Anstey* case (for that was a book which no one took seriously or described as 'inciting', but which was vulgar and obscene in a coarse sort of way). At any rate, the fact that the Professor chose 'means' for his amendment did not signify that his attitude had changed and that he was prepared to confine the scope of the Censorship in future. On the contrary: the rest of his definition was so wide and all-embracing that it was quite immaterial which verb he used and was comparable with that in the original 1928 Bill. Senator Kingsmill-Moore attacked the amendment on the grounds that it would be quite legitimate to say that gambling and drinking were injurious to public morals and that thus the Censorship Board would be given a sort of 'roving commission' . . . which was quite unacceptable. The amendment was withdrawn when the Minister announced his preference for the 1929 wording, saying that he was quite satisfied that, no matter what words were put in the definition section or in the Bill itself, they would still have some people objecting.

Senator Douglas, pointing out that under the Bill the only parliamentary control of the Censor's would be at the stage of appointments to the Board, moved that one member be retired each year, and in this amendment was very strongly supported by Senator Kingsmill-Moore, who thought that such a provision would keep the Board fluid and would prevent the members 'growing stale, losing touch with public opinion or being dominated by the strong personality of one of their number' (an obvious reference to Senator Magennis). Senator Sir John Keane (who was present at the debate but was noticeably quiet)[44] also supported this amendment. But Senators Magennis and O'Buachalla sided with the Minister who put paid to the discussion by saying that it was difficult enough already to get people to serve on the Board and that there had been in practice a considerable degree of fluidity in its composition.[45]

An interesting point was made by one senator who called attention to the fact that once a ban had been unsuccessfully appealed against, no way was provided in the Act for the uncensoring of a book.[46] On the question of the Appeal Board itself, Senator Magennis moved that there be five members on the Board; this was agreed to. The Minister recalled that his original intention had been to use the same arrangement for book censoring as for film censoring (a paid censor, and an Appeal Board), but that Senator Magennis had persuaded him to have two boards instead; he was not attached to the figure three.[47]

Speaking to an amendment moved by Senator Douglas, Senator Kingsmill-Moore reiterated his suggestion that one member of the

Appeal Board should be nominated by the Irish Academy of Letters—
the very idea of which provoked an animated protest on the part of
Senator Magennis who saw in it 'an insidious attempt' to have a
voluntary body recognised by legislation; he went on to reveal how
unpalatable in his view the Academy really was: out of 34 members'
names given in *Thom's Directory* no fewer than nine had had books
banned and 'I notice that [its] honorary Secretary is Mr Lennox
Robinson'.[48] The debate grew more and more heated until Senator
Magennis made a veritable apologia for the censorship system and
civilisation. 'Is Ireland to be Irish' he asked, 'or is it to be subjugated
again by a foreign printing press by means of a spiritual defeat? That
is how I regard the situation.'[49] Eventually it became so clear that he
and Senator Kingsmill-Moore were liable to come to blows that Senator
Douglas felt obliged to withdraw his motion.

Another point of interest concerned the *scope* of appeals. Senator
Magennis was reluctant to allow the Appeal apparatus to be retrospective; he felt that no book banned under the 1929 Act should be the
subject of appeal (he would thus condemn them to prohibition for
eternity). In some cases, he suggested, it would be against justice to call
such an appeal fair 'because the members of the Appeal Board would
have their opinions coloured by previous controversies'. In any event,
the books banned under the 1929 Act had had their chance of appeal:
they could have been the subject of appeal to the Minister. (But the
Minister immediately rejected this argument on the grounds that people
could not really have been expected to appeal to the authority which
had censored the book in the first place.) Actually, when the relevant
clause came up in debate, doubt was expressed by many senators as to
whether it read in such a way as to give the Appeal Board retrospective
powers. But they agreed that the Board should have these powers. The
discussion on the point was indicative of the care which the Senate took
of the Bill as a whole.

The question of who should be given the right of appeal was also
thoroughly discussed. Many senators spoke with annoyance of the
provision whereby any five members of the Oireachtas might appeal
to the Board: (later experience confirmed the Minister's opinion that
it would involve them in no extra work). One amendment to increase
the number (of Oireachtas petitions) from five to ten was put and
negatived; then came an amendment from Professor Magennis which
would have removed the provision altogether. 'There is joy' said the
Professor 'in the camp of those who wish to destroy censorship alto-

gether, because of the introduction of this provision . . . an unnecessary excrescence (on the Bill)':[50] perhaps the Professor meant that if the right of appeal were confined to the author and publisher (who were required to pay a deposit to guard against frivolous appeals) there were likely to be few appeals simply because these would not go to much trouble to liberate a ban imposed in a country where their sales were negligible; if, however, members of the Oireachtas were to be given the right to lodge a complaint before the Board without paying a deposit, it was quite possible, Professor Magennis envisaged, for five Kingsmill-Moores to be found[51] who would bring many books before the Appeal Board which otherwise would never have reached it. One gets the impression that Professor Magennis was interested in appeal only as a sort of 'advertisement for the sale of *appearance* of justice'. His amendment was however lost by 14 votes to 23.

As a sort of compromise arrangement Senator Douglas proposed for Section 8, ss 4, that besides the author and publisher, the following should have the right of appeal:

(a) any Archbishop or Bishop of the Holy Catholic Apostolic and Roman Church;

(b) any Archbishop or Bishop of the Church of Ireland;

(c) any person acting on the authority of the governing body of any religious denomination existing in Ireland;

(d) any person acting on the authority of any association in Ireland, which in the opinion of the Minister, was formed for the promotion of culture or the study of literature;

(e) any person acting on the authority of a trade union.[52]

One reason he gave for this amendment was that there was 'a strong feeling . . . that certain books have been banned ostensibly under the head of indecency or obscenity, but actually because the doctrines put forward were considered to be so far to the left as to be subversive from a political point of view'. This amendment was withdrawn at the Committee Stage and re-introduced at Report, on which occasion Professor Magennis insinuated that the mention of the 'Archbishop of the Holy Catholic Apostolic and Roman Church' was mere window-dressing. Before leaving the Appeal question mention should be made of an amendment by Senator Kingsmill-Moore designed to give the appellant or his representatives right to appear before the Appeal Board. He argued that this right was due him because it was not the book which was condemned but the reputation of the author himself. The amendment was not accepted.

As in 1929, the greater part of the debate was concerned with the minutiae of the Bill. Attention should be drawn to this fact—to show the care the House took of the measure.[53]

It remains only to consider the Fifth Stage of this debate to discover the attitudes of various senators to the Bill as modified by this house.

Senator Hayes, a former Chairman of the Seanad, felt that the Minister 'under duress of long speeches at the Committee Stage' had changed things too radically.[54] Senator Kingsmill-Moore took this opportunity to speak on the principle of censorship. He had, he said, examined various bibliographies of censorship (including one issued by the University of Oregon[55] and another published in the Encyclopaedia of Social Sciences) and had read every book available in the main libraries in Ireland dealing with censorship from the abstract point of view; he assured his colleagues that from 1916 onwards there was no book available in the public libraries which had 'one good word to say in favour of the principle of censorship'; he concluded by making the mischievous observation that, in upholding censorship, Ireland was like Russia, Spain and Germany.

Senator Douglas, who must surely have been one of the most amicable of senators—and both realistic and principled—complimented the Minister on his endeavour to treat the Bill as a non-Party measure.

To Senator Magennis the Bill appeared vastly improved. It would, he thought, make censorship easier, more effective and more acceptable even to some of the disgruntled critics of the past. He, also, congratulated the Minister. And Mr Boland in turn congratulated the House on its treatment of the Bill: it had given it 'a far closer examination and was more helpful than the house to which I belong. There is no doubt about that. I did not try to rush the Bill in the other house but there was very little debate on it there'. It is quite true to say that the 1946 Act,[56] in its details, owed very much to the Seanad, though one is obliged to say that probably it would have been a very different story if Senator Magennis had been a member of the lower house; not that Senator Magennis himself 'made' the Bill but that the discussion which it needed and deserved if it was to be a worthy measure necessarily centred around the person of Professor Magennis who was in so many ways the personification of Censorship.

As an indication of the importance given by the Senate to the Bill reference may be made to an incident which occurred towards the end

of the debate, when one Senator suggested that it was outrageous that
the Bill had occupied two full days of the House's time. He was promptly
upbraided by Professor Magennis with the words: 'If it were a question
of the standing price of a bushel of wheat there would be no objection
to giving a lot of time to it. The spiritual requirements of the nation are
at least as equally important.' This attitude of Senator Magennis was
one which in different ways characterised the Seanad as a whole. It was
an important Bill.

4 STATUTORY REGULATIONS

The *Principal Regulations*[57] issued in 1946 referred mainly to the forms
on which complaints were to be made. There was no substantial change
in the complaint procedure as compared with that arranged for the 1929
Act: except that only three recent issues of a periodical were required
for a formal complaint. The CTS could no longer criticise the Minister's
regulations as enabling newspapers to 'dodge' the censorship.[58] The
suggestion that the complainant indicate some passages 'in support of
my view' was retained.

Provision was also made in the *Principal Regulations* for the appeal
procedure. A form together with six copies of a periodical as the Appeal
Board might reasonably require, was to be sent to the Appeal Board
and 'an appellant or applicant to the Appeal Board may submit, in
addition to the prescribed form, a written statement of the grounds
upon which the appeal or application is based. The Appeal Board may,
if they think fit, afford to any person an opportunity to appeal before
the Board and make oral submissions in relation to an appeal or application to the Board'. The requirement that appellants furnish the Appeal
Board with six copies of each book weighed particularly heavily on
members of the Oireachtas (an author or publisher being able to suppy
copies to the Board at a fraction of the retail cost). In view of this and
because of the reference to 'marked passages' in the complaint forms
Senator Kingsmill-Moore tabled a motion[59] to annul the regulations.
The motion was moved in his absence by Senator Johnston; Sir John
Keane spoke to it and Mr Boland intimated that he was inclined to
modify the regulations so that members of the Oireachtas need not
submit copies of books. The debate was then adjourned and when it was
resumed on 12 March 1947[60] Senator Kingsmill-Moore explained how
the modification was in fact necessary:

'When the Bill was being debated, it was suggested that

English publishers would be anxious to flood the Irish market with books of a type which would not appeal to the Censorship Board. . . . As a matter of fact, the Irish market does not matter in the least to the English publisher. That is proved by the fact that, in the year in which this Act has been in existence, although there have been over 1,000 books on the banned list, the English publishers did not think it worth their while to appeal one single book.'

Accordingly, the whole onus of appeal—especially in the vital first year of the 1946 Act (after which it would not be possible to appeal books banned before 1946)[61]—fell on members of Parliament. In fact, the Minister altered the regulations on 8 February 1947 (*before* the debate on the motion was resumed).[62] The 1946 Act became law on 13 February 1948: thus Senator Kingsmill-Moore and Senator Fearon, who organised the hundred-odd Oireachtas appeals made at this time, had only five days in which to do so.[63]

VI

Censorship 1946-58: Special Aspects

The period between 1946 and 1958 constitutes a distinct second phase
of censorship. The Act passed in 1929 had been worked for fifteen years,
during which time the Censorship Board had met with sufficient opposition to warrant the 1945 re-assessment. As has been seen, the debates
on the second Bill could not be described as constituting an 'agonising
re-appraisal' of the whole censorship question; the general principle of
a preventive censorship still stood. But the establishment of the Appeal
Board destroyed the utter permanence which had hitherto been the most
irksome characteristic of the decisions of the Board. Mistakes, justifiable
or otherwise, would be made again—of this everyone was sure; but now
the Court of Appeal was not a Minister (who had never in fact acted in
that capacity), but a body of five other men who, it was hoped, would
exercise a moderating influence.

However, it was not the period of calm and right reason which the
improved legislation was expected to usher in; on the contrary, the
censorship was to have a much rougher passage than it had before 1946.
There was of course no repetition of the comedy to which the public
was treated by the Seanad in 1942: the fact that the Minister was no
longer responsible for the banning of books, and the presence of the
Appeal Board, meant that individual decisions of the Censorship Board
would not be examined in the Oireachtas. Public debate was now confined—if that be the word—to newspaper controversy, articles in
journals, discussions and lectures, the activities of various pressure
groups against censorship and others as enthusiastically but less ener-
getically in defence of it. An examination of these sources yields a wealth
of material I have tried to confine to two chapters, one dealing with
internal or special aspects, and another with general aspects of the
censorship. In Appendices 6 and 7 notes are given on individual books
which, for one reason or another, were particularly bound up with the
censorship controversy.

1 THE CENSORSHIP BOARD AND ITS MEMBERS

On 27 March 1946 the Minister for Justice appointed the first Censorship Board under the new Act; it consisted of four members of the previous Board (Professor Magennis [Chairman], Father Deery, Professor Shields and Professor Wigham), and one newcomer, Mr C. J. Joyce.[1]

However, these five men never met around the same table, for some days after his appointment, Professor Magennis died suddenly. There was a certain irony in the event; Professor Magennis had been for many years the very personification of the Censorship, and by far the most prominent speaker in the debates on the 1945 Bill; one would have wished, at least for curiosity's sake, to see how the new Act would fare in his hands.

The position of Chairman of the Censorship Board is not in itself powerful: the Chairman is a *primus inter pares* and holds no casting vote. However, in the Board as in any committee, the chairman can be a leader, and in fact Professor Magennis, who had been chairman since 1942 when he took the place of Mgr Boylan, was a very forceful leader indeed. Narrowminded though he may have been, his undoubted intellectual qualities combined with a native energy to enable him to control the Board very effectively.

His successor, Father Joseph Deery, was a Dublin curate; he does not seem to have been a man of Magennis's calibre, although his views on censorship were certainly as conservative as those of previous chairmen. At this time, to be sure, he was an 'unknown quantity'; his short experience in censorship was confined to 1945, a particularly unsettled year for a Board living in the shadow of change: in that year only 60 books had been banned—fewer than the previous year, and considerably fewer than the previous annual average. Father Deery was the second senior member on the Board at Professor Magennis's death, having had a year less service on the Board than Professor Wigham, the 'Trinity representative'.[2] At any event, the Board now suffered from a marked lack of experience, of continuity in its membership, a fact which should be taken into account when examining the drastic upward trend of bannings during the ten years of Father Deery's chairmanship.

The vacancy created by the death of Professor Magennis was filled by Professor J. J. Pigott, Professor of Education at St Patrick's Training College, Dublin.

Thus constituted, the Board worked without change of membership until February 1949, when Professor Wigham resigned and was replaced by Dr J. D. Smyth, a lecturer in biochemistry at Trinity College. Dr Smyth proved to be the Lynn Doyle of the new Act, for he resigned in protest some six months later: in a letter to the Minister for Justice dated 1 July 1949[3] he explained that he 'did not see eye to eye with his colleagues on the interpretation of an important clause of the Censorship of Publications Act' (Section 6, ss. 2a, which instructs the Board to have regard to the literary and artistic merit of each book). He referred to the application of an internal rule of the Board to the effect that it must pay more attention to the offensiveness of a book than to its other qualities, and also complained that he had not been given adequate time to come to a decision on each book. He was bitterly opposed to the 'marked passages' method. The Board for its part replied to Dr Smyth by way of a letter from the Secretary to the *Irish Times* explaining that there was no such ruling,[4] but that certainly the Board regarded as relevant to its decisions certain remarks from the 1929 debates which indicated the intentions of the framers of the Act. It went on to deny that Dr Smyth had not been given sufficient time in which to judge books fairly.[5] Later, in reply to a letter from Dr Smyth alleging that books had been banned at one meeting without his having read them,[6] the Secretary of the Board agreed that this did occur but showed the vote was quite in order (three of the four members present voted in favour of banning).[7] The correspondence then changed to the subject of venereal disease.

And so, after a lapse of twelve years, another member of the Board made a public complaint about its procedure. It is difficult to establish whether (or not) Dr Smyth was justified in making these charges. At this time the Board was examining only about 300 books per year, which made an average weekly reading of six: this is a fact which Dr Smyth must have known before he accepted the Minister's invitation to take up the unrewarding and burdensome appointment of censor. On the question of marked passages, Dr Smyth's was not a new revelation; Lynn Doyle had said it all before; one might agree that the censor was tempted to take the easy way out and simply 'read around' the marked passages: but on the other hand, no censor was *required* to decide on the basis of reading these passages; if he disagreed with the method he had the alternative of reading the book through. The fact that he could not cope with the volume of work expected of him was a very worthy reason for resigning, if not for protesting; but there was nothing necessarily objectionable in the banning of a book which one member had not read. Certainly the other members could have agreed to postpone the final decision on the book in question until Dr Smyth had examined it: but they could do this in exceptional cases only, for otherwise a 'slow' member could hinder the work of the entire Board.

The vacancy caused by Dr Smyth's resignation was filled one month later by Mr District Justice T. G. O'Sullivan.* A year later, in September 1950, another change took place when Professor Shields resigned and Dr P. T. Breathnach joined the Board. After 1949, the number of bannings steadily increased. Having remained around an annual figure of 160 for the 1946-1949 period, it showed a 100 per cent increase in 1950, and by 1954 it was six times the 1949 figure.

The second Board under the 1946 Act, appointed in February 1951, was extremely stable. Its five members had all belonged to the outgoing Board, and only two changes occurred durings its life: one due to the death of Dr Breathnach (in whose place Professor C. J. O'Reilly, also from St Patrick's Training College, was appointed in June 1951), and the other caused by the resignation of Mr Joyce in May 1952 after six years of service (his place was now taken by Mr D. J. O'Flynn).[8]

In this period the volume of bannings increased phenomenally; the mounting figures of 500, 600, 700 and 1,000 bannings per year rendered all pre-1946 bannings pale by comparison.[9] And as the lists grew, so too did public opposition to the Censorship: not simply because the public was perturbed at the scale of bannings, but because the Board seemed to make no distinction between books by established authors and the rest; Hemingway and Mickey Spillane appeared side by side on the lists which were published regularly on the instructions of the Board. When the total number of books examined had been small—a matter of two or three hundred a year—people who had entertained misgivings about the 'marked passages' method could still hope that serious literary works received special consideration before the decision to ban was taken; but the figure of 1,000 books (and 80 periodicals) prohibited in one year (1954) meant that the censors examined an average of twenty books a week,[10] and even if the Board did in fact take the trouble of *reading* the serious works, there was a very natural suspicion in the public mind that this was unfortunately not the case.

* Previous to this, it had been the custom to appoint at least one member of the staff of Trinity College, Dublin to the Board. In Mr Paul Blanshard's view 'since Dr Smyth's resignation the Government has been unable to persuade any Protestant professor of Trinity College to co-operate in such proceedings' (*The Irish and Catholic Power*, p. 72).

Mr O'Sullivan was a Catholic, which meant that there were only Catholics on the Board from the time of his appointment. This situation prevailed until December 1956, when Mr R. R. Figgis, a Protestant, was appointed.

In 1955 there was a distinct drop in these figures to 494 books examined and 434 banned. There is no external evidence to indicate why this was so. It is unlikely that it was due to differences of opinion within the Board. The secretary has spoken of some 'hitches' in the machinery around this time, and from an examination of the statistics it would appear that the customs authorities were responsible for the drop, in that they forwarded a smaller number of books to the Board.

Figure 2

CENSORSHIP BOARD: BOOKS: PROHIBITION GROUNDS 1946–1964

year	total number of books examined	obscenity	birth control	obscenity and birth control	total number of books prohibited
1946	285	106	9	1	116
1947	317	160	4		164
1948	329	170	11		181
1949	304	157	9		166
1950	671	401	9		410
1951	717	534	5		539
1952	838	627	11	2	640
1953	1023	755	11		766
1954*	1217				1034
1955*	494				434
1956*	342				278
1957*	223				102
1958	911	462	25		487
1959	797	385	16	1	402
1960	518	282	9		291
1961	631	399	9		408
1962	569	381	8		389
1963	687	443	11		454
1964	537	345	16		361
TOTAL	11,410	5,616	163	4	7,622

* Detailed statistics not available for this year.

This tendency would probably have been corrected in the following year had the Board been given a free hand. But this was not so. The early months of that year saw the *Observer* Incident, the Mansion House

Meeting and the Civil Liberties petition to the Taoiseach: events (dealt with in the next chapter) which had an inhibiting influence on the Board; while, from within, the Board suffered the loss of two long-serving members. District Justice O'Sullivan died in March 1956 (a month before the *Observer* Incident), while in June, when the storm of opposition was more or less over, Father Deery also resigned. The reason given for his resignation was that his new duties as Vicar General of the Archdiocese of Dublin (he now became Monsignor) rendered him unable to devote to the Board the time it demanded.

These two resignations rendered the Board legally unable to act, and in contrast to all other occasions when vacancies arose, the Minister for Justice delayed the appointment of new members to the Board: a fact which the *Irish Times*, with its usual alertness, pointed out.[11] This delay was interpreted as a sign that the Minister (Mr Everett) was grateful for the opportunity to put a curb on the censorship, and to choose new censors with the greatest care. It is equally likely that various persons influenced by the unpopularity of the censorship refused his invitation to act on the Board.

The Censorship Board remained unable to function until December 1956 when Mr A. F. Comyn[12] and Mr R. R. Figgis[13] were appointed. The news was welcome in certain quarters: Mr C. Gore Grimes of the Civil Liberties Association was quoted in the *Irish Times* as being very pleased at the news.[14] His pleasure was not shared, however, by Professor Pigott, who had become Chairman of the Board in succession to Mgr Deery.

The attitude of Professor Pigott and the two other older members of the Board towards Mr Comyn and Mr Figgis did not become apparent until over a year later, when Professor Pigott issued a public statement first published in the *Irish Independent* on 5 December 1957:

> 'In June 1956 two vacancies occurred on the Board. These were not filled until the following December. In the meantime it was common knowledge that the Civil Liberties Association were seeking to have persons who favoured their outlook appointed to the Board. The Civil Liberties Association have been the traditional enemies of censorship, and they have been fear-conditioning the mass mind to prevent the proper operation of the Censorship Act.
>
> 'In the result two reputable professional gentlemen were appointed to fill the vacancies. At first I refused to believe that these two men shared the views of the Association, but two

matters caused me to change my mind. First of all, the vitriolic criticism of the Board's decisions ceased, and in actual fact, the Board was praised by those who formerly abused it; the Board's good sense was attributed to the two new members.' Mr Gore Grimes challenged Professor Pigott to prove his accusation that the Civil Liberties Association was concerned with the two appointments[15]; but no further information was given by Professor Pigott. This episode is referred to below, but before examining it, mention should be made of the other changes which occurred between the appointment of Mr Comyn and Mr Figgis in December 1956 and the end of the period.

The story is easily told. In May 1957, exasperated by the behaviour of the new members, who refused to ban certain 'omnibus editions', Professor Pigott suspended the meetings of the Board: 'I, as Chairman, adjourned the meetings (8 May 1957) with a view to placing the matter before the Minister[16] for his decision.'[17] When the Minister received Professor Pigott in June, the Professor suggested that he would have to ask either the two mew members or himself to resign; the Minister however, pointed out that he had no power to demand the resignation of a member unless he were absent from a number of meetings without a valid excuse, or because he proved unsatisfactory. The Professor claimed that the two members were unsatisfactory because they were making the literary, scientific or artistic merit of a book the final consideration.

> 'The Minister did not commit himself at that meeting . . . I refused in the meantime to authorise the Secretary to the Board to call a meeting of the Board until the Minister's decision in the matter reached me. In September, the Minister asked me to meet him again, and at that meeting we travelled over the same ground. I still refused to call a meeting. The Minister then said that he would reluctantly have to ask me to resign.'[18]

Professor Pigott then received a letter, dated 9 September, from the Minister to the following effect:

> 'I was sorry to find at our interview of September 5th that your mind had not changed, and that you were not prepared to convene a meeting of the Censorship of Publications Board while it remained constituted as at present. That being so, I feel that I have no option but to ask for your resignation.
>
> 'I am taking this step with the greatest reluctance, but I feel that there is no other course open to me to set in motion again

the machinery of censorship established by the Censorship of
Publications Acts.'[19]

Professor Pigott then resigned,[20] stating that he could have no patience
with a man (the Minister) who refused to obey a directive of the Attorney
General (see page 127). Mr Traynor accepted his resignation very
graciously. At the same time the two other older members of the Board,
Mr O'Flynn and Professor O'Reilly, resigned in sympathy.[21]

With the minimum delay Mr Traynor now reconstituted the Board,
appointing in October 1957 Judge J. C. Conroy (Chairman), Mr F. T.
O'Reilly, a retired civil servant, and Miss Emma Bodkin, ACA, a practising accountant.

None of the new members appears to have had very radical views on
censorship. None was 'exposed to the influence' of an Old Guard on the
Board: Mr Comyn and Mr Figgis had attended meetings only for five
months so far, and, if anything, had been running against the traditional
censorship tide. The only link with the past was through the Secretary
and staff of the Board; the former, whose vast experience of the censorship machinery must have made him indispensable, could not, even if
he had wished to do so, have maintained much of the atmosphere of the
old Board. The new Board was something of an unknown quantity, and
there was no telling whether Mr Comyn and Mr Figgis would find
themselves in agreement with the attitudes of the other members.
However, some eight months after the reconstitution, Mr Traynor (in
reply to a question suggesting that the Board's powers were inadequate)
went on record as saying:

> 'From my own personal experience the Board is working
> smoothly, effectively and efficiently. These are the qualities
> that I have been looking for in the Board, and now that I have
> got them I do not propose to interfere with them.'[22]

The change in the censorship after 1957 was not revolutionary; the
machinery of censorship was maintained and used to the full; but the
attitude of mind of the Board seemed to be quite new.[23] None of the
members shared Professor Magennis's view of the Board as a bulwark
protecting the minds of Irish men and women from the evil influences
of materialism emanating from post-Christian England and America.
Rather, one could say that they regarded their task in the same way as a
British or French board would have regarded it: as one of making it
difficult for the average person to read books which were pornographic
and had no literary merit.

Figure 3

CENSORSHIP BOARD: PERIODICAL PUBLICATIONS: EXAMINATIONS AND
PROHIBITIONS (INCLUDING GROUNDS) 1946–1964

year	No. exam- ined	No. pro- hibited	prohibition grounds				No. of order		
			ob- scenity	birth control	crime	obscen- ity and crime	1st	2nd	3rd
1946	4	1	1				1		
1947	9	8	6	2			4	2	2
1948	13	7	7				2	1	4
1949	4	3	3				1	1	1
1950	71	58	56	2			49	8	1
1951	114	97	97				71	22	4
1952	35	32	29		3		21	9	2
1953	73	60	50	1	2	7	41	15	4
TOTAL	313	266	249	5	5	7	190	58	18
1954	84	77							
1955	59	45							
1956	31	27							
1957	10	7							
1958	157	124	87	3	34		103	20	1
1959	82	54	46	1	10		34	23	
1960	83	66	60	1	5		38	28	
1961	52	43	42	1			29	14	
1962	33	26	24		2		14	12	
1963	38	27	23	1	3		17	10	
1964	31	21	18	2	1		14	7	

In 1958, the first full year of its activity, the new Board banned some 480 books out of a total of 900 which it examined, and although the latter figure was quite substantial, the fact that the proportion of bannings to books examined was of the order of one to two did indicate that the Board was selective. Two other factors should be borne in mind—(1) over one hundred of the prohibition orders were 'repeat orders', the books they referred to not being examined by the Board, and (2) some of the Board's industry must have been provoked by the backlog of complaints accumulated during the period when the censorship was not functioning.[24] As is pointed out elsewhere, this Board was extremely energetic in its examination of periodical publications (see page 168).

If lack of controversy implies public confidence and support, this Board was indeed more successful than any previous Board had been. The few censorship controversies which did arise concerned decisions of previous Boards. Few new bannings were being objected to[25]; and with the exception of the evil literature campaign of December 1957—June 1958, the Board received little criticism from those sections of the community which are normally concerned about the effects of reading on moral conduct.

2 THE RESIGNATIONS OF 1957

Having considered the Board's progress during these years, it remains to focus special attention on the disagreement which took place in 1956-1957 between Professor Pigott, Mr O'Flynn and Mr O'Reilly on the one hand, and Mr Comyn and Mr Figgis on the other. It is the only internal dispute of the Board for which we have a considerable body of evidence from public and private sources.

Very soon after their appointment Professor Pigott realised that the views of Mr Comyn and Mr Figgis on the nature of censorship differed radically from his own. 'The almost invariable decision,' he tells us, 'was three for and two against banning, except in the case of purely pornographic books, which were unanimously banned. According to the Act, if more than one member objects to banning, the book cannot be banned. So two can defeat three.'[26]

This basic disagreement came to a head in February 1957 when the question arose of banning some 'omnibus volumes', i.e. volumes containing two or more unabridged books, one of which was already banned. According to Professor Pigott, 'the invariable practice of the Board, acting on the advice of the Attorney General, was to ban such a book, but this did not mean that the other books in the volume, except the one already banned, were considered objectionable and, of course, if published separately they would not be banned'.[27]

Among the private papers of Professor Pigott are minutes of a meeting of the Board (attended by Messrs Pigott, O'Flynn, Comyn and Figgis) held on 28 March 1957. One of the minutes (No. 6569) reads as follows:

> '*Read*—the Attorney General's opinions on a question raised at last Board meeting (Minute 6560).
>
> '[Without a prohibition order in respect of the omnibus volume booksellers *might* be misled. Alternatively, they *might* evade the prohibition for a while on the pretence that they did

not appreciate that the prohibition on part of an omnibus volume covered the whole volume.

'The only safe course it to make a prohibition order in respect of the omnibus edition.']²⁸

'Mr Comyn was of the opinion that the Attorney General had not given a definite reply to the question, and at the request of the former [it was decided to ask for an explicit direction from the latter on the following point:

'Where a book which is already prohibited is republished as a component part of an omnibus volume is the Board obliged to ban the omnibus volume automatically, or must it examine the volume, and having examined it, is the Board entitled to come to a different opinion ?].'

On 15 April, in reply to a minute of the Board (embodying this query) dated 3 April, Mr P. Berry, Secretary of the Department of Justice, sent the following letter to the Secretary of the Board:

'I am directed by the Minister for Justice to refer to your minute of the 3rd April and to say that while the Attorney General has the duty of advising the several Ministers on matters of law and legal opinion, it is no part of his duty to advise statutory bodies such as the Censorship of Publications Board, and that the Minister is not disposed to ask the Attorney General to advise him further on the specific points upon which a direction is sought for the following reasons, viz., firstly, that it is not for the Minister to give directions to the Board; secondly, that the circumstances in which the Board are obliged to make a prohibition order are set out in Section 7 of the Act of 1946 in clear and unambiguous language which admits of no doubt; and thirdly, that it is no less free from doubt that [the Board would be acquiescing in a futility if, having duly examined an omnibus book which included a prohibited book, they were to decide not to prohibit the omnibus book, since it appears from a previous opinion of the Attorney General that a publication which incorporates a prohibited publication clearly identifiable as such, is *ipso facto* itself a prohibited publication.]'

Despite 'that very definite reply'²⁹ Mr Comyn and Mr Figgis refused (at a meeting on 8 May 1956) to ban two omnibus volumes, and Professor Pigott adjourned the meeting, intending to return the matter to the Minister.

In his statement to the press Professor Pigott himself gave a short account[30] of his two meetings with the Minister, in June and September; among his papers are two incomplete typewritten notes which would appear to have been compiled for this meeting and which it is interesting to reproduce here:

> '. . . censorship where any loophole or means of evasion can be found. They [clearly the new members] take the view that literary merit in a book justifies all else, that artistic considerations must override moral considerations, and they base this claim on Section 6, Sub-section (2) of the 1946 Act. It is obvious to us that no such rule could hold in a Christian country, but fortunately we have in addition concrete evidence of the intention of the Oireachtas (see attached extract No. 1).[31]

> 'They hold that a book, no matter what its nature, must be read out to the bitter end. The other members consider that if the indecency they have seen at any stage of the book is sufficient in nature and extent to convince them that no literary or other merit could excuse it, then there is no need to wade further through it. For their justification in this conviction: they have again the direction of the Oireachtas (extract No. 2).[32]

> 'The Minister is no doubt aware of their refusal to accept the ruling of the Attorney General to the effect that an omnibus volume which contains a prohibited book or story is *ipso facto* prohibited. To us, hair-splitting on this point is nothing short of obstruction. Successive Boards have always loyally accepted the decisions of the various Attornies General. Whether they happened to be in full agreement with them or otherwise, but in this case, above all, it is clear that any course other than that recommended would stultify the Censorship of Publications Act.

The above notes are typed and, as has been said, were probably used by Professor Pigott for his meetings with the Minister, and for the preparation of his statement to the press. His papers also include some handwritten notes, which are not available for publication. They contain further criticism of the new members and of the Civil Liberties Association, and an elaboration of his views on the treatment of sex in literature. Apparently Mr Comyn[33] suggested that the Revenue Commissioners cease forwarding books to the Board.

Only when he realised that he could not influence the Minister in favour of his point of view did the Professor agree to resign.

It would be a very facile assessment of this complicated affair to see Professor Pigott as the villain of the piece. On the precise point of omnibus editions, it would appear that the Professor had merely followed standard practice; and the letter from the Minister on the matter, while in general discounting the opinion of any Attorney General on any censorship problem, does seem to favour the Professor's views. Mr Comyn tried to take advantage of the omnibus edition to reconsider the original decision of the Board on the banned book contained in that omnibus edition: it would seem this is a function proper to the Appeal Board, and not to the Censorship Board. The Minister, by his action in calling for the Professor's resignation and not that of the two new members, would seem to have sided with the latter.

Possibly the most startling feature of the disagreement was Mr Comyn's proposal that the Board no longer accept informal complaints from the Revenue authorities. To anyone at all favourable to censorship this proposal would be nothing less than shocking. For it was—and is—an incontrovertible fact that without such informal complaints the Board would be paralysed (see pages 71 and 171f). Indeed, anyone who interviews one of the 'old members' of this Board can easily be persuaded that Mr Comyn's clear intention at this time was to make use of any opportunity to hinder and render ineffective the working of the censorship. It may well be that the new members saw no hope for censorship as they understood it until the Board had been cleared of all members who followed the tendency to discount literary merit—which had been a feature of all Boards since 1930: and so, in order to provoke the resignation of the old members, Mr Comyn, with Mr Figgis as his consistent supporter, was prepared to force the issue.

Thus the division in the Board went very deep, being based on different attitudes to the importance to be given to the literary merit of books coming before the Board. Professor Pigott put his finger on the nub of the problem when he criticised the fact that the new members were against banning all but 'purely pornographic books'. The *Irish Times* saw the situation in the following light:

> 'The foolish and humiliating Act . . . still stands. On Professor Pigott's admission, however, an attempt was made, with some success and for some months, to administer it in the proper spirit. Two members of the Censorship Board, anyhow, tried to confine it to its reasonable function, which is the

prohibition of "indecent and obscene"—or, as Professor Pigott prefers to call them—"purely pornographic"—books. Their attitude has nothing to do with the charge, so frequently made, that bundles of frankly salacious publications are on sale on the streets of Dublin: it is conceded that the two members of the Board offer no defence to this kind of stuff. Professor Pigott, in fact, makes it clear that the majority on the Board during the early part of this year sought to preserve the traditional defiance of the spirit of the Censorship Act, against the opposition of a minority that preferred to accept the law, and to make it acceptable in the process to normally intelligent people.'[35]

Was the issue as clear-cut as this? According to at least one of the old members it was not: the motto of the old school was 'when in doubt, ban'; that of the new, 'when in doubt, release'. The conservative view was tempered by the attitude: 'There is an Appeal Board; better therefore for the Censorship Board to be slightly strict than for it to decide categorically against banning'. If such an attitude was taken, it would be unjust to say that it acted in defiance of the Act.

Mr D. J. O'Flynn's view of the record of the reconstituted Board is worth reproducing here. Addressing the U.C.D. Law Society on censorship on 25 February 1960,[36] he said:

'In the last two years the present Board has adopted a more liberal attitude. This new policy, we are told, is due to an enlightened Public Opinion. This I would not accept. Merely because a minority have ceased to write letters of complaint to one particular daily newspaper does not entitle us to offer this as evidence of a substantial change in Public Opinion. . . .

'I am convinced that the new policy has created bad results, shown by the type of reading material now granted permission to circulate freely in the country. . . .

'In an effort to appear broadminded the pendulum has now swung too far in the opposite direction. Now the intellectuals are pacified, but the immature are exposed to new dangers and they have no second court of appeal. . . .

'If the powers of Church and State agree that the new broadminded liberal policy of Censorship should persist, then we have a duty to say so clearly and honestly to our parents, teachers and youth leaders, to enable them to realise that Preventive Censorship here is now a dead letter.'[37]

3 THE APPEAL BOARD

As might be expected, the Appeal Board from its very beginning has had a relatively sheltered and tranquil existence. It had the best of both worlds; if it granted a revocation order it could not fail to be popular—at least with the appellants, and in fact scarcely anyone has protested against such a decision—and yet if it rejected an application the public continued to regard the Censorship Board as the villain of the piece.

With the exception of its second year—when it received some 130 applications—it never suffered from the condition of overwork which has been the lot of the Censorship Board. There was never the sheer physical need to resort to the system of marked passages in its examination of books. The fact, too, that most if not all of the works submitted to it were of some supposed literary value was an additional reason for its giving each book a more careful examination than that given by the Censorship Board. And the fact that someone—publisher, editor, author or members of the Oireachtas—had inconvenienced himself to the extent of making application for appeal, was an indication that the book deserved a re-consideration; whereas it would be argued that the Censorship Board, with respect to a certain range of books, would have no fore-knowledge of the public's reaction to a ban, and might for this reason, tend to make decisions with less circumspection.[38]

The first Appeal Board, appointed in 1946 for the statutory three-year period, was composed by Mr Justice K. Haugh (a High Court—later a Supreme Court—judge) as Chairman, Professor James Hogan (Professor of History at University College, Cork), Dr Fitzroy Pyle (reader in English at Trinity College, Dublin), Dr Richard Hayes (the Film Censor) and Mr H. B. O'Hanlon (a Dublin solicitor). Only two changes occurred in the Board during the period: Professor Liam O Briain (Professor of Romance Languages at University College, Galway) took Professor Hogan's place in the 1949–1952 Board; and in October 1954 Professor J. J. Hogan (Professor of English at University College, Dublin) took the place of Dr Hayes, who resigned for health reasons. This stability of tenure is in marked contrast to the many changes which occurred in the Censorship Board over the same period.

Scarcely had the Appeal Board begun to function than it, or the provision referring to it in the 1946 Act, met with strong criticism in the *Irish Times*. Mr Frank O'Connor, whose book *The Midnight Court* was the subject of an unsuccessful appeal, complained that it 'excluded appellant, counsel, witnesses',[39] while another correspondent spoke of 'a purely arbitrary tribunal, bound by no rules of law, no rules of any sort, no authority. . . . The most amazing aspect of the matter is that our authors and publishers agree to the principle of despotic censorship. Their periodic outcries have not been against it, but against particular findings'.[40]

The general tone of the correspondence was, however, academic: particularly so after Professor James Hogan chose to write to justify the Board's decision on the grounds that Mr O'Connor's was a faulty translation, untrue to the original. Professor Hogan accused Mr O'Connor of 'gross mistranslation' and referred to 'his indulgence in the game of searching for what he would like to find in the way of scandalous and offensive passages'. The vast correspondence on this point makes entertaining reading.

On the more general question of the 'openness' of the Board, another member, Dr Pyle, later joined in the controversy to point out that there did exist the possibility of the appellant making submission to the Board in writing, or at the discretion of the Board, in person.

A leading article in the *Irish Times* welcomed this observation, but suggested somewhat mischievously that Dr Pyle's delay of almost a fortnight in writing his letter was due to his 'thinking up' this excuse. The correspondence continued and it was interesting to see Dr Pyle urging the public to make application for appeal of books banned under the 1929 Act:[41] for, under the terms of the new Act application with respect to these books had to be made within a year of the passing of the Act (Section 8, (1)).[42] Dr Pyle did strive to present the public with a good image of the Board and made a sincere appeal for public confidence in the new institution.[43]

Over a year later the Board came in for criticism from Mr Sean O'Faolain, who complained of the Board's 'private way of working'.[44] Once again Dr Pyle (whose manner of dealing with his critics was in sharp contrast with that of the Censorship Board—see page 134f) spoke in defence of the Appeal Board, pointing out that up to that time 85% of the applications made to it had resulted in revocation orders:[45] to which O'Faolain replied that the unbanning was of little use due to the fact that the freed books were out of print and unobtainable.[46] Again Dr Pyle exhorted the public to appeal to the Board. (Rather ironically, the issue of *The Bell* for the same month (January 1948) paid the Appeal Board the compliment of saying that it had 'begun to show flashes of adult good sense';[47] this journal was now under the editorship of Mr Peadar O'Donnell).

Before leaving this subject reference should be made to one other criticism: that contained in Mr Austin Clarke's article on Irish censorship in the *New Statesman and Nation* in 1953, when he said of the Appeal Board that it 'has proved of little use as a corrective. . . . (It) consists mainly of lawyers known for their orthodoxy, and they have shown the traditional caution of their profession'.[48] To most people the fact that 80% of the applications for appeal made between 1946 and 1953 were successful would scarcely indicate that the Board was 'cautious'.

There are extremely few instances of criticism of the Appeal Board on the grounds that it was over-lenient. A few references to such criticism are made elsewhere in this study. Mention might be made here of a protest by the Irish League of Decency (see page 232) in 1956, when that body passed a resolution disapproving of the Board's action in 'permitting periodicals banned for indecency by the Censorship of Publications Board, to re-appear in circulation'.[49] But never has a prohibition order revoked by the Appeal Board been re-promulgated by the Censorship Board.

The point which Dr Fitzroy Pyle made in two of his letters to the *Irish Times*, and on at least one other occasion[50]—namely that there should be more appeals—indicates the main difficulty which the Appeal Board encountered. With the exception of the year 1947, when a considerable number of applications were made (most of these relating to books banned before 1946) the number of applications bore no relation to the number of prohibition orders. The blame for this must be laid at the door of the author, publisher, editor or members of the Oireachtas— if one accepts as equitable the limitations imposed by the Act.

Taking the years 1946 to 1953 (consecutive years for which detailed statistics are available) out of 208 applications made to the Appeal Board, 2 were made by authors, 72 by publishers and 134 by Oireachtas members.[51] Bearing in mind the fact that author, editor or publisher is required to pay a deposit of £5 while an appeal is pending, it is not difficult to understand the relatively few applications from these sources.

Most authors, though paid on a royalty basis, leave the sale of their work entirely in the hands of the publisher; the latter is usually more concerned with the success of a book than the former, for his profit is generally larger. Foreign authors can hardly be expected to worry about the at best meagre sales their books might lose as a result of being banned in Ireland; while Irish authors might reasonably expect the Irish public to concern itself with the technicalities of application on their behalf.

Figure 4

APPEAL BOARD: BOOKS: APPLICATIONS AND REVOCATIONS
(INCLUDING SOURCES) 1946–1964

Year	A applications submitted by			Total A	B revocation orders issued in respect of			Total B	C applications dismissed			Total C
	1	2	3		1	2	3		1	2	3	
1946		1		1							1		1
1947	2	1	133	136	1		32	33				5	5
1948		8		8		8	31	39				6	6
1949		6		6	1	5	2	8		1	1		2
1950		16	1	17		12	1	13		4			4
1951		6		6		6	5	11			4		4
1952		14		14		12	11	23		3	3		6
1953		20		20		17	16	33		3	3		6
TOTAL	2	72	134	208	2	60	98	160		12	22		34
1954*				63				59					4
1955*				59				48					11
1956*				42				27					15
1957*				7				4					3
1958*				3				1					2
1959		3		3		1		1		2			2
1960		9		9		3		3		7			7
1961		8	1	9		1	1	2		7			7
1962		6		6		3		3		2			2
1963		13		13		5		5		6			6
1964		10		10		1		1		9			9
TOTAL		49	1	224		14	1	154		33			68

Key: 1=authors.   2=publishers.   3=members of Oireachtas.

* Detailed statistics for this year are not available; also: the figures in column 'Total A' are for applications considered, not 'total applications'.
For each year or group of years total of revocation orders plus the total of applications dismissed does not necessarily equal the total of applications. This is because not all applications are necessarily considered during the calendar year in which they are made.

Considering the publisher as a businessman interested in the profits to be derived from the Irish market, it may be reasonable to expect him to go out of his way to reopen that market in the case where a book by an Irish author is banned; he is much less likely to do so where books by foreign authors are concerned.[52] Granted this fact the publishers' showing appears to be satisfactory.

The large figure for Oireachtas-inspired applications ceases to be impressive on closer examination, for all but one of these applications were made in a single year (1947), and were due mainly to the efforts of two Senators—Mr T. C. Kingsmill Moore and Professor W. Fearon (a former member of the Censorship Board). Applications by members of the Oireachtas are not burdened with the inconvenience of paying a deposit in respect of each book or periodical; the only difficulty is that of obtaining the support of five Dail or Seanad members. The 1947 Oireachtas applications were made on the initiative of the members themselves; at least there is no evidence of lobbying on the part of the public or of authors or publishers. As presented in the *Reports* the Oireachtas' showing was poor. However, during the 1954–1957 period there was an increase in the number of applications for revocation orders (see Figure 4), and it is possible that members of the Oireachtas were responsible for some few of these.

If the members had made more use of their power to initiate appeals at times when the Censorship Board was under heavy fire, they could at least have demonstrated their interest in removing grievances and sources of public annoyance. They are under no obligation to read a book before applying for appeal: in the same way as it is not necessary to investigate grievances of any other nature before calling for a public enquiry. There is no evidence to support the view that some individual senators or deputies did try to start appeals, but failed to muster sufficient support among their number.

One notable feature of the *Reports* of the Board is that each included a list of books which were the subject of applications, but with which the Board had been unable to deal due to its inability to obtain the requisite number of copies. This drawback was caused by the fact that the book was out of print, or that the applicants did not furnish the Board with copies of the book in question. This and other similar technical matters are dealt with in Chapter Eight.

The remarkable stability of the Appeal Board's membership through-out the period might lead one to wonder whether the success of the Board—as witness much positive approval of its behaviour, and negligible

Figure 5

APPEAL BOARD: PERIODICAL PUBLICATIONS: APPLICATIONS AND
REVOCATION AND VARIATION ORDERS 1946–1964

year	applications	revocation orders granted	applications dismissed	variation orders
1946	4	4		
1947	6	6		
1948	3	3		
1949	3	3		1
1950	2	2		
1951	12	10	2	
1952	11	5	6	
1953	12	10	2	
1954	20	14	6	
1955	26	18	8	
1956	13	7	6	2
1957	3	1	4	
1958	3	1	2	
1959	1		1	
1960	7	2	2	2
1961	6	1	5	1
1962	5	2	3	
1963	3	1	1	
1964	2		3	
TOTAL	142	90	51	6

In those years for which detailed statistics are available (i.e. 1946–1953 inclusive
and 1958) all applications were made by publishers. All applications for variation
orders were made by publishers.

criticism—is not due more to the personal qualities and outlook of its
members than to the nature of the Board as an institution, its position
in the censorship machinery and relatively comfortable conditions of
work.

4 THE 'PUBLIC RELATIONS' OF THE CENSORSHIP BOARD

As has been quite evident throughout the course of this study, public
criticism of the Board was based on the grounds that it ignored those
clauses of the Acts which gave protection to work of literary merit: on

this score the Board was accused of 'formidable backwardness'[53] or of downright contempt for those provisions of the Acts. However, there were other aspects of the Board's behaviour to which objection was, or could be, taken.

One of these is that the Board, on one or two occasions at least, gave the impression that it was at odds with the Appeal Board, or at least disagreed with that Board's decisions. Thus, when the *Sunday Times* and the *Observer*[54] on one occasion reported that the Censorship Board had revised its opinion on a book, a week later a letter from the Secretary appeared in both papers. He wrote:

> 'I am directed by the Censorship of Publications Board to inform you that this is incorrect. The ban on the book in question was removed by the Appeal Board and not by the Censorship Board which originally imposed the ban and has not changed its opinion of the book.'

It will be remembered that in the 1945 debates, when the Appeal Board provisions were under discussion, Professor Magennis was very concerned that the Appeal Board should have at least the same number of members as the Censorship Board, so that there should be no danger of the Appeal Board being regarded as the more 'intelligent' of the two, the one to whose views more weight should be given.[55]

Another minor source of irritation was the delay involved in publishing the Board's *Annual Reports*. These reports were a welcome feature of censorship after 1946.[56] Prior to that time official information regarding the censorship could be obtained only through the *Iris Oifigiuil* and the *Register of Prohibited Publications*.[57] These *Annual Reports* (of the Censorship Board and of the Appeal Board) were published bi-annually after 1946, while the Register was published at irregular intervals either in full or in the form of supplements. Information included in the *Reports* gave statistics of the number of meetings held, an analysis of the sources of complaints, details of the number of books and periodicals examined, as distinct from the number banned, etc. Most of this information is incorporated in the statistical appendices and tables. However, grateful though the public must have been for this information, it was quick to complain[58] that there was a considerable delay in publishing these *Reports*. The *Reports* for 1952 and 1953, for example, were not published until August 1955,[59] a time-lag which rendered them relatively useless for the purpose of controversy. Criticism for this delay should probably be aimed at the Minister for Justice or his department or the printers responsible, for the *Reports* (addressed to the Minister) are usually dated the January after the end of each two-year period: in other words the Board itself was not to blame.

There is no statutory obligation on the Minister or the Board to make such reports available to the public; indeed, as it happened, no *Reports* were published for the years 1954 to 1957 inclusive. From the fact that the Office of Censorship of Publications has furnished me on two occasions with sets of certain statistics (for this period) which did not agree with each other, it would appear that the Boards did not even prepare *Reports* to the Minister in these years. The Secretary of the Board at the time has confirmed (in an interview) that this was the case, and states that it was due to the fact that the Minister did not ask the Board for *Reports* for these years.

Another and more important source of irritation lay in the nature of the letters from the Board which were published in the press.[60] On many occasions in reply to criticism, the Censorship Board made a public statement of its own case by way of letter signed by the Secretary on its behalf; these letters are useful as being indicative of the attitude and temper of the Board. Most of them were written in reply to attacks which constituted substantial criticism of the Board; they were not provoked by casual criticism of individual bannings. However, while they were effective in that they expressed the point of view of the very source of the censorship—and incidentally added fuel to the fire of controversy—the tone in which they were written was not calculated to help the Board's case.

At different times during the period members of the public complained that the self-righteous tone of the letters came ill from public servants. One letter in the *Irish Times*, for example, complained that 'some of the letters have . . . verged on the bad-tempered, the truculent and the obstreperous'.[61] An extreme instance of this was a letter from the Board to the *Irish Times* in June 1954. This letter was provoked by a third leader in that paper[62] which had praised Mr Justice Stable who, during a recent case of obscene libel in London, had instructed the jury to go home and read the book in question from cover to cover: 'Don't pick out the highlights. Read it as a book.' The *Irish Times* comment was that 'these sentences ought to be inscribed in letters of gold over the seat of the Chairman of our Censorship of Publications Board'. This mild remark drew an extremely strong letter from the Secretary of the Board:

> 'We would have had nothing to say to this fresh display by the *Irish Times* of its slavish worship of everything English and its ill-conceived hatred of all things Irish if only it had confined

itself to facts when pontificating on the subject of censorship of publications.'[63]

He went on to defend the Irish system as better than the English one; despite the fact that it was not the function of the Board to provide apologia for the Acts which had given it birth. Two days later a correspondent of the paper wrote to complain that 'we have been treated over the past few months to a childish, hysterical, semi-literate stream of personal abuse, in the McCarthy style, against anyone who questions the workings of the Act. . . . The Minister should teach the Board better manners'. Another letter called for the resignation of the Board for its 'scurrilous attack on a newspaper for merely giving ventilation to a matter of public concern'.

On other occasions the Board appeared to quibble. In May 1953, for example, when the *Irish Times* in the course of an article mentioned that Lynn Doyle 'sat on the Censorship Board' the Secretary took the trouble to write on the Board's behalf to point out that Lynn Doyle never sat on the Board or ever met any of its members.[64] Technically this was true, but it was calculated to have the average reader understand that Lynn Doyle had never been a member of the Board, which of course was quite untrue. In the same letter the Board claimed that it had won 'an absolute victory' in its correspondence in the *Irish Times* at the time of Dr Smyth's resignation.

An earlier example of the Board's reaction to criticism is its treatment of the Dublin *Evening Mail* in 1943. In an editorial on 15 November 1943 that paper, on the meagre excuse of a recent technical school debate on censorship, launched a ferocious attack on the Board: it spoke of 'the ramshackle machinery of censorship' and protested that:

> 'the censors do not know where their functions begin and end; it is a sad reflection on the Government that they continually overstep their powers and do so with impunity. . . . No one seems to care sufficiently that the Censorship Board is breaking the law and should be prosecuted.'

Two months later the editor of this paper received a letter from the Secretary of the Censorship Board, who remarked on this editorial's 'peculiar recklessness of statement' and would have it that it exhibited 'venomous malice towards the members of the Board'. The Board had had opinion of counsel on the article, he said, and had been advised that the publication of the editorial constituted a libel. The *Evening Mail* made reparation for its fault in the manner requested by the Secretary:

a full and unqualified apology was published together with the Secretary's letter.[65] And there the matter died.

Since these letters occur right through the period, and are all written in the same tone and style, it seems likely that they were composed by the same person. It is doubtful if this person was a member of the Board. It is more likely that they were the work of the Secretary, the principal full-time official of the Board. But whatever their origin, they were published as letters from the Board, and the Board as a whole accepted responsibility for their contents and tone. That they were objectionable seems beyond doubt. At any rate they had the effect of presenting the public with an unattractive image of the Board which increased its dislike for censorship.

Since 1956 the Board has seldom written to the press.[66]

5 CENSORSHIP AND BIRTH-CONTROL

Section 7 of the Censorship of Publications Act 1946 lays down the grounds on which books and periodicals may be prohibited; one of these has become almost a household phrase—'indecent or obscene'; its companion, however, is less well-known and certainly less controversial:

> 'That it advocates the unnatural prevention of conception or the procurement of abortion or miscarriage by use of any method, treatment or appliance for the purpose of such prevention or procurement.'

Since birth-control has been propagated on a large scale in modern Europe only in the past thirty or forty years, and since the authority of most churches was solidly against it for many years, it is relatively easy to understand how the proscription on the propaganda of its methods etc. was accepted in Ireland by almost all sections of the community in 1929 (in 1926 the B.B.C. could still give Julian Huxley a dressing-down for simply using the word birth-control). The matter did not really come up again at the time of the 1946 Act, which was an amending Act dealing mainly with the 'obscene and indecent' side of the censorship; only a few casual references were made to the question of birth-control. Even in the decade after the passing of this Act comment and controversy about this question are extremely difficult to find. This is both easy and difficult to understand; easy, because Catholics greatly predominate in the State and they might be expected to conform, at least publicly, with the doctrine of the Church on this subject—although they might support a campaign to drop this prohibition, on a 'public right–private wrong' basis; and difficult to understand, because the Protestant attitude to the question has certainly become much less fixed in recent years—one could expect the prohibition to weigh on Protestants more than on Catholics.[67] At all events the Protestant and non-religious sectors of the community remained extremely quiet, scarcely ever raising their voice in protest against the proscription; one can only deduce from that that they do not feel particularly irked by this restriction, or that they consider it to be very impolitic to attempt to change the Acts on this point.

The negative evidence in support of this view is most impressive. *The Church of Ireland Gazette*, for example, never once complained of the restriction during the post-1946 period: at least never in its articles on censorship, which in themselves were few and far between. In his book *The Face and Mind of Ireland*, Arland Ussher, a Protestant, could devote a whole section to the censorship question without once mentioning the birth-control restriction. At the Mansion House Meeting in 1956 no mention was made of it by the principal speakers. In an article in the *Spectator* dealing with the position of Protestants in Eire (23 September 1949) the question of birth-control or of divorce was not even raised.[68] In fact, I know of no sustained controversy centering on this point.

Positive evidence of disagreement with the birth-control prohibition occurred in letters to the papers on the occasion of the banning of particular books. In July 1946 one finds the banning of *Men, Women and God* by A. Herbert Gray, a book first published fifteen years before. The books was banned on the grounds of being indecent and obscene and of advocating birth-control. A letter to the *Irish Times* accused the Censorship Board of reading 'advocating' as 'mentioning'.[69] The prohibition order was later revoked, but the ban was the subject of some discussion in the controversy that ensued after the publication of Mr Paul Blanshard's *The Irish and Catholic Power*.[70]

When the *Report* of the Royal Commission on Population was published in Britain in 1949 the *Irish Catholic* protested vigorously against its recommendations, though it made no suggestion about banning it.[71] However, in October 1948 the *Report* was banned on birth-control grounds, a decision whose wisdom even the *Irish Press*—normally reticent on censorship matters—questioned. *The Leader* too, in an editorial on 'Our Censorship',[72] deplored this fresh example of the Censorship Board's 'excess of zeal'. It considered the banning 'an amazing decision' and suggested that 'proper directives should be given to ensure that works of a non-popular, scientific character should not be dealt with in the same way as vulgar or indecent publications intended for wide-spread circulation'.

The prohibition order on this book was revoked in January 1950, but shortly after the revocation there was a notable exchange of letters in the *Irish Times* (the 'Liberal Ethic' correspondence),[73] in which the revocation was challenged. The *Report* had been banned under Section 7 of the 1946 Act and revoked under Section 8 of the same Act; but the point was now made that it should still come within Section 16 of the 1929 Act which prohibits the sale, etc., of any birth-control book or periodical publication *whether or not* such book or periodical appears on the list of prohibited publications. The question of the mandatory nature of this Section was not, unfortunately, fully thrashed out in the correspondence. It is of course of great importance, and in fact, constitutes the legal background to the '*Observer* Incident'.

The birth-control book which cast the longest shadow was undoubtedly *Laws of Life* by Halliday Sutherland, which remained on the Register of Prohibited Publications throughout the period. It does not, however, concern us here because no artificial birth-control issue was involved in the book or in the debate concerning it.

The one major controversy which grew out of the birth-control prohibition was the *Observer* Incident of April 1956. The ins and outs of this curious affair are still a closed book to the Irish public, mainly due to the varied accounts given as to the facts of the case. In view of this I have tried to make a thorough investigation of the subject.

The morning newspapers of 2 April 1956 all carried news of the 'impounding' of the issue of the *Observer* of the previous day (Easter Sunday). The entire consignment of this paper was, the *Irish Times* understood, 'impounded'[74] because it carried an article on 'Family Planning', which had been advertised in advance in the previous issue. The comment and correspondence which grew out of this incident dealt with two distinct points: the responsibility for the 'impounding' and the desirability of banning birth-control publications, the former of these questions being decidedly the more important.

On 3 April no information was forthcoming from any quarter as to what actually had happened, and on 5 April the *Irish Times* devoted its first leader to an attempt to clarify the situation. Pointing out that the Censorship Act did not empower seizure of periodicals, it showed that either the Board had acted illegally or else the impounding had been carried out under another Act: the former it considered the more likely of the two hypotheses. However, in its news columns on the same day it reported that people were coming round to the view that the Customs were responsible; but still no definite information was available: the copies were still withheld from the booksellers and newsagents; the members of the Censorship Board were on Easter holidays, and the Government Information Bureau declined to give any information in reply to the numerous queries it received. With the announcement on 5 April by the Department of Justice that the Censorship Board did not make a prohibition order in respect of the *Observer*, attention was concentrated on the Customs officials and their powers in this area. However, the following day the Government Information Bureau stated that 'on enquiry from official sources it was ascertained that the Customs authorities did not seize or prohibit the circulation of copies last Sunday'. (In the same issue was a report that the Committee of the Irish Retail Newsagents, Booksellers and Stationers Association had issued a statement endorsing the action—unspecified—of preventing the distribution of the paper.) The *Observer* itself still maintained that the Customs impounded the papers[75] and its next issue (8 April) carried only the briefest account of the incident and an indication that readers could obtain copies of the 'impounded issue' from London, in view of the Minister for Justice's statement that no import licence was required.

Thus, a full week after the incident, the public was completely in the dark as to what had actually happened: both the Censorship Board and the Customs officials had denied that they were involved. Correspondence dragged on—in the *Irish Times* particularly—for another week or more, and no additional information was made available by the Government Information Bureau—with the notable exception of a statement to the effect that the matter was now one for the distributor.[76]

When the Seanad met on 18 April, Dr Owen Sheehy Skeffington brought the House's attention to the matter by asking for further information, complaining of the Government's failure to make an early and frank public statement on the matter, but the Chairman informed him that he had 'ascertained that no action was taken to prevent the distribution of this paper by, or on the authority of, any Minister. In these circumstances I must rule that Ministerial responsibility is not at issue, and therefore the matter is not suitable to be raised in this manner' [at the Adjournment].[77] When Dr Skeffington then said he was not satisfied that no action had been taken without the authority of the Minister he was rather abruptly told not to argue with the Chair. In passing, it may be noted that Dr Skeffington received little or no backing in the House on this, a matter which should have been pressed—Dr

Skeffington did try to have it debated—until the truth was made available. The *Leader*, to mention one periodical, protested against the treatment he had received:

> 'Surely, the case is one which asks something more of the authorities than a formal washing of hands, and the donning of a halo of self-exculpation? Thanks very largely to the efficient functioning of the Dublin grapevine, a good many people in the capital are better informed than they were three weeks ago of the background facts of the affair; but Dublin isn't Ireland, and as far as the majority of people, at home and abroad, are concerned, the main question is still unanswered.
>
> 'We have already committed ourselves to the view that— whatever may be thought of the *Observer*, or the article which caused the trouble—high matters of democratic principle are involved in this unhappy business. We see no reason to discard the judgment now. In all the circumstances, we feel that the authorities might properly have done more than they did to clear up the mystery and give the people the facts. For that reason particularly, we regret that the matter did not come to discussion in the Senate. Presumably, the Chairman was well within his rights in refusing Dr Sheehy Skeffington's motion on the ground that Ministerial responsibility was not an issue; but the uninstructed layman will find some difficulty in persuading himself that one of the month's biggest news "sensations" involved no element of "urgent public importance".'[78]

Thwarted in the House, Senator Skeffington now put before the public all the information at his disposal, by publishing in the *Irish Times*[79] his correspondence with the Revenue Commissioners on the subject. This only served to underline the atmosphere of mystery which characterised the whole affair.

This correspondence may be summarised as follows: On 5 April, four days after the event, Dr Skeffington wrote to the Revenue Commissioners asking for permission to import one copy of the previous, and one copy of the next issue of the *Observer*. The Commissioners replied that no permit was required. He then asked whether any one employed by them, or any department of theirs, took any action to delay or hinder the distribution of the issue in question. Their reply was that the issue was not seized or prohibited by the Customs authorities. Dr Skeffington then asked whether they had done anything other than 'seize' or 'prohibit': whether in fact any instruction or advice had been given to any of their officials. To this the Revenue Commissioners replied that they were not at liberty to discuss any matters regarding an individual importation with any person other than the importer or his authorised agent.

Here the matter rested until later in the month, when at the Mansion House meeting organised by the Irish Association of Civil Liberty, Mr Sean O'Faolain had the last word. In his summing up at the close of the meeting O'Faolain spoke of 'one point which had not been made':

> 'There is a case of censorship by fear—a sort of psychosis which is not easy to lay one's hands on. Reference has been made, for example, to the case of the *Observer* a couple of weeks ago. The actual truth of what happened seems to me to be both much more interesting and amusing than anything which has been forced into the press by the efforts of the press.
>
> 'A gentleman whose duty it was to collect the newspaper every Sunday morning went to Collinstown Aerodrome. He evidently had a certain fear as to the consequences if he distributed the *Observer*. And well he might, since there is a clause in the Censorship Act which imposes a possible penalty of £50, and a period of imprisonment for anybody who distributes any document advocating contraceptives. Mr Kirwan (the distributor) decided not to move the papers. It was the duty of the Government, which has imposed a form of censorship on the country and imposed these rules on the citizens, to inform citizens as to whether they may be entitled to distribute and receive certain newspapers. No such information was forthcoming. Eventually, it was elicited that no official ban lay upon this paper.
>
> 'So the position is that this psychosis, or this fear, exists all over the country.'[80]

Dr Skeffington has given me a slightly different version of the story. Around 4 April he received a call from a journalist who told him that he had been at Dublin Airport (Collinstown) when the distributor's carrier arrived to collect the consignment on the early morning of 1 April. But precisely at this moment the Customs official at the airport received a telephone call 'warning' him about the paper, and asking him to impound it (or such was the journalist's interpretation). Then followed a series of telephone calls (one to the Censorship Board, it was suggested). Eventually the carrier left—without the consignment *and* without any document to the effect that a seizure had been made. Dr Skeffington later approached the distributor, Mr Kirwan, for information, but while he thanked Dr Skeffington for his interest he refused, almost apologetically, to comment. Then Dr Skeffington, in a last attempt to discover the truth, proposed to the *Observer* that they bring the matter to the Courts: but they were not prepared to do so, since this would have meant prosecuting their distributor with whom they were on excellent terms, and whom they did not want to put in an awkward position. And there the matter rested.

Of these two versions the one which has gained the greatest credence is O'Faolain's: the distributor called at the airport; there a Customs official casually remarked that if he distributed the paper he, and all his retailers, might leave themselves open to prosecution; the distributor was unwilling to undertake that risk, preferring to have a clear-cut view of his legal position. This uncertainty on the distributor's part (whether spontaneous or provoked) was a natural consequence of the mandatory nature of Section 16 of the 1929 Act, and there is every possibility that something similar may happen in the future—a repetition of the *Observer* Incident could be avoided only by an amendment of the Act which would require a birth-control publication to have been formally prohibited by the Censorship Board before its distributor could be proceeded against. All this having been said, it remains true that this was an unpleasant affair, mainly because of the secrecy which characterised it. For our present purpose it should be pointed out that, though it does form part of the general censorship story, there is no proof that the Censorship Board was, in fact, in any way concerned.[81] It is also true that free discussion and advocacy of birth-control even in the Irish press in recent years makes the whole incident rather like a fairy-tale.

This incident did provoke one reader of the *Irish Times* to protest in the following manner about the whole birth-control prohibition: He wrote:

> 'It is characteristic of life for the religious minority of this democratic Republic that they are bruised into accepting an endless series of restrictions on their . . . liberty—minor jabs of the needle into the skin so inured to such treatment that it no longer responds. One lives and works here; one accepts, for the most part, battered into resignation. One tries, almost subconsciously, to avoid becoming constantly aroused,'

and went on to suggest that books dealing with birth-control should be available for purchase, but that a warning should be shown making clear to Catholics their Church's proscription. As it was, the 'religious minority . . . was being denied its civil liberties *in order to protect* the majority from itself'. Protestants were 'not afraid of family planning'.[82]

Although birth-control literature is not on sale in the country, private individuals who order it from British booksellers and publishers can usually get it by post, since the Customs authorities are not addicted to opening small parcels of books, especially if they do not carry a publisher's label. The same holds good for birth-control appliances. Individuals can, furthermore, obtain advice from their doctor on this subject. In the course of an interview with the author on this subject, a leading Dublin firm of medical suppliers has indicated that it does obtain books on birth control for married couples directed to it by a medical doctor. Upon receipt of a prescription, the firm orders the book and its experience is that never once has the order been stopped. If ever it were, the firm would try to obtain a permit for importing the book. The firm in question is a reputable one, and it is suggested that parcels addressed to certain other firms and containing such books would be more likely to be examined and stopped.

In summing up we can merely reaffirm our finding that birth-control censorship has never been a major issue, and shows no immediate sign of becoming one: this may be partly because birth-control discussion and advocacy are now quite free in the country and there is a growing access to chemical contraceptives. To the average Irishman, censorship of publications still means the banning of books and periodicals as indecent.

VII

Censorship 1946-58: Public Opinion

This chapter deals with public reaction to the Censorship Board and its decisions in the period under review. Only casual reference is made to the supporters of the censorship, for these were by and large lost amid the host of its critics. Vocal support for the Censorship Board as such was almost always the effect of criticism; it rarely appeared spontaneously; no one wrote to the papers lauding a decision of the Board: many wrote to register their alarm at the banning of this or that particular book. Real evidence of the support which the censorship received is to be found in that acquiescence in its decisions which characterised the great majority of the public; and it is necessary to bear this acquiescence in mind when reading the paragraphs that follow.[1] This section avoids, in so far as possible, those specific controversies dealt with in other sections and in Appendices 7 and 8.

1 THE BOARD ATTACKED

The period opened with two noisy controversies hinging on the newest aspect of censorship, and specifically on its decision on Frank O'Connor's *The Midnight Court* (see page 53 and Appendix 7). Dr Pyle and Professor Hogan of the Appeal Board, Frank O'Connor, Sean O'Faolain and the Secretary of the Censorship Board exchanged vast letters in the *Irish Times* in the familiar manner. This was followed by a lengthy controversy in July 1949. Dr J. D. Smyth resigned from the Censorship Board in protest against the method followed by the Board's staff of marking doubtful passages in books before they were read by the censors. The Censorship Board, to whom he had given no forewarning of his resignation, immediately made public its denial of and resentment at his charge that the Act was being maladministered, and asked him to make a public withdrawal of his allegation; in its letter to the *Irish Times* (14 July) it quoted liberally from the 1929 censorship debates, using particularly the remarks of the then Minister for Justice as a gloss on the

Censorship Acts, a practice which was followed by the Board in many other controversies in which it took part. The method of marking passages was a favourite point with critics of the Board and was mentioned often in the years which followed; it was met equally often by the Board and by individual members of it.[2]

In 1950–1953 criticism of censorship was relatively scattered and it is not until 1954 that there was another energetic attack on the Board. This was occasioned by the publication in England of Mr Paul Blanshard's *The Irish and Catholic Power*.[3] Mr Blanshard was a staunch upholder of a liberal ethic and, as such, two of his particular enemies were the Catholic Church and censorship. He had already published a book dealing with the threat to democracy which the Catholic Church offered in America, and another on *The Right to Read*, a pamphlet on literary censorship in America.[4] In Ireland he found censorship in a Catholic state, so to speak, and one of the most virulent chapters in his book deals with the official and unofficial censorship in the country. Like all his writing, his account of censorship was a curious mixture of facts, half-facts, emotion and personal opinions. The following quotations are chosen at random:

> 'If two of the five members (of the Board) consider the work printable, it is saved from condemnation; perhaps this is one reason why the Board has never at any one time had more than one non-Catholic member.' (p. 76). ['Publishable' not 'printable' is the correct word to use in this context ('printable' implies licensing). For some months in 1937 there were two Protestants on the Board: Professor Fearon and Lynn Doyle.]
>
> 'Complaints against books usually come into the Censorship Board from small semi-fanatical Catholic groups' (p. 79). [In fact, the vast majority of books received by the Board are and were sent by the Customs authorities.]
>
> 'The sessions of the Board, presided over by a priest [he refers to the period during which Dr Smyth was on the Board] were technically free for frank discussion, but in practice the Catholic members did not dare to express "anti-Catholic" opinions in the presence of the priest' (p. 78). [With the exception of Professor Magennis's term as Chairman (1942–1946) this position had since 1930 been occupied by a Catholic priest. See Appendix 4].
>
> 'Irish Catholics are not permitted under canon law to read

them (his books *American Freedom* and *Communism, Democracy and Catholic Power*). Seminary students have no way to get the offending volume unless they commit a mortal sin by purchasing it at a non-Catholic bookstore' (p. 102). [Mr Blanshard's books were never on the Index. In so far as they attack the Catholic Church they might come under the general ban of Canon 1399, par. 3 and 4. The point about the bookstore is quite ridiculous.]

In his book Blanshard claimed that he had 'interviewed' the Secretary of the Censorship Board and had consulted 'handwritten records of the Board'; it was on this claim that the most substantial, and the most amusing, part of the ensuing correspondence turned: the Secretary insisting that he had never met Blanshard and Blanshard insisting as vehemently that he had. An impasse was reached until Mr Blanshard gave his definition of 'interview' as a 'formal or informal, casual or arranged' meeting,[5] and stated that he had not given his name when he called at the Board's office. The Secretary of the Board remained unconvinced of his sincerity. During this angry correspondence Dr Sheehy Skeffington added fuel to the fire by quoting the Jesuit weekly *America* as saying that 'Censorship . . . is always fraught with danger. It easily leads to abuses. It has led to such abuses in Ireland'.[6]

Early in 1956, a new controversy was sparked off by an address which the Chairman of the Censorship Board, the Reverend J. Deery, gave to the Dublin Institute of Catholic Sociology. As reported in the papers, he said he was of the opinion that 'one page in a book could be more dangerous than fifty in another if it took the form of an attack on the Catholic faith'[7]—a remark which strongly suggested that the Board might use specifically Catholic criteria in coming to its decisions.[8] The correspondence which followed[9] continued almost up to the *Observer* Incident —which in turn was followed by a noteworthy debate on censorship sponsored by the Irish Association of Civil Liberty, and held in the Mansion House, Dublin.

This Association, which held its first public meeting in October 1948,[10] had always kept a close eye on the Censorship Board and had become so critical of the decisions of the Board that in March of 1956 it had organised a public petition[11] to the Taoiseach (Mr J. A. Costello), calling on him to set up a commission to investigate the workings of the Board. The Mansion House Meeting was organised to attract public attention to the censorship question, and incidentally to the petition.

The meeting is of interest because of the attention it received and also because the opinions voiced at it are in some way a cross-section of the various attitudes to censorship in principle, and censorship as it was being practised at the time. The principal speakers were Mr Thomas Finlay, TD, Professor J. D. Smyth, Mr Denis Johnson and Father Roland Burke Savage, SJ; Mr Sean O'Faolain[12] was in the Chair.[13]

Mr Finlay accepted the principle of censorship, especially on the grounds that the great mass of the people were literate but uneducated (a modern phenomenon):

> 'The output of literature created by us or directed by us or inspired by us is only a drop in the ocean of the literature published in the English language. It seems to me that this being so, and there being an undoubted advance in what I might describe as evil literature, an increase in its distribution, its attraction and in the variety and energy of its method of distribution, all these things mean that if you expose a person who can read, but is of immature judgement, to all forms of literature on the basis that if he can read the good he can read the bad as well, and if he can read the bad he can read the good as well, you will not give him freedom to develop, to create his own judgements and make his own choices; that, in fact, as things stand at present you are not giving him a fair freedom.'

He went on to point out what appeared to be the three main charges being made against the Censorship Board: (1) that it was not representative of the generality of opinion in the country and did not have a sufficiently broadly-based accepted or common standard of morality; (2) that it neglected to observe Section 6, ss. 2 (1) of the 1946 Act; and (3) that it did not read books *in toto*. While suggesting remedies, he warned that unforeseen disadvantages might attend the introduction of modifications in the law: 'if we should even in error cut down the real effectiveness of censorship of literature in this country in an attempt to improve the machinery, it is not in our own generation, but in the next generation that we would reap the rewards of that fatal act.'

Professor Smyth gave an account of the practical working of the Board, based on his personal experience. Father Burke Savage suggested the setting up of three or four boards, each to deal with specific groups of publications such as American periodicals, British periodicals, novels or more serious works. Other speakers objected to: the presence of a Roman Catholic priest on the Board; the presence of laymen on the Board; the absence of women on the Board; the banning of books by

Margaret Mead (these were banned in 1944); the fact that Customs officials banned books (which they do not); the '*Observer* mystery'; and State-imposed virtue. The meeting was closed by Mr O'Faolain, who spoke of the seven censorships existing in Ireland:

1. Censorship by fear (shades of the *Observer* Incident).
2. Censorship by the bookseller (on behalf of libraries).
3. Censorship by librarians.
4. Censorship by library users.
5. Censorship by library committees.
6. Censorship by the Censorship Board.
7. Censorship by the public (especially clergymen) exercised on book-shops particularly.

'Censorship was,' Mr O'Faolain said, 'an obstacle race which books have to go through before they reach you. They might be considered as horses and better put before the N.S.P.C.A. than the Censorship Board.'

This meeting, and the petition organised by the Association (signed by university professors, authors, members of the clergy, professional people and others) did not succeed in bringing about the appointment of the committee of enquiry as desired, but it is likely that they were instrumental in causing the Minister to delay the appointment of new members of the Board to the vacancies created by the death of District Justice O'Sullivan and the resignation of Mgr Deery, which occurred in March 1956 and June 1956 respectively. Mr A. F. Comyn and Mr R. R. Figgis, the new members eventually appointed—after six months, during which period the Board did not function—were certainly accept-able to the Association: Professor Pigott later described them as 'its candidates' (see page 120).

May of the following year brought an interesting correspondence in the *Irish Times* in which the playwright Sean O'Casey was a protagonist. O'Casey protested violently that Customs officials stopped copies of a book of his from getting into the country: 'every copy sent to a customer was unceremoniously returned to the publisher. This had been done so often that the publisher has decided to forward no more of this book to any customer's order'. O'Casey did not say whether the book in question was on the banned list; presumably it was. He went on to attack the whole idea of literary censorship and to affirm that 'A word or action is obscene only when the mind thinks it to be so.'[14] In reply another reader asked:

'Whose mind? That of a Christian? A pagan? A sex-maniac? A Manichee? An existentialist?'

which in turn induced Dr Monk Gibbon to remark rather more soberly:

> 'I should imagine . . . that it was fairly clear that reading can influence outlook and that outlook eventually determines conduct. Before we put dust and ashes upon our heads for the many past absurdities of our censorship, let us at least remember that there is such a thing as social decadence. . . . While France is horrified by the number of her 'teen-age alcoholics, while England contemplates with dismay a rapidly mounting graph for juvenile crime, and the U.S.A. imposes a death sentence for drug-pedalling, we have the less disagreeable task of regretting our prudery, our lack of moral courage, and the fact that one of the dirtiest and most denigrating books of modern times had its origin in Dublin.'[15]

O'Casey replied:

> 'Here we have bishops, priests and deacons, a Censorship Board, vigilant librarians, confraternities and sodalities, Duce Maria (*sic*),[16] Legions of Mary, knights of this Christian order and knights of that one, all surrounding the sinner's free-will in an embattled circle. . . . The banning of bombs is more to the point than the banning of books, and Christians should know this better than anyone else.'[17]

Even O'Casey himself admitted that contributions of the type to which he is addicted are not calculated to produce results. The most they have done has been to keep the censorship question alive during those—few—periods when things were quiet.

With the exception of this correspondence 1957 was a singularly quite year for the censorship, until the month of December; but it was this apparent calm—itself a product of the reduction in the number of books banned—that determined Professor Pigott, the former Chairman of the Board, who had resigned the previous October, to publish his statement explaining the reasons for his resignation and criticising the 'two recalcitrant members' (Mr Comyn and Mr Figgis) who were, in his opinion, hindering the work of the Censorship Board.[18] In a very strong editorial on 6 December the *Irish Times* criticised 'the foolish and humiliating Act which is probably without parallel in any democratic country', and took Professor Pigott severely to task for complaining that the new members of the Board would vote in favour of the banning only of 'purely pornographic books'. It went on to criticise the 1946 Act on the grounds that the words 'in its general tendency' (qualifying the label 'indecent or obscene') were removed from it, thus constituting an 'Act of Indemnity' for the past mistakes of the Board.[19] 'From that time onward . . . any crank could make a case against a book; and as things turned out, the exercise of censorship became wilder and less discriminating than ever'. The correspondence between Professor Pigott and Dr Skeffington hinged mainly on this question of standards, on what weight the Board should give to the literary, artistic and scientific merit of a book. Professor Pigott, replying to the editorial, explained what he meant by 'pure pornography':

> 'books that openly deride chastity and advocate sexual license as trial marriages and the like. . . . None but a moral moron would refuse to ban them. The same unanimity was not, however, always manifested when the Board came to deal with examples of that Freudian-inspired fiction which delights to portray, in the name of realism, details of seductions, adulteries and free-love orgies.'

He insisted that the censorship was 'primarily a moral censorship. . . . Hence books, written by whomsoever, must be judged by purely moral standards, unless people are prepared to regard literary merit as of greater importance than moral rectitude'.[20] In support of his views he quoted liberally from Mr Fitzgerald-Kenney's speeches in the 1929 debates. Dr Skeffington replied with other sections of the same speeches which seemed to support the opposite view and followed up with an attack on six decisions of the Censorship Board, spread over the previous fourteen years (these included *Laws of Life*). The correspondence then turned to the more doctrinal theme of belief in original sin (which Dr Skeffington denied) and was in danger of being interminable, until a mistake by Professor Pigott brought it to an ignominious close. This mistake concerned the prohibition order on *Laws of Life* which Dr Skeffington said applied to all editions of the book. Professor Pigott insisted it applied to only one edition, and asked whether Dr Skeffington's persistence in this matter was due to 'ignorance, crassness or lack of common sense'. But Dr Skeffington was right, and eventually Professor Pigott unhesitatingly withdrew all that he had said about the 1941 ban[21] on this book, and elegantly apologised to his opponent. Another strand in the exchange dealt with the alleged influence of the Civil Liberty Association in the Board through the appointment of Mr Comyn and Mr Figgis to it (see page 120).

All that can be said about this correspondence is that it was at times in bad taste, and did little to win support for the previous Boards, or indeed for Professor Pigott's case.

Professor Pigott was heard in public various times during 1958, notably at a debate on 12 January, where he suggested that, in view of the amount of books it had to deal with, the membership of the Board should be a full-time, paid (but not pensionable) job for selected persons, not drawn from the Civil Service, who would be removable by the Minister if they proved unsatisfactory, and that either the Censorship Board or the Appeal Board should be composed entirely of women, 'because women were more affected by immoral literature';[22] he also called for an increase in the number of customs officials engaged on 'censorship' work, and advocated that majority rules should operate in both Boards. In March he repeated his claim that the deciding factor in a censorship decision should be a moral and not a literary one; he also suggested that the provision in the Act for a book being referred to the Appeal Board at the request of five members of the Oireachtas should be amended so that it would be necessary for the members to have read the book before doing so.[23]

In addition to *The Irish and Catholic Power*, criticism of the censorship is to be found in various other books and articles published during the period. Sean O'Faolain, in *The Irish*, wrote with eloquence of the 'plight' of the Irish novelist and put censorship in its social context (1947):

> 'Literature is naturally one of those things which the peasant looks upon with the greatest suspicion. That the poor fellow's defences are meanwhile being utterly undermined by the vulgarities of the cinema, the radio, trashy books, cheap amusements, "foreign" fashions of every sort, and the chase for easy money, and by the effects of a hand-over-fist emigration to industrial Britain under the worst social conditions, he does not realise in the least. He thinks himself safe behind formal religion, formal censorships, and an emotional nationalism that is at least a quarter of a century out of date' (page 139).

In an article in *The Month*, the English Jesuit publication, on 'The Dilemma of Irish Letters' (December 1949), O'Faolain wrote in the same tone, criticising the banning of 'almost every Irish writer of note', and painting a gloomy, poet's picture of Irish life: 'Our sins are tawdry, our virtues childlike, our revolts desultory and brief, our submissions formal and frequent. In Ireland a policeman's lot is a supremely happy one. God smiles, the priest beams, and the novelist groans.'

Mr Arland Ussher devoted a small part of *The Face and Mind of Ireland* to this subject, writing in a milder vein: Ussher was not opposed to censorship as such, which he described as 'lamentable in its operation as it is praiseworthy in its presumable intention' (page 130). His protest was tired and sad, and expressed a desire to see his country 'show the world a really fine example of Censorship and How to Do It'. Brian Inglis wrote frequently in the *Spectator* and almost invariably managed to include some instance of the Board's 'latest inanity'. In one article on 'Smuggled Culture'[24] he reviewed the activities of the Board and the public reaction thereto, spoke favourably of the Appeal Board ('a more enlightened body of citizens'), and found that 'no real demand existed for the abolition of censorship in Ireland'. Austin Clarke, three of whose books had been banned, wrote a strongly worded article in the *New Statesman and Nation* in 1953;[25] he spoke of the 'quietly increasing menace' of the censorship and was of the opinion that the Appeal Board had 'proved of little use as a corrective'. In particular he bewailed the plight of writers in Irish (who could not reach the safe position of having an English publisher): 'The position of the new Gaelic literature is precarious, for its writers must depend on Government publication or on the new Gaelic Book Club. What chance would they have if they wrote with the candour, say, of Liam O'Flaherty or Frank O'Connor?' Clarke was probably exaggerating here. It is a fact that no book in Irish has ever been banned. Indeed, one could make out a good case to prove that writers are permitted greater freedom of expression in Irish than in English. The 'vulgarity' of some of Brendan Behan's plays, for example, was not objected to until they were performed in English.

Apart from these criticisms by Irishmen published abroad, there were some instances of an outsider reviewing the Irish censorship. Thus, the *Bookseller*, the organ of the British Booksellers Association, published on 23 January 1954 a letter from an English publisher, who spoke of the 'continuous defamatory insult to British publishers' offered by the Board, and asked 'what possible standard of judgement has been applied that brands practically every leading British publisher as a purveyor of pornography? . . . The wholesale banning of even good books is both a denial of the adult status of the Irish people, and a libel on the good name of British publishers'. Correspondence on the subject continued for some weeks. In another letter[26] an English publisher who had attended the PEN Congress in Dublin in 1953, spoke of Ireland's 'thought-controlling bureaucracy' and stated that he had discovered with the help of 'Irish colleagues' that offending passages in books need not be obscene, but may deal with politics or be critical of the Roman Catholic Church, or even of social evils which form part of the Irish 'way of life'.

This last accusation was refuted by Mr Donal Giltenan, the President of the Dublin PEN Congress, who neatly pointed out that books by Paul Blanshard and Honor Tracy, extremely critical of the Irish way of life, circulated freely in the country.[27]

Two other instances of criticism which may be cited are, firstly, a survey of freedom of the press throughout the world, published in Zurich in 1956[28]—this described the Irish censorship as extremely drastic 'both in its terms and in its application'—and secondly, Dr Norman St John-Stevas' *Obscenity and the Law* published in the same year. This book, which has become a standard text-book on the general subject, contained a chapter on the Irish censorship.[29] St John-Stevas had very little to say in favour of the Irish practice and received a very severe dressing-down for his remarks from Professor J. J. Pigott, who reviewed his book in the *Irish Independent*.[30]

None of these criticisms by Irish writers and others abroad appears to have influenced public opinion at home, which was in any case well aware of the shortcomings of the system or of the men who ran it. However, it should in all fairness be pointed out that very many articles published abroad by Irish writers during the period—articles dealing with modern Irish literature—contained no comment, adverse or otherwise, about the censorship: from which one might conclude that they were not unduly worried about censorship practice (which is unlikely), or that they did not wish to criticise their country in the foreign press.

2 THE ATTITUDE OF THE CATHOLIC PRESS

Before examining public opinion as expressed and influenced by the 'Catholic Press' in Ireland during this period it is necessary to describe briefly what this phrase is taken to mean. In some sense all newspapers and periodicals, with the important exception of the *Irish Times* group and a few denominational publications such as the *Church of Ireland Gazette*, can be said to reflect Catholic public opinion. This is in marked contrast to England, where the Catholic viewpoint is found in a restricted number of publications: the secular press containing Catholic comment only incidentally.

The vast majority of the secular papers, including all the dailies, apart from the *Irish Times*, and almost all the provincial weeklies are run by Catholics and are very much aware of the fact that their readership is Catholic and that they are expected to provide comment which conforms with Catholic principles. However, while they do give considerable and perhaps over-generous coverage to ecclesiastical news (papal and episcopal pronouncements; ordinations, anniversaries and deaths of priests; openings of clerically-controlled schools; and so forth) they have always tended to reserve comment on controversial 'mixed' questions, such as censorship, the Mother and Child Bill in 1951, the Fethard-on-Sea episode in 1958, the Hierarchy's ban on Trinity College, etc.

The consequence is that Catholic opinion on the subject of censorship is mainly to be found in periodicals which have, or had at the time, a specifically Catholic character. According to their intellectual standing these periodicals fell into three categories: (i) *Studies, Christus Rex, Irish Ecclesiastical Record, Furrow*;[31] (ii) *Doctrine and Life,* the *Irish Monthly, The Leader* and *Hibernia*;[32] and (iii) the *Irish Rosary,* the *Irish Catholic* and the *Standard.*[33]

(i) The most interesting fact to be mentioned regarding the first group is the lack of comment on censorship. *Studies* carried no article on the subject during the period. In its literary articles it did deal with some novels which had been banned (works of Graham Greene and Hemingway, for example), but even in these articles there is no mention or criticism of bannings. The *Irish Ecclesiastical Record* likewise contained no comment, although this is more understandable for it specialises in church history, theology and canon law. The two other periodicals both started publication during the period under review. *Christus Rex,* a review of sociology, began in 1947, while *The Furrow,* a review of pastoral theology, was founded three years later.

The Furrow published a few articles on censorship[34] though none dealt specifically with the Irish phenomenon. The most interesting of these was by Father Courtney Murray, the American Jesuit.

Starting not from the theoretical problem of freedom of expression, but from the fact that the State has always claimed a police power in this field as an attribute of government, Fr Murray saw the central issue as that of striking a right balance between freedom and restraint in society. His proposition was that:

> 'censorship in the civil order must be a juridical process. In using the word "juridical" I mean that the premises and objectives of the program should be defined in accord with the norms of good jurisprudence, that the forms of procedure should be properly judicial and that the structure and workings of the process should be sustained by the consent of the community.'

He emphasised the basic principle that morals and law are differentiated in character and are not co-extensive in their functions:

> 'Law . . . looks only to the public order of human society. . . . The moral aspirations of law are minimal. . . . The net of all this is that no society should expect very much in the way of moral uplift from its censorship statutes. . . . In the civil sphere . . . the less we have of moral indignation and the more we have of professional competence and an unclouded faculty of judgement, the better it will be for the juridical nature of the censorship process.'

In conclusion, he appealed to Catholics especially not to choose the side of the Philistines unconsciously (an exhortation which many were making at this time to the Censorship Board). The article did not concern itself with particular instances of censorship, but its argument seems to have been aimed at the NODL (National Organisation for Decent Literature) quite an influential body in the United States, where the article was first published.

During the period covered by this chapter *Christus Rex* did not devote any space to the censorship question, but the summer issue of 1959 published a very valuable article[35] on the subject. Written by Fr Peter Connolly, Professor of English Literature at St Patrick's College, Maynooth, the article is in many ways the best on the problem of censorship in Ireland written during the whole period from 1926.

In a concise introductory account of ecclesiastical censorship, Fr Connolly asked that the issue be not clouded by such remarks as 'the Catholic is committed to the principle of censorship. . . . To my mind the Catholic Church is officially not concerned in the choice of means which faces a State as between one form of book control and another.' He examined the *Index Librorum Prohibitorum*, pointing out that it does not attempt to cope with the mass of modern literature,[36] and went on to survey the Irish censorship from the time of the Committee on Evil Literature, examining especially the definition of the word 'indecent' in the Acts. He had great faith in the author's *intention* as providing a clear dividing line between literature and pornography, and roundly criticised the censors for banning books on the strength of one or two frank passages.

Narrowing his attention to certain banned books which had some literary claims, Fr Connolly came out on the side of O'Faolain, Frank O'Connor, Mr Justice Kingsmill-Moore, and many others who have been critical of the Board. His list has a familiar ring about it: Faulkner,

Graham Greene, Kate O'Brien, O'Faolain, Huxley, Proust, Hemingway, Erskine Caldwell, Halliday Sutherland. . . . He suggested that 'the test of "general tenor" and "artistic intention" was applicable to such novels and had not been applied'.

> 'However, we must expect—unless our vision is Utopian—some clash at all times between changing social and literary standards and the law. No law or censorship can move very far ahead of majority opinion and usually lags just a stage or two behind the spearhead of advanced opinion. But the rest of the moral also follows, namely, that it is unwise to lag too far behind contemporary taste. More harm than good results. Today, for example, books cannot be censored in a reasonable manner on the assumption that this is not a post-Freudian age. To hold away from our reading minority serious novels which reflect this fact is equivalent to concealing from them the latest in physical sciences or philosophy. It would be foolish to make extravagant claims for the novel, or to claim that the intellectual march of the nation had been halted for lack of a few hundred banned novels. As we know they can still be obtained by any reader by hook or by crook. But a society should not be bereft of the salutary criticism of some of its own most passionately aware members, and the reaction to so many of the literary bans is harmful—a cynicism about the Act and contempt for Censorship in general. The new novels and the new ideas will seep through in any case, but into a negative atmosphere in which the sense of intellectual adventure has gone stale and embittered. This is an aspect of the common good which we might reconsider at greater length, particularly if the problem of an intellectual Catholic elite is one which faces us in Ireland today.'

This article has done or should do much to clarify the ideas of Catholics on the censorship question, and to present clear evidence to other members of the community that there is nothing intrinsically *Catholic* about the censorship. Many people have seen in Fr Connolly's article the justification of the more liberal attitude of the Board after 1958.

(ii) All the periodicals in the second group are reasonably serious in character, though not as intellectual in content as those of the first group. Because of their greater periodicity they are in a position to involve themselves in specific and topical censorship controversies. *Doctrine and*

Life (first published in 1951) did not, however, take any interest in the question, and the same is true of the *Irish Monthly*.[37] The *Leader* on the other hand did comment at various times on specific censorship questions. The magazine combined a down-to-earth belief in the need for, and efficacy of, the censorship as a whole with intelligent comment on the practice of the Boards.

At the time of Dr Smyth's resignation from the Board it suggested that the Minister should give a clear public directive to the Board to have regard to the literary and artistic qualities of each book, and asked that the author be given the right to attend meetings of the Censorship Board.[38]

In 1955 it published an article devoted to criticism of the fact that the Act instructed the Board to 'examine' (not 'read') each book, maintaining that the censors were unable to cope with the amount of books which came before them (unless they were content with this 'examining'—which necessitated the marking of passages) and suggesting the reconstitution of the Board by having it composed of three full-time censors drawn from the higher ranks of the Civil Service. The article also argued in support of the Irish 'prevention' method of censorship, as against the English prosecution method.[39] In 1956 *The Leader* joined in the mounting criticism of the censorship, coming out strongly in favour of the petition of the Irish Association of Civil Liberty for an investigation of the workings of the censorship.[40] In 1958, at the height of the evil literature campaign (see page 165f), it asserted that 'responsibility for the choice of reading rests primarily on the adult individual and on the parents or guardians of the young', but was guilty of making an unfortunate suggestion that the Irish censorship learn from the ecclesiastical censorship, and ask for the submission of a manuscript before publication: (though this was an unrealistic proposal, it would be one method by which Irish authors and Irish publishers could get the lie to the land before publication).[41]

It should, however, be pointed out that the golden age of *The Leader* lay far in the past; nowadays this journal has very little influence.

(iii) This brings us to a consideration of the part played by the *Irish Rosary*, the *Irish Catholic* and the *Standard*.

The first-mentioned, published by Dominican Publications, relied for most of its effect on rallying cries for the preservation of the Catholic religion and of Irish culture. A few excerpts from its columns will reveal its general attitude and tone (the title of the article precedes each quotation):

[Public Indecency] 'Hence censuring Public Authority for having a Board of Censors to safeguard the general public against publications that pander to unchastity is senseless. And screaming against the mere idea of Censorship of unchastity in printed matter is simply immoral madness. And what does all the twaddle about the "backwardness", "intolerance" and "narrow-mindedness" of a Board of Censors indicate? Simply this, that persons . . . are blear-eyed in the matter of chastity, like owls in the tropical sunlight, blinking blindly in the face of the Sun who is Life Itself, and therefore cannot see the duty of a Christian State to make effective Christian teaching regarding unchastity—the Christian teaching that public unchastity is one of the most awful public calamities, pestilence from the lust of the flesh and the lust of the eyes, like salt upon Sodom' (September–October 1946).

[About Indecency] 'A novel, therefore, that because of its lack of proper restraint regarding things connected with sexual matters arouses such sentiments or incites people to sinful actions, or to both, is out of moral bounds for a man of right living.'

'The criterion of whether any such novel is indecent is— the way it presents such sinful things' (September–October 1948).

[Judging Indecency] It does not object to novels which deal with indecency provided 'the impression on the reader may be one of loathsomeness and abhorrence to such sordid things, not of sympathy or incitement towards sexual sin. . . . The novels rightly banned by the Irish Censorship Board are obviously indecent. . . .' (July–August 1952).

[Literary Indecency] 'There is a woolly-headed section of the community devoted to censuring the Censorship Board for damning the flow of literary indecency into this country' (March–April 1953).

In a few articles there is a mild admission that some of the findings of the Board are not justifiable.

The *Irish Catholic* suffered from the same simplistic approach as the *Irish Rosary*. At best uncritical, one finds the Censorship Board described in its editorial columns as 'fair' and as having behind it 'the support of all but the most negligible section of the population. . . . The censorship is reasonable which forbids the publication of matter that, in the estimation of the majority of the citizens, constitutes a threat to the values cherished by the public opinion of the country. Our censorship satisfies this criterion, though the ninety-nine per cent who favour it are less vociferous than the tiny group whose testimony is at once suspect by reason of the fact that they are financially interested in the subject at issue.'[42] The newspaper was particularly vocal during the period of the thrashy literature scare in 1957-1958 (see page 166f), and commented from time to time on the activity—or rather inactivity—of the Censorship Board.

The *Standard* took a more serious and independent line. On the one hand it vigorously supported the Bishops' call to clean up the bookshops and bookstalls (31 January 1958: see page 167), while its commendation of the work[43] of the Irish Association of Civil Liberties showed that it had a discriminating approach to the question. At the time of the Mansion House Meeting it was slightly afraid that the opponents of censorship were trying to get at the birth control clauses (this it would not permit), but it favoured erring on the side of freedom and emphasised that it was 'neither our duty nor our intention to defend the workings of the Censorship Board'.

The Catholic press in Ireland does, then, reveal a whole range of opinions on the question, but while no uniform attitude emerges, it may be interesting to consider the *extent* to which it interested itself in the censorship. The most significant answer to this question is that the volume of space which it expended on the subject was greatly inferior to that given by the *Irish Times*: if not physical volume (column inches), then most certainly that persistence without which little impression can be made on public opinion generally. Many of the Catholic press's articles and editorials coincided in timing with controversies in the *Irish Times*, and one gets a strong impression that it felt itself called on to defend the Censorship Board from the attacks it received from that quarter. Thus it tended generally to apologise for the Board; and it never voiced the extreme opinion that the whole censorship system was objectionable. If the *Irish Times* had been absent from the scene, it could be argued that the Catholic press would have acquiesced even more in the actions of the Board: but on the other hand, a strong case could be made that it would have felt a need to adopt a much more critical attitude towards the question—in which case the full range of Catholic opinions on this mixed question might have been more apparent.

3   OPPOSITION FROM THE RIGHT

In general, most of the criticism directed against the Censorship Board, whether in the pre- or post-1946 period, was aimed against its strictness, its alleged disregard for literary merit. To the simple question 'Why was the Censorship criticised?' the simple reply is 'Because it banned Hemingway, Huxley, O'Connor, O'Faolain and other such writers.'

However, on certain occasions the press and private and public bodies and individuals complained of the inadequacy of control over periodical publications, and that the Board was failing in its duty to keep objectionable publications out of the country. Examples of this type of criticism were numerous in the periods 1950-1951; 1953-1954 and 1957-1958, while there was mild and unsustained criticism during the intervening years.

In 1949 Father Richard Devane SJ, who had always taken an interest in the question of objectionable publications, began what might be called a 'campaign' against the imported press.[44] Reference to and support of this campaign is found in all papers of the time, notably *Hibernia*, the *Standard* and the *Irish Catholic*. It could not be fairly called a campaign against the Censorship Board, because Father Devane and his supporters were not interested in obscene publications as such, but rather in the imported press in general;[45] the importation and sale in Ireland of English and American newspapers and magazines which showed an almost complete disregard for Christian values. The Government action sought was not the admonishing of the Censorship Board, but the imposition of higher tariffs drastically to reduce the circulation of these publications in the State[46] and subsidise struggling Irish publications in the same category: popular newspapers, comics and magazines. An interesting article by Father Devane on 'Press and Propaganda in Ireland', with comments by Lord Killanin, Benedict Kiely and others was published in *Hibernia*[47] and similar or more exhortative features appeared in the press for some two years. Fr Devane himself produced a pamphlet[48] on the subject and was largely responsible for the campaign until his death in May 1951.

In this pamphlet Fr Devane made a meticulous examination of the size of importations of books and periodicals into the country. He produced the comparative figures which are quoted on the following page:

YEAR	IMPORTED BOUND NOVELS	DAILY PAPERS	TARIFF-FREE SUNDAY PAPERS
1933	756,353	2,631,121 dozen	668,750 dozen
1934	914,957	1,581,785 „	746,518 „
1935	710,037	1,345,349 „	897,082 „
1936	760,568	1,331,248 „	1,013,465 „
1937	653,982	1,232,587 „	1,059,629 „
1938	560,901	1,166,696 „	1,133,691 „
War years	Not available	Not available	Not available
1947	450,800	380,963 „	1,308,749 „
1948	567,973	343,786 „	1,439,256 „
1949	742,678	444,585 „	1,689,030 „

Confronted with these statistics, Fr Devane asked rhetorically, 'What should the feelings of a patriotic Irishman be?'* and proposed that a tariff of one shilling per bound book be imposed, and that a quota for imports of newspapers be fixed at 60% of the 1949 import figures.

A few extracts from articles will give an impression of the general tenor of the campaign. For instance, the *Standard*, reporting the address of a priest to pilgrims at Knock shrine:[49]

> 'The Republic of Ireland import nearly 50,000,000 copies of assorted papers, magazines and periodicals, an alarming number of which contain subtle propaganda of the new paganism, recently condemned by the Pope. Where is the dumping ground—the Irish homes.'

The *Irish Catholic* wrote in much the same vein:

> 'The Sunday newspapers with their lurid headlines, magazines and books with veiled or open sex appeal vauntingly displayed on our bookstalls and numbering their readers in tens of thousands . . . a flood of evil literature. . . . The imported press is but one manifestation . . . of the challenging spirit of secularism. It is nothing about which to be indifferent. . . .'[50]

---

* In the course of his article Fr Devane quoted the following lines, based on Tennyson's *Locksley Hall.*

'Authors—essayist, atheist, novelist, realist, rhymester, play your part,
Paint the moral shame of nature with the living lines of Art.
Rip your brothers vices open, strip your own foul passions bare;
Down with reticence, down with reverence—forward—naked—let them stare.
Feed the budding rose of boyhood with the drainage of your sewer,
Send the drain into the fountain, lest the stream should issue pure.'

The only practical effect of the campaign was to increase the number of periodicals prohibited. Since all complaints made to the Censorship Board in respect of periodicals have to be formal complaints (i.e. coming from members of the public) the effectiveness of this censorship depends far more directly on the general public than does the censorship of books. This seems to have been realised, for in comparison with 13 complaints in 1948, and four in 1949, the number rose to 71 in 1950 and 114 in 1951, and the net result was that in these two last mentioned years a total of 155 periodicals were banned for varying periods of time (see Figure 3, page 123).

However, the call on the Government to control the imported press by increasing tariffs and reducing quotas fell on deaf ears, and after the death of Fr Devane (May, 1951) this call became less and less articulate.

Campaigns and controversies cannot easily be squeezed between dates—of month or years—and for some time afterwards one finds traces of this attack on foreign publications. Blanshard's *The Irish and Catholic Power* told of priests who 'combine hostility to sin with an appeal to anti-foreign prejudice' and mentioned posters which appeared in Dublin in 1953 announcing 'THE FOREIGN PRESS IS A NATIONAL MENACE'. In August 1953 the Taoiseach received a delegation from Cosg Ar Foillseacháin Gallda (Boycott on Foreign Publications), an ephemeral organisation, but in reply to its plea for Government action Mr de Valera intimated that the campaign would need to have much more support of public opinion if it were to succeed in any noticeable way.[51] The Cosg, for its part, rounded up support in the county councils and similar bodies: many items appear in the press of this time (notably the *Irish Independent*) to the effect that this or that county council or county vocational committee had come out strongly against foreign publications. But no Government action was taken.

After this time the attack on foreign publications was concentrated on horror comics imported from England and America.[52] Already, in 1952, the *Irish Catholic* had objected to the free availability of 'comics' in the shops; in 1953 *Hibernia* took up the cry; and in the autumn of 1954 the battle was drawn. Complaints were lodged that the Censorship Board was not doing its job (that it should be banning these 'evil comics'), and suggestions were made that the censorship laws should be amended. In October 1954 a Fianna Fail Deputy did ask the Minister for Justice whether 'he intended to amend the Censorship of Publications Acts in order to deal with the flood of undesirable magazines, Sunday newspapers and comics coming into the country', to which the Minister replied that 'the Acts did not of course provide for the prohibition of reading matter which might be undesirable in the sense of being vulgar or materialistic or unsuitable for children', but he doubted if many Deputies on full consideration of the problem would support legislation for the prohibition of reading matter merely on those grounds.[53]

This rather unsatisfactory statement by the Minister induced county vocational committees, the Cosg and the like[54] to renew their protests;[55] the lesser Catholic papers wrote editorials on the subject insisting that 'something must be done', but were not very realistic when it came to making concrete proposals.[56] Even readers of the *Irish Times* were pleased to direct the Censorship Board's attention to horror comics, hoping probably that these would help to distract it from other, more adult, fields.[57] The net result of these protests was that at the end of 1954 the Censorship Board did ban some, though not many, of these comics;[58] and, as during the 1949–1951 campaign, there was a distinct increase in the number of complaints sent to the Board and in the number of periodicals banned (77 banned in 1954 and 45 banned in 1955).

In March 1955, on the publication in England of an American sociologist, Dr Frederic Wertham's, *Seduction of the Innocent*, the *Irish Times* carried an article on horror comics which reported that Dublin quayside shops were by then quite clean: they had only *Superman* and such comics; the stallholders and booksellers replied to the writer's request for horror comics with 'We don't get any of them now.' It would seem then that the protest against these publications did produce a reduction in their circulation; but it is impossible to judge to what extent the campaign was really a storm in a teacup. At all events, in Ireland the distribution of horror comics was controlled by the force of public opinion alone, whereas in England remedial legislation was deemed necessary to cope with this problem.

Of the three campaigns the last was certainly the most intense and most widely felt, and the one most closely connected with the Censorship Board.

As is noted elsewhere all did not run smoothly within the Board itself in the years 1956–1957, when it was inactive for two rather long periods: from June to December 1956 (due to lack of a quorum), and from May to October 1957 (due to Professor Pigott's refusal to call meetings of the Board). As a result of this inactivity it is reasonable to suppose that some publications were admitted into the country which would otherwise have been excluded. At all events, the Catholic Archbishop of Dublin, Dr McQuaid, was satisfied that this was so, for at the beginning of

December he addressed a conference of youth leaders of 20,000 girls at which a resolution was passed condemning the influx of evil literature[59] and soon all the newspapers in the country, the *Irish Times* being the main exception, had taken up the cry, affirming that the bookstalls[60] in Dublin and elsewhere were in an appalling state, and that the Censorship Board was largely responsible for this.[61]

The *Irish Independent* was particularly vocal on the matter. Examining the situation in an editorial ('New Wave of Vicious Books'), it suggested that:

> 'The inactivity of the authorities can be explained in only one of three ways. First, they may not be aware of the gravity of the problem; if this be so they are singularly out of touch with what is happening on the streets of Dublin.[62] Secondly, they may be satisfied that their powers to intervene are inadequate; if this be the true explanation it is the plain and urgent duty of Parliament to give them the necessary powers. Thirdly, they may feel that although their powers are adequate, the higher authorities will not encourage them to take action. . . . Of course it is futile to expect the present system of censorship to grapple with this phase of the problem. The censorship is so slow-moving that that mischief is done before any ban can be issued. Indeed, it would be expecting too much to look to a small and sharply divided body of censors, necessarily giving only their spare time to the work, for the speedy and stern action that alone can meet the case. . . . But the public should insist that immediate measures be taken to remove a growing menace to the youth of the country.'[63]

It should be noted that many of the articles dealing with the need to take stern measures to stem the inflow of evil literature made no mention of the Censorship Board; this may have resulted—to some extent at any rate—from a desire not to embarrass the Board. Blame for the inflow was placed rather at the door of the Gardai.

The campaign was not confined to the newspapers; voluntary bodies from all over the country,[64] vocational education committees and innumerable county councils and their sub-committees passed resolutions calling for Governmental action, many proposing impracticable solutions for the control of objectionable literature; the Irish Retail Newsagents, Booksellers and Stationers Association even issued a statement, asking that the publications in question be stopped at point of entry[65]—their main complaint and reason seems to have been that prosecutions occurred in a very arbitrary fashion (one bookseller might be prosecuted for selling a book, while others got off scot free, though they were selling the same book). [66] The Association was quoted as saying that the 'Censorship Board was partly responsible for the influx of these publications'. . . . One view put forward (to explain the lack of governmental action) is that there may be political doubt about having what might appear to be too much censorship activity'' because of the impression it might create in the North. [67]

One colourful event in the campaign was the action of a Dublin parish priest [68] (in Ballyfermot, a lower-income district) who organised a protest to the effect that 'the people of Ballyfermot' demanded (1) that no censors be appointed who, 'from their association are opposed to censorship as we wish it', (2) that two censors be unable to control the decisions of the board, and (3) that the Gardai play their part properly. The 'association' referred to was the Irish Association of Civil Liberties, which had welcomed the appointment of Mr Comyn and Mr Figgis to the Board. This protest followed immediately on the publication by Professor Pigott of his reasons for resigning from the Board.

When the campaign was already in full swing it received an added impetus in the form of a statement from the Catholic Bishops, issued to the Press on 31 January 1958: [69]

> 'There have been widespread complaints confirmed by the strongest evidence that our country is being flooded with enormous quantities of books and magazines which are detrimental to public and private morality. These publications describe in vivid, suggestive manner, and often with illustrations, crimes of violence and unchastity; they have no literary value whatever, and are simply a form of profiteering on the corruption of the young . . .'

The Statement went on to warn the 'small minority who put private profit or pleasure before the law of God and the public good', and reminded parents to safeguard their children; it ended with a stern admonishment that 'booksellers and newsagents incur grave sin if they sell such books and magazines'. Judiciously, it contained no mention of the Censorship Board or of censorship. [70]

During these months various questions were put to Mr Oscar Traynor, Minister for Justice, in the Dail. On 12 February 1958 Mr Traynor reported that the Censorship Board had been put in a position to function again, and that he 'was glad to say that the members of the Board are now working in complete harmony.' [71] Some days later in a reply to a question by Dr Noel Browne he gave figures of the numbers of books and periodicals submitted to the Board by the public in the years 1954–1957;[72] these figures show that he had cause to complain that critics of evil literature were not themselves helping towards a solution by submitting books and periodicals to the Board. They seem to have taken this remark to heart, for the number of final complaints to the Board regarding periodicals rose from 10 in 1957 to the all-time record in 1958 of 157 (of which 124 were banned). This increase is a clear repetition of the *practical* effect of the two earlier campaigns.

Two weeks later, in reply to another question, the Minister reaffirmed his opinion that the law to deal with obscene publications was adequate 'if the general public are prepared to co-operate.'[73] If the necessary co-operation was not forthcoming, he would be ready to consider further measures. On 12 March[74] he told another deputy that he did not think it necessary or desirable to act on the Newsagents Association's resolution in favour of a system of licences to wholesale importers and distributors of periodicals and paperback books so that responsibility would rest with the importers and distributors: 'it would' he said, 'have the effect of weakening the sense of responsibility of the actual seller, which was the best protection against the sale of objectionable publications that the public had'.[75] In May, in reply to a question about delays in censorship, Mr Traynor stated that the Board was functioning 'with as much expedition as is consistent with a conscientious discharge of its duty',[76] and Dr Ryan, Minister for Finance, in reply to another question, said that he was satisfied that the examination of book-parcels etc. at point of entry was adequate. On this occasion General S. MacEoin suggested that importers should be asked to submit in advance a list of what publications it was proposed to import (i.e. a system such as that practised in the Department of Industry and Commerce). Finally—for it really marks the end of the campaign—on 10 July we find the Minister assuring the House that he has no intention of changing the law on obscene publications, and refusing to accept the implications that the Censorship Board had inadequate powers.[77]

At no stage in the campaign did the Minister show signs of yielding to extravagant demands made on him; he did, however, pay attention to the complaints, and in addition to encouraging the Censorship Board by giving it his full support, he did use the customs authorities[78] and the police to control the flow of objectionable literature.[79]

VIII
The Censorship Process

The present chapter largely consists of an ordering of information which the reader may well have already absorbed in earlier parts of this study; but for all that, it is a necessary chapter, and in many ways the most objective of all. For it prescinds from the controversial and concentrates on the undramatic day-to-day workings of the censorship machinery. In this account the protagonists are the Censorship Board, the Appeal Board, the Customs and Postal authorities, the Minister for Justice, authors, editors,[1] publishers, booksellers, libraries and in the last place, the public at large.

It would cause confusion rather than illumination to examine here the censorship process over the whole period from 1929 onwards; for this reason I intend to describe how the censorship has functioned in recent years, indicating here and there points on which a change of procedure has occurred over the years. The sources used in this enquiry include the Censorship of Publication Acts, 1929 and 1946, and various peripheral acts and statutory regulations, but much of the most interesting information has been gleaned from conversations with persons who have been, or are still engaged in the activities of the censorship.[2]

I shall deal first with the censorship of books and then with that of periodicals, insofar as it differs from the former.

1 THE MINISTER

Taking the process chronologically, the first move is that of the Minister for Justice, whose function it is to appoint the Censorship and Appeal Boards, and see that they perform their respective tasks according as the law prescribes. The Minister has, then, a very important function—as has indeed always been recognised by those members of the public who have been concerned over the leniency and strictness of the Censorship Board. When the 1929 Act was passed the *Irish Times* and the *Irish*

Statesmen were prepared to bide their time to see whom, in fact, the Minister appointed to the first Board before they adopted any very pronounced attitude to it; as it happened, they registered extreme displeasure at the choice Mr Fitzgerald-Kenney made. At many times in the post-1946 period the *Irish Times* too, when criticising the activity of the Board, affirmed its belief in the Act itself, and campaigned not for modification of the Act, but for reconstruction of the Board by the resignation of existing members and the appointment of others who could be expected to adopt a more broadminded attitude. Certainly the reconstruction which took place in 1957 is an instance of how the Minister has exercised his power to influence the whole trend of censorship. Nor was this the first instance. The resignation in 1937, for example, of Lynn Doyle was, we are reliably informed, requested by the Minister—although at the time it appeared that Lynn Doyle had resigned on his own initiative (see page 72f). The Minister took this action because the other four members of the Board at the time refused to sit with Mr Doyle until he had either withdrawn or substantiated accusations which he had made previous to his appointment.

On other occasions, notably in 1956, the Minister has influenced the pace of censorship by delaying the appointment of new members, thus preventing the operation of the Board.[3]

Once the Censorship Board has been constituted, it is unable to function until it is furnished with books for examination purposes. The Board has the right to examine books on its own initiative,[4] but in fact it has done so in relatively few cases[5] over the years. The main reason for this—apart from the excessive amount of time that such 'inviligation' would consume[6]—is that it has never been furnished with funds adequate to this purpose. In one year during Professor Magennis's chairmanship it received some £30 for the purchase of books, only after an inordinate amount of negotiation with the Department of Finance. I understand that in recent years hardly anything has been devoted to this purpose. On this score it should be mentioned that the Board has always held some few library subscriptions which it avails of when it wishes to examine books on its own initiative. Indeed this very fact was a thorn in the side of many of its critics, and on one occasion at least, in the 1940's, a body of citizens (The Council of Action) actually approached the Times Book Club in London with a view to persuading it to forbid its associate, Switzer's Lending Library in Dublin, to lend books to the Censorship Board. (It received a polite refusal.)

The second source of complaints reaching the Board is the general public. Members of the public are required to send the Board one copy of the book in question, together with a complaint form (Form A) which encourages the complainant to mark passages on the text in support of his view. The total number of these 'formal complaints' has never exceeded 80 in a single year—a fact which indicates that the Board would for all practical purposes cease to function if it were to depend on the public as its main source of books. The complainant is entitled to have the book returned to him whether it is banned or not, although, as one might expect, if he thought strongly about the objectionableness of a book he would have little or no wish to claim it. However, on occasions the copy of the book which is sent from the private complainant is not his own copy, but rather one which he has borrowed from a public or circulating library and which must be returned thereto. If such be the case, the Board usually tries to come to a quick decision.

2 CUSTOMS OFFICIALS

The last and most prolific source of books for the Board is the Customs authorities. As has been mentioned earlier, the role of the Customs in censorship was one which 'just grew'. Little or no mention was made in the 1928 debates about the activity of the Customs in the field of indecent literature; the 1929 Act provided that the Customs should deal with prohibited publications in the manner laid down in Section 42 of the Customs Consolidation Act 1876 (i.e. they would be forfeited, 'destroyed or otherwise disposed of as the Commissioners of Customs may direct'). However, from the moment that the 1929 Act began to operate, the Customs authorities sent books and periodicals to the Board for examination and the 1946 Act contained a complete section (Section 5) confirming and regulating this practice. Section 5, ss. 3 forbids the detention of a book, not being merchandise, (and not being prohibited under the Acts) which is carried by, or forms part of the personal luggage of an incoming traveller. This practice of the Customs did not, it should be pointed out, start in 1930; the Customs Consolidation Act 1876, which the new Free State retained and which is still in force, constituted an important means of excluding obscene matter from the United Kingdom and from the Free State.[7] The Customs officials kept a type of black list based on matter which had previously been detained under the 1876 Act; there had been, for instance, an 'exclusion order' in respect of James Joyce's

Ulysses, and this order was still in force in the Free State after the passing of the first Censorship of Publications Act, and not allowed to lapse until around the year 1934. The appearance of the Censorship Act meant merely that the Customs authorities instead of themselves deciding as to the objectionableness of a publication, now left the Censorship Board with this unpleasant task, simply by submitting to it publications for which they thought there was a *prima facie* case for exclusion.

Thus the first phase of the censorship process is not in the hands of the Board. This may not be a cause for concern when the Board in power is known to be lenient; but if the Board is strict—in the superficial sense of banning a large proportion of the books which come before it—the role of the Customs assumes a special significance.

The Customs examination of books functions in the following manner. In Parnell Square, Dublin, there is a joint department (called the 'Bookscale') of Customs and Postal officials who examine parcels of books coming into the country by post; the books covered by this examination include about 80% to 85% of book imports from Britain, and the parcels concerned are easily identifiable as containing books by the customs declaration forms which are affixed to them. The number of parcels examined per day varies, according to one customs official, from 500–600 in the autumn, to perhaps 200 in the summer months; this does not include parcels of religious books, which would generally not be of interest to the Censorship Board, and whose publishers can normally be expected not to send any prohibited publications into the country.

These parcels are examined by a customs landing officer, who is helped by a post office sorter; but not all the parcels are opened.[8] If a particular publisher is 'going well' his parcels would get the green light; whereas all parcels coming from some other firms known to be inclined to carry a somewhat more risqué line would undergo a thorough examination. The customs officer examines the books, some of which he has been on the look-out for as a result of reading reviews of them in the English press; he may examine them on the spot or bring them home after work to read them at greater leisure, and possibly ask his wife for her opinion in a particularly doubtful case. Once a consignment is stopped a detention note is sent to the consignee to that effect, and the officer sends, by special messenger employed for this purpose, one copy of each book to Division 2 of the Revenue Commissioners at Dublin Castle, with a note drawing attention to, for example, chapters 24–25 (which would possibly indicate erotic detail but not a pornography-pattern) or to chapters 7–8, 11–12, 15–17 (which would suggest that the book was probably objectionable).

Certainly one former official of the bookscale was of the opinion that these notes accompanied the books when they were sent to the Board but according to the Secretary of the Board this is not the case: the books are casually examined at Dublin Castle by senior officers[9] and the notes are not passed on to the Board deliberately.

According to the officials of the bookscale there is no delay at their stage of the process; yet members of the Censorship Board have said— rather involuntarily—that they do not receive books from the Customs with the efficiency they would like; it would then appear that the Revenue Commissioners are responsible for some delay, though this may not be more than one week.

Larger consignments of books and periodicals are imported by sea in crates, and are examined by Customs officers or postal officials, mainly at the ports of Dublin, Cobh and Limerick. The great bulk of this trade comes through Dublin and consists of books and periodicals printed in the United States. Any doubtful books which are noticed are forwarded to Dublin Castle: and if they have to be sent from Limerick or Galway, the delay involved before they reach the Board is correspondingly greater.

As well as detaining books for examination purposes the officers of customs and excise also try to prevent the import of publications which are already on the *Register of Prohibited Publications*. Such publications if imported, are seized and the consignee asked why they should not be destroyed immediately. It would seem that prohibited periodicals *are* burned summarily, while the practice is to keep books for a month before burning; usually arrangements are made for such books to be returned to the publisher unless he has a reputation of trying to run the gauntlet of Customs and Board (perhaps by including a limited number of banned books in a large consignment of otherwise safe publications). Banned publications in the possession of incoming travellers are confiscated if discovered; some Southern customs officers on the border between Northern Ireland and the Republic of Ireland are noted for their vigilance in this matter. However, by way of reminder, it should be pointed out that the Customs are specifically refused the right to detain an unbanned book, not being merchandise, which is carried by, or forms part of, the personal luggage of an incoming traveller.

It is certainly a fact that private individuals can import by post[10] banned books without detection—in the great majority of cases—for the bookscale and other customs officers rather understandably concentrate on larger consignments to booksellers.[11] The safest and only legal way of importing a banned book is to seek the permission of the Minister for

Justice. However, in practice members of the public are not inclined to take this trouble—according to the Department of Justice only some half a dozen permits are issued each year; there is no evidence for supposing that this is due to strictness on the part of the Minister.[12] (When a permit is granted one copy of the permit is sent to the importer[13] and another to the bookscale). According to one officer of the bookscale *bona fide* reviewers for such newspapers as the *Irish Times* or the *Observer* are allowed to import banned books for review purposes without special licence; this practice would appear to be quite legal, as according to Section 19, 1, of the 1946 Act 'the Minister may at his discretion grant permits for the purposes of this Act, and may grant any such permit subject to such conditions as he thinks fit to impose and specified in the permit.' Booksellers are not aware of these 'general permits' to which I refer. The Censorship Board takes no interest in the number of permits granted.

In regard to periodical publications, there is no clause in the Acts which makes explicit provision for the reference of these to the Board by Customs officials. The 1946 Act contains a section which provides for this in the case of books, and indeed the framers of that Act avoided the inclusion of periodicals in this section on the grounds that the delay necessarily involved in sending publications to the Board could mean serious financial loss for publishers and newsagents, in the case of periodicals which would be later cleared by the Board. However, one subsection of Section 5 states that 'nothing in this section shall be construed as affecting the operation of the Customs Consolidation Act, 1876, as amended or adapted by or under any subsequent amendment' and the relevant section (Section 42) of that Act provides for the detention and forfeiture etc. of 'indecent or obscene prints, paintings, photographs, books, cards, lithographic or other engravings, or any other indecent or obscene articles'; in other words the Commissioners of Customs have the power to detain any periodicals which they consider obscene. It would appear that this power has seldom been used for the Customs authorities are very wary and are anxious to avoid mistakes which could lead to a public outcry, or to representations on the part of those financially concerned in the sale of these periodicals. The outcry occasioned by the non-distribution of the issue of the *Observer* for 1 April 1956 easily justifies their caution in the exercise of these powers: in fact, according to the *Reports* of the Censorship Board, all complaints regarding periodicals are formal complaints (i.e. from members of the public).

Many critics of the censorship have objected to the part played by the

Customs in the control of books, because they realise that without their co-operation the Censorship Act would very soon become a dead letter. However, if the principle of censorship is accepted it is relatively simple to justify their activity—provided the Censorship Board itself is operating in accordance with the Acts; but when the Board is noticeably strict and is inclined to prohibit a large proportion of the books it receives from the Customs, this activity can very definitely be a mixed blessing. One official (interviewed) has, so to speak, complimented himself on the fact that '83.7% of the books sent by me to the Board were eventually banned', and that 'two appeals were allowed' (this percentage is really a percentage of the books sent by the official to the Revenue Commissioners; but the high percentage suggests that Dublin Castle forwarded to the Board the vast majority of the books it received from the bookscale). Booksellers too are aware of the role of the Customs, and managers of more than one firm express the wish that the Customs officers employed on the bookscale had better qualifications for the work they are doing; and although the bookscale maintains that it is on good terms with publishers and booksellers, we know of at least one instance of a prominent British publisher travelling to Dublin expressly to upbraid the customs for sending an innocent book to the Board and thus hindering its sale in Ireland: not that the public heard that the book was sent before the Board and for that reason were reluctant to buy it, but because any delay in getting a new book—especially a novel—to the Irish shops means that some part at least of the early publicity it receives by way of reviews and advertisements in English periodicals is thus wasted.

One final point: the Censorship Board says that it returns to the Revenue Commissioners the copy it has received from them; this is then repacked in the parcel which is either delivered to the consignee (if no prohibition order has been made), or returned to the consignor. This is done because there is a post office regulation which requires that any packages opened by the bookscale must be either returned or delivered intact. It means that the Censorship Board cannot easily maintain a library of prohibited publications, and so the Appeal Board, in the case of Oireachtas appeals, has to forage for a copy on its own behalf.

In the last analysis responsibility for the treatment of books must be placed squarely on the shoulders of the Board; in theory, such terms as 'strictness' or 'leniency' should not be applied to Customs and Postal officials whose work consists solely of forwarding books to the Board—a task which is nothing more than a condition *sine qua non* of that body's activity.

3 THE CENSORSHIP BOARD

The office of Censorship of Publications is located in a large Georgian house in Upper Pembroke Street, Dublin, which it shares with other government agencies. Its premises are at best cramped, and are little in the way of an improvement on its former offices in Ely Place and Fitzwilliam Square.

The staff of the office, which serves both the Censorship Board and the Appeal Board, consists of a full-time Secretary, one staff officer, four clerical workers and a messenger. From the beginning of the censorship until his retirement on reaching the age limit on 4 October 1962, Mr B. MacMahon occupied the position of Secretary.

Mr MacMahon was not a civil servant prior to his appointment and had no interest in censorship until that date. On occasions members of the Board have complained of inadequacy of staff (Professor Magennis spoke of this, for example, in the 1945 debates), but currently this does not present a problem. Indeed, in recent years the staff has been reduced by two to the present size: no replacement was made when one officer was promoted in the Service and when another died. Similarly, complaints that the Office is not adequately financed have not been made in recent years, whereas they were in Professor Magennis's time. The monies allocated to the Censorship in the Annual Estimates are mostly devoted to the payment of salaries to the staff (all of whom are full-time employees); the remainder is spent on library subscriptions, the occasional purchase of a book, travelling expenses of members, etc.

When a book reaches the office it is examined by a member of the staff who marks on a card the numbers of the pages which he thinks are objectionable—in the case of formal complaints (from members of the public, most of whom mark passages) or the occasional book from the Customs, in which the note sent to the Revenue Commissioners has accidentally been left, he is facilitated in this work. However, I am given to understand by the former Secretary of the Board that the marking by members of the public is sometimes of no help whatever because they may draw the attention of the Board to attacks on religion, for example, and overlook erotic passages.

Figure six

The following information regarding the financing of the censorship is taken from the *Annual Estimates* and *Appropriation Accounts* at five-yearly intervals:

YEAR ENDED 31 MARCH	GRANT (a) £	AMOUNT SPENT £ s. d.
1931	400 (b)	210 12 8 (c)
1936	258	280 4 10
1941	620	683 16 7 (d)
1946	933	942 4 3
1951	1,985	2,002 8 2
1956	4,071	3,870 0 0
1961	4,494	4,378 0 0

(a) In the Estimates no distinction is made between monies allocated to the Appeal Board and to the Censorship Board (this is because the same staff serves both Boards).

(b) The appropriations given above are for the payment of staff. Travelling expenses of members of the Board and library subscriptions and book-purchase allowances were estimated separately and usually included in a general appropriation for incidental expenses of the Department. Monies spent on library subscriptions etc. have varied from £15 in 1935–1936 to £60 in 1959–1960.

(c) For some years at the beginning, the Secretary was the only member of the staff.

(d) The increase in the figures given above are due entirely to increases in salary scales and in staff.

At this point I might mention that occasionally publishers send books to the Board on their own initiative—perhaps before publication, in order to avoid possible delays when the book appears; such books are treated in the manner normal for formal complaints. On one or two occasions manuscripts have been submitted to the Board, but it refused to give a formal opinion on them because to do so would mean that it acted in a licensing capacity, which is not its function according to the spirit of the Acts: indeed its powers are limited to the examination of *printed publications* (Section 1). It was of interest to enquire on this point because such licensing might be of help to Irish publishers who stand to lose more than foreign publishers in the event of a book of theirs being prohibited.

I comment below, when discussing the Appeal Board, on the precise coverage of prohibition orders on books; however something should be said of this question at the level of the Censorship Board. Under the 1929 Act (Section 6, ss. 8) a prohibition order was to refer to all editions of the book, unless the Board limited it to cover more particular editions, or unless the Minister excluded a certain edition or editions by making amending order (no such order was ever made). The 1946 Act contains no such clause, but it is assumed that the Board has the right to decide which editions shall be covered by its order (the Appeal Board is, of course, given the right to make a 'variation order' which is equivalent to the old 'amending order' of the Minister).

Normally the Censorship Board made out its prohibition orders to cover 'all editions'; this was the established practice for some time. However, according to the Secretary of the Board, at some time after 1946 the Revenue Commissioners (in a position to stop the importation of prohibited books) began to interpret the 'all' as meaning 'all editions by the publisher mentioned'; the Board consulted the Attorney General on the point, and changed its formula to 'all editions published by this publisher or any other publisher'. For some time the Board was including in its lists, published in the *Iris Oifigiuil*, new editions of books long since banned ('repeat orders'): this was, to say the least, somewhat embarrassing, for often it meant re-opening the old wounds of criticism. In recent years the Board has reverted to the 'all editions' formula. It would appear that different attornies-general give different criteria on this and other points. Here I might add that there are no books or periodicals in languages other than English on the *Register*, and that in the case of prohibited books by non-English-speaking writers the prohibition order is almost always limited to 'all English versions by this publisher or any other publisher'.

Once the Board's staff has examined it, the book, together with the card indicating certain pages, is then forwarded, usually by post, to one member of the Board, who returns it when he has examined it; the Office then sends it to a second member and the process continues in the same manner. The 'marked passages' are not always of great help to the members of the Board. In the first place, the staff is not inclined to give the book the benefit of the doubt and might, for example, mark a passage containing the innocent information that a woman became pregnant. Then again, some members do not pay any attention to these passages. In fact, of course, the censors are under no obligation to take them into account. At least one censor's procedure in examining a book is as follows: he first reads one or two chapters to get an impression of its literary value, and if the book is serious he feels obliged to read it completely; if however, it is worthless from the literary point of view, he then turns to the marked pages. Having examined the book in this manner, he fills in a Comment Form which contains headings for: the title of the book; author; the member's recommendations re banning; and his comments. Almost invariably he fills in the first three sections; the last section which, during the life of the 1958–1961 Board at least, was filled in often by two members and rarely by the others. These forms are designed to be a help to the staff to check which books have been examined by which censors; they are also useful to the censors themselves, especially at times when many books are under review. I understand that this is their only purpose; they are not regarded as a substitute for a censor's voice in the event of his inability to attend a particular meeting of the Board: in accordance with Section 11 of the 1946 Act—'(b) four members shall constitute a quorum at any such meeting . . . (c) a prohibition order shall not be made unless *at such meeting* (my italics) three at least of the members vote in favour of the making of the order and not more than one member votes against it.'

The physical size of the task carried out by the censors has varied considerably; the number of books examined was around 60 in 1930, whereas it reached 1,200 in 1954 (see figure 2). The higher the figure the greater the uneasiness of the critical member of the public. The examination of 1,200 books by each member of the Board would mean an average of twenty-five books a week: a very sizeable number, even allowing for the fact that many deserve no more than a superficial examination. Taking 500 books a year as the average, one can readily appreciate that the examination of these demands a considerable dedication of a censor's leisure time—given that he is professionally employed during working hours. It is quite possible that this is more than can reasonably be asked of a person who accepts the disagreeable public service which membership of the Board implies: but it is difficult to venture an opinion, since one has no precise information as to the degree of thoroughness with which the Board examines the books that come before it. One clear fact is that members of post-1946 Boards are required to do much more work than were the Boards operating under the first Act (these Boards banned 171 books in their most energetic year and probably examined as few as 250 to find them). It was with this problem in mind that Professor Pigott suggested in 1958 that membership of the Board should be full-time, and should be paid but not a pensionable post.[14] That this would be a practical solution to a practical problem of time there is no doubt, but it might be a change which would harm the censorship in the long run. For it could lead to the formation of a very closed, introverted Board whose whole business and time would be spent on the control of pornography, and who would not benefit from the ordinary social and professional life which part-time members have managed to combine with their task.[15] In effect, the problem is not easy of solution.

The censors are in general men and women who have taken no more than a layman's interest in censorship before their appointment. The majority have been people still actively engaged in their several professions; in recent years for instance, meetings of the Board have been held outside office hours at 5-30 p.m. and may last an hour or less. The meetings, formerly held once a month, are now fortnightly, but are not on a fixed day. In general the keynote of the proceedings is efficiency.

One point of interest is whether all the members of the Board do in fact examine each book. According to the Act the Censorship Board is instructed to examine each book, and the quorum for a meeting is four members; it would then appear that the members are required to have examined, or to examine on the spot, all the books upon which each expresses his opinions at a meeting. However, I have it on good authority that one member at least, because of pressure of time, may read only one book a week; this is usually one which the others have already read but about whose banning they do not agree. If this is the case, that member would appear to hold a balance of power in some sense: he would seem to be a super-censor on whose decision or indecision the fate of a book would depend. Such behaviour would be objectionable if the other censors were inclined to extend their powers to books not legally censorable; if however, they have a reputation for conscientiousness, it is not so reprehensible. Considered in the abstract it is not undesirable; thus the need is seen for the Department of Justice to make sure that those appointed to the position of censor are in a position to devote all the time necessary for an examination of all books; common sense and balanced judgement, however admirable they may be, can hardly be regarded as an adequate substitute for compliance with the letter as well as with the spirit of the law.

Under the terms of the 1946 Act (Section 6, ss. 3) the Board may communicate with the author, editor or publisher of the book, and may take into account any representation made by him; in practice, according to the Secretary of the Board, the Board does not exercise this right. Occasionally a plea is made that the author etc. should himself have a right to appear before the censors. In respect of appeals provision is made for him to appear before the Board (at the Board's discretion), and in view of the experience of the past fifteen years—when few authors have appeared in person—there could be no serious objection to allowing it to operate in the case of the Censorship Board also. It would probably be availed of by some Irish authors and their English publishers.

Currently, over 95% of books on the *Register* are banned on the grounds of indecency; the remainder, except for some five or six titles banned on both grounds, are banned on birth control grounds (see Figure 2). It should be noted that the distribution or sale of birth control literature is forbidden under the unrepealed sections of the 1929 Act, and the prohibition of these by the Censorship Board is merely a second line of defence, as it were: it is designed to make quite clear that certain specific books do contravene the law.

There are no statistics readily available of the distribution of prohibited books on the basis of country of the publisher or author. An examination of the *Register of Prohibited Publications*' Supplementary List for the year 1958 shows that some 250 of the 487 books mentioned were published in the United States and Canada. However, the more than 100 'repeat orders' made in that year referred to U.S. editions (mainly paperback) of books which were British-published when first banned.

In the present examination of the machinery of censorship it is irrelevant to examine where and whether the books banned as 'indecent or obscene' have all in fact fallen into that category. But perhaps it is relevant here to say that the Board is noticeably intolerant of that type of paperback which makes its sales appeal on the basis of a lurid and suggestive cover and blurb, but whose contents are not classifiable as 'obscene', no matter how frivolous they may be. In such cases the practice of the Board has often been to ban on the strength of the blurb if it gives them the most meagre excuse. A classic example of this was the case of an American paperback edition of Daniel Defoe's *Roxana*. Strictly speaking, this type of decision is not within the Board's power to make. It might be argued however, that there are sound social grounds for such decisions; and there has been no evidence of criticism of these bannings.

When the Board decides to prohibit a book[16] it causes its prohibition order to be published in the *Iris Oifigiuil*; the order is effective from the date of publication, which normally occurs within a week of the decision of the Board.

The process for the censorship of periodical publications is in most respects the same as that for books, but there are important differences between the two.

In the first place, the Board examines at least three recently published issues of the periodical,[17] which it receives from members of the public. It is empowered to prohibit for all or any of the following reasons: that issues—

'(a) have usually or frequently been indecent or obscene, or

(b) have advocated the unnatural prevention of conception, etc. or

(c) have devoted an unduly large proportion of space to th publication of matter relating to crime' (Section 9, ss. 1).

The vast majority of prohibition orders in respect of periodicals are made on grounds of obscenity (see Figure 3).

These publications are banned for varying periods of time, ranging from twelve to three months[18] depending on the lesser or greater periodicity of the publication (Section 9, ss. 3). However, the practice of the Board appears to be and to have always been that if, after the expiration of the first prohibition order in respect of a particular periodical, that periodical continues to offend, then it is prohibited again and this second prohibition is permanent, being renewed automatically when it expires. Thus, there are on the *Register of Prohibited Publications* papers and magazines which have been subject to a prohibition order since the very first years of censorship, and it is quite possible that some of these have never been re-examined since that time. At first glance this would seem to be grossly unfair to the publications in question but in fact what it means is that the onus of 're-opening the case' is on the publishers. For the publisher may apply for a revocation order, or a variation order, at any time provided that three months have elapsed since the Appeal Board considered an earlier application in respect of the same publication.

4 THE APPEAL BOARD

The Censorship of Publications Appeal Board is appointed by the Minister for Justice under the terms of Section 3 of the 1946 Act. Its chairman must be a Supreme, High or Circuit Court Judge or a practising barrister or solicitor of not less than seven years standing. Since its inception in 1946 the Board has had as chairman Mr Justice Kevin O'Hanrahan Haugh, who was a High Court Judge at the time of his appointment, and became a Supreme Court Judge during his fifth term of office. One other member, (Mr Henry O'Hanlon, who has also been on the Board since 1946) is a member of the legal profession (though he need not necessarily be so), while the other members have always been associated with the arts to some extent, some at an academic level. As has been mentioned elsewhere, the Appeal Board membership has been noted for its permanence; there have been only two changes since 1946, and the Minister has never availed of the opportunity of replacing members when their term of office ends after each three-year period (see Appendix 5). The Board meets, on average, five times each year.

With the exception of the first years of its existence the Appeal Board has received few applications from authors, editors, publishers or members of the Oireachtas—who constitute the persons who have a right to make such application. For the three first-mentioned there is a statutory regulation requiring them to submit six copies of each book with their application, and to lodge a deposit of five pounds, recoverable if the Board considers that the application is not frivolous. I understand that only three or four applications have been deemed frivolous since 1946. Applications by five Oireachtas members are not required to be accompanied either by a deposit or by submission of a copy or copies of the book.[19] One result of this fact has been that the Appeal Board has experienced difficulty in obtaining the requisite copies of the books whose appeal is thus applied for. Even in 1961 one application lodged in 1947 was still pending. This is indicative of two facts—firstly, that many of these prohibited books have gone out of print (and so even if the appeal is allowed, the public has not much opportunity of reading the book) and secondly, that the Board has not considered it proper to go out of its way to obtain the copies itself. The *Annual Reports* of the Board for the years 1950 and 1951 contain two long lists of books for which applications were made in 1947, and copies had not yet been obtained. One might have thought that if the Board were actively interested in its task it might have taken the initiative to find books and avoid this considerable delay. The books in question included titles by Somerset Maugham, Maura Laverty, John Steinbeck, Marcel Proust, Aldous Huxley, Robert Graves, T. F. Powys, Samuel Beckett, copies of which could have been readily obtained by an intelligent use of library subscriptions.[20] This is particularly true in view of the absence of pressure of work on the Board; rarely were more than five meetings held each year, and the number of books considered at each meeting was small: thus one copy of each book would be quite ample—one copy is all that the Censorship Board receives, and that body could well do with more.

As was mentioned earlier, the 1946 Act provides that when examining a book the Censorship Board may communicate with the author, editor or publisher, and may take into account any representation made by him in relation thereto (Section 6, ss. 3), but curiously enough, there was no equivalent provision for the Appeal Board. This anomaly was remedied by a statutory regulation included in the Principal Regulations made in 1946, shortly after the Act became law.[21]

This regulation has been availed of by various appellants; indeed according to a Secretary of the Board appellants have in certain instances employed a solicitor to represent them. In a certain sense the Regulation can be compared with the provision in the British Obscene Publications Act 1959, whereby the defence is permitted to argue the literary merit of a book as a reason for which it should not be suppressed. This regulation, joined to the fact that the Chairman of the Board is in fact a Supreme Court Judge, means that a book can be given an *in camera* trial.[22]

When the Appeal Board receives a first application in respect of a prohibited book it may affirm or revoke the prohibition order, or vary it so as to exclude from the application thereof any particular edition. If it confirms the prohibition order, this means that the book is for ever banned (this is true when the prohibition order covers 'all editions'), and no other appeal can be made unless it is in respect of a *particular* edition for which an application has not previously been made. To the Board's mind an 'edition' means a version of the book in which there are textual changes: the mere fact that a book has been reset, published in a different format, with different jackets etc.: neither does the inclusion of a foreword, for example, make for a new edition, or the inclusion of the prohibited book in an omnibus edition along with non-prohibited material.

Although this interpretation of the word is not that in normal use by the publishers, it is easy to see that it is the only logical interpretation possible. It would be pointless for the Board to take into account mere physical changes in the appearance of a book. This having been said, it is nevertheless necessary to point out that, since different 'editions' of books (in the publishers' sense) rarely vary materially one from another, once a prohibition order has been affirmed by the Appeal Board, the book is to all intents and purposes banned *in perpetuam*. This is unfortunate: because it in some way refuses to recognise that public standards, especially standards of reticence, do vary—in the sense that what would have shocked in 1930 may only provoke a mild reaction forty years later. The only way to avoid this 'permanent' character of Appeal Board decisions (assuming that its interpretation of 'edition' is satisfactory) would appear to be the introduction of an amendment to the Act providing that application for appeal may be renewed (for a new printing), say ten or fifteen years after the first application has been rejected. There is no reason to think that such a provision would be abused for only such books as had withstood the test of time would still be in print after such an interval.

With regard to appeal relating to periodicals, the Board has similar powers as for books to make a revocation order or a variation order (Section 10).[23] In fact, most of its orders relating to periodicals have been straightforward revocation orders (see Figure 5). However, occasionally the ban has been lifted by a variation order. This means that a particular edition is permitted to circulate in the country while all other editions continued to be prohibited. The explanation for this procedure is that some periodicals undertake to publish a special edition for the Irish market; a recent example of this is the case of the newspaper, *The News of the World* which was banned in November 1930, and was the subject of a variation order in 1961 when it undertook to publish a special edition for Ireland. According to a Secretary of the Board, the editors of some prohibited periodicals actually submitted to the Board sample copies of proposed special Irish editions which they prepared at their own expense for the Board's examination. To some people the behaviour of the publishers (mainly British) is two-faced: it may take the form of serialising in the Irish edition the edifying, and probably sensational, life history of some pious person, while publishing in the English edition a 'frank' expose of London brothels. Hypocritical such behaviour may well be, but it could be more mildly described as the mere expression of financial interest.[24]

5 LAW ENFORCEMENT

The task of the Censorship Board and of the Appeal Board is limited to the examination of books and periodicals with a view to deciding whether they should be permitted to circulate in the country. Once a prohibition order has been made in one case, or sustained in the other, the Boards have no further function with regard to the particular publication involved. In other words, the enforcement of the law is not in their hands, but in those of the Customs and the police. The Customs have the right to seize and destroy any prohibited book they discover, whether in packages etc., or on the person or in the luggage of an incoming traveller. It is not, however, their duty actively to look for prohibited books, but when they do discover them, they seize them. One has no grounds for suspecting that they are negligent in this matter. No statistics are available of the magnitude of the Customs' activity in this field.

Since practically all the publications on the Register are published outside the country, this examination by the Customs (and by Post Office officials) does mean that control is not a very difficult task. This is undoubtedly true of large consignments of banned publications, whether sent by post or shipped; as has been mentioned earlier, small packages containing one copy of the publication would very likely escape detection unless they were among a number of small packages selected at random or carried very blatantly the label of a doubtful publisher.

Once a banned publication is smuggled into the country to a private individual the Censorship authorities or the police have no interest in it; however, if it were to find its way into a lending library or bookshop or newsvendor's stall, the person responsible would be guilty of an offence, for under Section 14, ss. 1, of the 1946 Act a person is forbidden to (a) sell, or expose, offer, advertise or keep for sale, or (b) distribute or offer or keep for distribution, any prohibited publication. I have enquired of the Department of Justice as to the number of prosecutions annually brought under the Censorship of Publications Acts, and have been informed that these statistics are not available, and that to compile them would require an inordinate amount of research. The Secretary to the Department suggests that prosecutions under these Acts are 'uncommon —perhaps not more than six per annum on average'.[25] From our perusal, of Irish daily newspapers over this period, we are not surprised by this estimate, and should say that probably the figure is less than the number given. There have been no spectacular cases in the sense of vast quantities of banned books being discovered. And there is one case on record of a bookseller being fined for selling an insignificant prohibited book which some two or three weeks later was removed from the Register by a revocation order!

It is interesting to recall that to obtain from a district justice a search warrant in respect of prohibited publications, the police are not required to prove that prohibited publications are being kept for sale or distribution on the premises in question: 'reasonable ground for suspicion' (Section 17, 1) is sufficient. In England there is an onus of *proof* on the police: this procedure is the cause of much inefficiency in the task of controlling the sale of indecent matter.

In addition to prosecuting in respect of the sale or distribution of these publications the police have also at times used their powers under common law to bring before the Courts persons who deal with indecent publications, not already banned. Unfortunately no statistics are available of the extent to which this is done, but it is doubtful if there is a case more often than once every two years.

The Irish daily and Sunday press do not take any very important part in the censorship process. Of their differing attitudes to the behaviour of the Boards and to the Acts, I have treated elsewhere. However, it may be convenient to recall here that the *Irish Times* is the only daily paper which publishes lists of prohibitions, revocation and variation orders; the other papers merely give the number of orders and the grounds on which they are made. But there is no evidence that any paper goes out of its way to advertise these bannings or the banned books themselves; only very rarely is a prohibited publication reviewed in the Irish press.

With the exception of the members' rights to appeal against a prohibition order, the Oireachtas has only a tenuous connection with the censorship. At different times during the operation of the 1946 Act questions have been put to the Minister for Justice on the subject: and there has been one motion—that of Senator Kingsmill-Moore in 1947 to annul the Principal Regulations; but the amount of time devoted to censorship in either Dail or Seanad has been minimal.

If one compares the few occasions on which the censorship question was raised in the Oireachtas with the comparatively large volume of criticism which the Board received from the general public, one is inclined to the view that deputies and senators have only the most meagre interest in censorship, and that even those who delight in being outspoken find better outlets for their temper in more popular issues, such as the travelling expenses of Presidential suites.

6 NEWSAGENTS AND BOOKSELLERS

Of all the institutions connected with the publication and distribution of the printed word, bookselling (and its associate, the selling of periodicals) seems to have the greatest single financial interest. One might then expect the Irish bookseller to be critical of the censorship, but surprisingly enough the contrary would appear to be true. The Irish Booksellers Association, and more especially the Irish Retail Newsagents, Stationers and Booksellers Association have staunchly supported the Censorship Board, and an examination of their trade magazines reveals only a very occasional criticism as compared with many laudatory references which are particularly to be found in the speeches of Presidents at annual general meetings.

At all events, the relations between the Censorship Board and booksellers in recent years have been nothing less than amicable. This may be due in part to the leniency of the Board, but it is accounted for mainly by the fact that the booksellers approve of, and do not merely acquiesce in censorship. This is certainly true of the more established and respectable booksellers and newsagents, and it is easy to understand. These shops deal with the public to an extent that no other individual or institution in the publishing business does; their wares are constantly in the public eye, and the Irish public is a conservative body which dislikes and refuses to be exposed to publications of doubtful moral value; it pays the bookseller to be conservative in this sense.[26] This is not to say that he does not criticise some aspects of the machinery of censorship. A particular bookseller is now and then annoyed to find that the Customs have detained his consignment of a certain title, while they have overlooked another consignment of the same book which was dispatched at the same time; but there is no simple way to avoiding this inconsistency: it could only be done by having the Customs and postal officials examine all parcels which pass through their hands, and this would be impracticable.[27] Again, as has been mentioned earlier, some booksellers, realising the importance of the Customs' role, have suggested that the officials devoted to this work should be required to have higher educational qualifications than is at present the case.

Booksellers have no formal relationship with the Censorship Board, but it is by no means unknown for members of the Board, especially the Chairman, to 'pop into' the Dublin bookshops particularly to soothe any bookseller whose consignment may have been held up for some time pending the Board's decision. This treatment is appreciated by booksellers: it is clearly practicable only in a country such as Ireland, where the important bookshops are of the order of ten in Dublin, two in Cork, and a few others in Galway, Limerick, Waterford and towns of a similar size.

Dublin booksellers will point out that the Censorship Board very often 'misses' paperbacks in the sense that, because they sell very fast, by the time a ban is announced average sales have already been achieved. There is little doubt that this is the case, for the standard of paperbacked books (especially as indicated by their covers) in Dublin shops has deteriorated considerably in recent years. It is still a far throw from Charing Cross Road.

All that can be said on this point is that the Board's desire to ban these publications must be backed by quick decisions. The Customs authorities, for their part, could maintain a stricter vigilance during the period in which the book is in the Board's hands.

While on the subject of paperbacks and periodicals, I should refer to the large and growing number of businesses which specialise in these publications. Many of these deal in a cheap type of publication at cheap prices; they can then be expected to 'feel the pinch' of censorship more. Some wholesalers dealing in these publications certainly do, for they buy in large quantities from larger wholesalers in Britain, and are not able to choose the titles they receive: they have to take what they get, the bad along with the passable, and very often hampered by Customs examination. The only books which the English wholesalers do not include in their consignment are those which are on the *Register*; but, with some at least of the other titles, it is crystal clear that the only reason they are not on the *Register* is that they have not yet come before the Board. This procedure—of Irish wholesalers having to take what they get, willy-nilly—also holds good for the central branches for Ireland in Dublin of English circulating libraries; one Customs official has told me that often 90% of the contents of a consignment for one firm would be detained on examination, and that the Dublin manager and Customs officers have often had heated arguments on the point.

Summing up the relationship of the retail and wholesale trade to the censorship, one may say that there has never or seldom been articulate criticism from this quarter; that the degree of discomfort suffered increases as one goes from the more expensive to the more ephemeral agents and sellers, and that on the whole the trade co-operates with the censorship.

Conclusion

I have tried in this study to gather, order and present facts about censorship in Ireland, avoiding the value judgements which a subject such as this so easily provokes.

It is not easy to estimate public opinion on the censorship issue: opinion sampling methods have rarely been used in Ireland and have never been used in this particular field. One is therefore forced to rely largely on articulate opinion as found in the press, trying to weigh correctly the opinions expressed by various individuals and groups, as also the unexpressed opinion of the large sector of the population which is either indifferent to, or aquiesces in, censorship as it is practised. Given that the *Irish Times* has been a protagonist in this account, one is exposed to the criticism that from the mere fact that a few individuals write (or desist from writing) to a particular newspaper, one ought not infer that 'public opinion' is critical of the censorship (or supports it, as the case may be). A valid criticism in the abstract, this is an over-simplification in the present context. The *Irish Times* (I use it as an umbrella word to include a scattered and growing public criticism of the Establishment) undoubtedly has its faults and still labours under a well-founded suspicion that the Ireland it represented was a landed, Protestant ascendancy which looked to Britain not only politically but also culturally and spiritually. But paradoxically it was by fighting a rearguard action in the 1920's to defend many political and social values to which few Irish men would today publicly subscribe, that it acquired its habit of freedom of expression. It is, certainly, liable to misuse that freedom but any incidental harm is outweighed by its acting as a release valve for otherwise frustrated opinion—a device which the country needs if it is to avoid the dead hand of subtle clericalism and the abuses of political machinery.

I might go on from here to discuss how acceptable is the principle of censorship and how effective the system. To my mind the acceptability of censorship in a general sense does not present a problem. To a great extent every educational system is based on the assumption that reading conditions one's personal development: and character and general outlook largely determine both individual and public acceptances of moral standards, which, in turn, affect the well-being of society. There is a wide agreement in theory in most societies on the prohibition of 'hard core pornography' but constant controversy as to whether particular books fit in this category. The incidence of grundyism has at times so frustrated the freedom of writers that liberal opinion has maintained that all censorship goes wrong in practice and therefore no legal or social control should be admitted. This view has been shattered by the great traumatic experience of twentieth century conscience—the inhumanities of nazism.

Certainly that obscene literature is objectionable is a judgement generally accepted in Irish society, and for this reason alone there is a *prima facie* case for controlling its sale and distribution in some way: a control exercised on behalf of 'the immature', and though this group-designation can include adults as well as young people, for practical purposes the State must take the protection of the young as the main justification for its action. I do not mean that it should apply *virginibus puerisque* criteria, providing a fairy-tale culture, but simply that the malformation which pornography produces in young people is the strongest reason for prohibiting its circulation. Certainly, young people have a right to a balanced formation; censorship of reading matter by parents too often defeats its own end; by exercising control of ponography the State or other organs of society can play a useful role.*

The distribution of pornographic literature may be regulated in two ways—by prior censorship or by post-publication control. The former of these would mean in effect State licensing of the press, a procedure which in a modern democratic State would be quite impracticable, even if it were acceptable; of its nature it tends to be secret or semi-secret and any injustices done to writers or publishers can only with difficulty be redressed by society.† Post-publication control is of two main types: by a censorship system which prohibites the sale and distribution of books

---

* In a recent book, *On Iniquity* (London 1967), Pamela Hansford Johnson develops these grounds for censorship by examining the direct and indirect influence of reading on the defendants at the Moors Trial (Chester 1966). Dr George Steiner of King's College, Cambridge is another attractive exponent of forms of control. In such views there is no shade of grundyism. They are based on reasoned personal convictions on the effects of reading on conduct and are accompanied by a plea for scientific research into the effects of reading.

† A recent elaborate study of licensing is Richard Findlater, *Banned: a review of theatrical censorship in Britain*, London 1967: a fact-filled book written on an anti-censorship thesis.

which are considered to be objectionable, or by a general prohibition on objectionable matter. In Ireland both methods are employed. There is a general prohibition on publications advocating birth control, whether or not they appear on the *Register*; and it is still possible to bring a prosecution for obscene libel under common law. But the principal method employed is the exercise of censorship by a five-man Board. One of the main reasons for the establishment of that Board in 1929 was that the prosecution method had become clumsy, wasteful and ineffective due to the fact that most publishers were outside the jurisdiction of the Courts.

The 1929 Act was not a hasty measure but a reasonable solution to a real problem. It was accepted enthusiastically in some quarters, with indifference in others, and with reservations in still others—adequate support for any political institution. Forty years later, these attitudes prevail. In the meantime, however, sections of opinion critical of the censorship as practised brought about a certain liberalisation: in the early forties an influential movement produced changes in the censorship machinery; in the mid-fifties another force—relying for the most part on the same personalities—moderated censorship practice.

Was censorship in fact conducted in accordance with the law? This question could be answered only by the legal decision of a judge or jury; in fact the Censorship Board has never been legally indicted (the closest it came to this was a Seanad debate in 1942). The only real grounds for a decision against the Board would be that it banned books which it clearly had no right to ban—books of definite literary merit which no reasonable man could describe as 'indecent' according to the Acts' definition. On the assumption that I am a reasonable man I might, for example, accuse the Boards which banned Sean O'Faolain's *Bird Alone*, Halliday Sutherland's *Laws of Life*, Walter Macken's *The Bogman*—to mention only a very few.

Less clear is the case of those serious works of literature which do contain some 'marked' passages (this is an unfortunately quantitative description which I use only as a metaphor).* The Acts do instruct the Censorship Board to take into consideration the literary merit and the class of reader which may reasonably be expected to read each book. This

---

* Necessarily a metaphor, otherwise the whole question is viewed naively: see Peter R. Connolly, 'The Moralists and the Obscene', in *Irish Theological Quarterly*, vol. xxxii, 3, pp. 116-128 (April 1965), a valuable investigation of literary considerations affecting the moral evaluation of obscene writing.

implies, negatively, that cheapjack pornography will get summary treatment. However, there are books of literary value which one knows will have the same social effects as pornography. (D. H. Lawrence's *Lady Chatterley's Lover* is a case in point. Certainly no Irish jury would have qualms about prohibiting this book—in which case it would in effect be deciding that moral and social considerations must outweigh literary and cultural ones.) The great problem is that contemporary literature, in reaction to the hypocrisy and discretion of other times, has become absorbed by sex and the incidence and permissiveness of the type of writing one finds in *Lady Chatterley* is currently increasing. If the Irish censorship now bans books of this type (as is its right according to law) will it in twenty or thirty years' time be held up to ridicule as earlier Boards have been or will it be praised for unique discernment of the intrinsic dangers of a passing fashion? The following excerpt from an editorial in the *Times Literary Supplement* (8 July 1965) echo my own doubts on this point:

> 'Novelists who busy themselves with sex can be divided into two groups. There are those who bring in sex because it sells; who put in salacious passages only for inflammatory purposes. In this case it is to be hoped that their novels will not sell, or at least that they will be recognised as belonging to a genre which needs this kind of underpinning, and will consequently be treated with the lack of seriousness, even derision they deserve. Then there are those who wish for serious reasons, honourable reasons, to write about sex. Such reasons include the study of human relationships, in terms of tragedy, comedy, satire and what you will. Obviously it is a little late in the day to institute some form of Inquisition about the presentation and treatment of sex in every kind of novel; it is more a matter of combating the acceptance of sex as the master metaphor for problems of existence: the notion that with it the writer may drill through to the undiscovered deposits of the collective unconscious and tap the *Zeitgeist*. There have been writers—D. H. Lawrence is the most obvious example—who have done this, disrupting an old and to some extent forging a new climate of feeling. At least part of the shock caused by Mr William Burroughs's contribution is that often he uses sex as a metaphor for his pre-occupations, but, forced by its translation to common literary usage, he rends it in Gothick pieces, flees from it. The naked lunchers sit in a litter of dead metaphors . . .

'Every writer can talk with truth of his need to issue memoranda on the current state of society but the use of sex in the memoranda writing so often ignores the dangers of the positivist fallacy. That is, that if you describe people copulating rather than kissing, you have inevitably said something of greater profundity about man's estate. Stendhal knew better and achieved a wonderful insight into the passions of Julien Sorel when he made him promise himself to take Mme. de Renal's hand at the stroke of ten.

'Those who reply that if writers are to discuss the issues of the day and age they must treat of such topics as, say, homosexuality in direct terms and that not to do would be to shirk the issue, should be reminded that here the novel finds itself staring documentary in the face and that if it stares too long it will turn to stone. Documentary exists to report the world; the novel has further tasks. It was said in the nineteenth century that the thing is not just to understand the world, but to change it; one of the grizzliest relics of late romanticism has been the notion, both in writing and in criticism, of the essential otherness of art, its basic irrelevance to life. It should not be forgotten —and how often it is forgotten—that novels are read by people, affect people, change people . . .'

On the grounds that people in their formative years should not be exposed to material for which they have not critical apparatus for mature appraisal censorship of books of this type may be admitted provided adults are given some satisfactory, if awkward, legal method of access to such literature.

Aside from books which use this sex metaphor in an obsessive way there is no doubt in my own mind that the literary merit and general tenor criteria ought to be applied to 'save' a book: the practical prudence of this judgement should be obvious from the history of censorship in Ireland. The possible danger to public morality which a 'marginal' book might offer is outweighed by the constant danger of heavy-handed censorship turning Ireland into a cultural ghetto—indeed, into something worse than a ghetto for, in addition to warding off foreign influences it also has expelled its own nonconformists and rejected invaluable criticism of its own social norms and customs.

In pleading for freedom in this area one realises that once a censorship system is admitted it is impossible accurately to define the scope of its operations. We are in the area of opinion and compromise: compromise which will never satisfy all interested parties and opinion ranging from that of the Minister for Justice or of the Boards which he appoints to that of the general public. One may regret certain decision of the Boards and try to rectify them; from the point of view of the public rather than the writer it would be an exaggeration to regard them as tragic; but it could well be argued that a strict censorship breeds scepticism and disrespect for state and society and that for this reason alone the Censorship Board particularly would be well advised to exercise a prudence which errs on the side of freedom. A relevant consideration is that in a world which is being steadily integrated by the means of social communication many forms of censorship are simply ineffective—a situation which would indicate that greater stress should be laid on positive action in the field of education: it is probably true that the teaching of literature in Irish schools is carried out in such a rarefied, censored atmosphere that the child is not being properly equipped to deal with the strong reading matter which he will later certainly meet—he is being artificially protected, not educated. Yet Dublin is still a pleasant place to walk in where sex is embodied in living persons, not sidewalk hoardings and neon-signs.

Has the censorship been effective in its attempt to control the sale of 'pure ponography'—of trashy, obscene books, and of periodicals which are obscene or specialise in crime? It is difficult to venture an opinion at first, for one tends to be distracted by the almost continuous controversy on the issue of literary merit. On closer examination it would appear that thirty years of censorship have at least controlled the influx of rubbishy publications. For years newspapers of the *News of the World* variety were excluded from the country; horror comics too have been effectively prohibited; and the vast majority of the books on the *Register* are of no cultural value whatever. As I have pointed out, the pressure of public opinion has sometimes been needed to make the Board prohibit these publications, but they have been prohibited, and since they are the type of publication the legislators were aiming at in 1929, the censorship may in this sense be described as 'successful'. If numerous periodicals escaped the net, the blame must be laid at the door of the average member of the public, who alone is responsible for registering complaints regarding periodicals, and without whose co-operation the censorship of periodicals would be ineffective. Certainly the censors whould be well advised to spend more of their spare time browsing in newsagents' shops than in booksellers', and they would do well to bear in mind the far-reaching effect which a ban on a periodical publication has, as compared with one on a book. Although far fewer periodicals are published than books, these bans are, as it were, renewed and actualised each week or month, and affect a much larger section of the public. It may very well be that if the Censorship Boards had not misdirected their energies by prohibiting works of literary value they might have exercised a more effective control on these cheaper publications; the opportunity still awaits them. But one has the impression that the advent of the paperback has offered the system its gravest threat—the sheer physical task of reviewing the constant flow of new titles is outside the scope of five part-time workers.

Over the years numerous suggestions have been made for the improvement of the censorship machinery. I have no special brief for adding to these, but some observations are called for.

In view of the need for censors to reflect in some way the moral standards of contemporary society a strong case can be made for an upper age limit of sixty for membership of either Board: in some instances men over seventy have been appointed.*

The requirement that complaints regarding periodical publications be accompanied by copies of three recent issues appears to act as a deterrent. Since the Censorship Board is dependent on formal complaints (from members of the public) in respect of periodicals as distinct from books, the statutory regulations could be modified to require simply that a deposit be made to avoid frivolous complaints, the Board procuring the necessary copies.

The causes for the paucity of appeals have been examined elsewhere. In view of the reluctance of authors, publishers and members of the Oireachtas to make application for appeal, there could be no serious objection to extending the right of appeal to ordinary members of the public. This would still not put appeal on a par with complaint (since the Customs are the source of most complaints), but it would go a long way to rectifying an imbalance which has always existed between the two boards. And instead of requiring a deposit (not to be found among

---

* It is difficult to select good censors: cf Mr V. S. Pritchett's remarks in an article on the censorship of plays in the *New Statesman and Nation* (20 April 1958): 'The second defect of such an office as the Lord Chamberlain's is that its readers are well-bred, cultivated, tolerant and experienced men. They are, doubtless, gentlemen. To know them must be a pleasure. That is to say, they are exactly the type unfitted by education or habit of mind for judging the unscrupulous curiosity, the necesary daring and restless intelligence of artists of any kind." The writer exaggerates but he has a good point which can help one to understand why the Irish Board should give a book the benefit of the doubt.

censorship requirements) the provision of one copy of the book would be quite adequate.

Arrangements should be made for the re-opening of appeals after a fixed period of time has elapsed since the rejection of a first application for appeal. Usually such a facility is not required, for worthwhile books are kept in print and new editions may be submitted to the Appeal Board even if applications in respect of earlier editions were rejected. However, some interesting books still on the *Register* twenty or thirty years after their prohibition are an unnecessary source of embarrassment to the Irish intellectual. In particular I refer to works by Irish authors whose sale in Ireland was restricted by prohibition and which are not likely to be republished. The lifting of an old ban on such books would have at least the effect of removing them from the *Register*, and of permitting the distribution of copies long withheld from circulation in library stacks. (It might even encourage the re-publication of these books by an enterprising Irish publisher: it is too much to expect an Irish publisher to risk investment in a new edition which he might be unable to offer for sale in the country.) Thus, a strong case can be made for a total revision of the *Register*—at least on the grounds that some prohibitions reflect judgements which no contemporary board would sustain: and rejected appeals, for example, could be reopened every ten years, at new appeal. An unsatisfactory but less difficult means of revision would be the issue of a general permission to sell and distribute specific banned books (under Section 14 of the 1946 Act). Under the same section permits for library distribution could open up a restricted circulation of titles on the responsibility and initiative of particular libraries.

The prohibition on importation of banned books which form part of personal baggage (included under Sections 5, 1 and 18, 1) appears to be an infringement of personal freedom and could be repealed.

Authors and publishers could be given a regulated right to appear before the Appeal Board. At the moment they must seek the Board's permission if they wish to argue their case before it.

The custom of publishing Reports of the Boards might be regulated in a legal form and both Reports and Registers issued at regular, frequent and specified intervals: at present it is difficult to acquire up-to-date information except through scattered references in the *Iris Oifigiuil*.

These are particular improvements which do not affect the underlying principles of the Censorship Acts. The need for a more radical reform is not indicated by the state of public opinion in Ireland at present.

There is really no 'conclusion' to this study—neither in the sense of *finis*, for censorship continues to be a feature of Irish life; nor in the sense of significant discoveries, for I have assumed throughout that it is not possible to dogmatise on the solution to particular censorship questions: these are very much a matter of opinion, though the opinion of many is rigid to the point of intransigence.

Minor findings there have been in plenty, due mainly to the exhuming of facts buried in the files of Irish newspapers and journals, and to the access I have gained to certain private sources of information. These findings are significant, for the story of censorship is one of small incidents, each of which is insignificant in itself, but which taken together, go to make up one of the most controversial aspects of Irish social and cultural life.

Postscript

In April 1967 Mr Brian Lenihan, Minister for Justice, introduced in the Dail a Censorship of Publications Bill which would limit to twenty years the life of obscenity bannings on books, provide for the rebanning of released books, and remove the time limit of twelve months for the taking of an appeal against a prohibition order. In the course of debate the Minister brought in an amendment which reduced to twelve years the duration of a prohibition order, and with this single modification the bill became law in August 1967.

In one grand gesture over 5,000 titles were released from limbo. Some of them, it is true, would be rebanned but almost all the controversial books of the pre-1956 period and particularly the work of the many Irish writers rejected as unsuitable for their own society are now free to circulate in the country. And never again will a banning carry the sting of finality.

The 1967 bill provoked little public or parliamentary debate — reminding one that dry legal technicalities never have the drawing power of, say, a prohibition of the latest Edna O'Brien. Indeed, except for worthy campaigners such as Owen Sheehy Skeffington, inured to misunderstanding and suspected of fanaticism, controversy in Ireland is of the 'instant' variety — fast, random, with little staying power. Of the hundreds who attended the first meeting of a Censorship Reform Society in Dublin in December 1966, less than ten came forward to subscribe and the lonely committee with its cautious programme watched on the sidelines while Mr Lenihan cut the ground from under its feet.

The 1967 Act is undoubtedly an improvement in Irish censorship legislation. It involves no fundamental change and no erosion of censorship. And it is an immediate reminder that times do change.

Notes to Chapters

NOTES TO CHAPTER I

[1] A. V. Dicey, *Introduction to the Study of the Law of the Constitution*, (8th ed.), London 1915, pp. 241-242. For a good general account of the development of English law on obscenity, see Norman St John-Stevas, *Obscenity and the Law*, London 1958. Cf also *Minutes of Evidence* taken before the Select Committee on the Obscene Publications Bill, London (H.M. Stationary Office) 1958; also the *Report* of this Committee (H.M.S.O.).

[2] From the Evidence submitted by the Association to the Committee on Evil Literature, 1926 in the private papers of the late Professor R. Donovan (subsequently referred to as RDP).

[3] Cf R. S. Devane, SJ, 'Indecent Literature: some legal remedies' in the *Irish Ecclesiastical Record*, fifth series, vol. 25, pp. 182-204 (February 1925).

[4] Fr Devane took a lively interest in the problem of objectionable literature. He published numerous articles on the subject and was the only individual—as distinct from association—that was invited to give evidence before the Committee for Evil Literature (1926). Shortly before his death in 1951 he organised his last campaign—against the imported press.

[5] 1869-1946. First Chairman of the Censorship of Films Appeal Board and Chairman of the Censorship of Publications Board 1942-1946. Professor of Metaphysics at University College, Dublin.

[6] The information contained in this and the following paragraphs is taken from communications of the CTS forwarded by the Bishop of Galway to the Minister for Justice (RDP).

[7] *Parliamentary Debates* (Official Report), fifth series, vol. 62, cols. 142-143, (16 July 1925).

[8] *Parliamentary Debates*, fifth series, vol. 194, cols. 790-800 *passim* (16 April 1926).

[9] *Parliamentary Debates*, fifth series, vol. 65, col. 159 (14 December 1926).

[10] *The Times*, 16 October 1928. Mr A. P. Herbert promptly wrote to 'assure the Home Secretary that my wife and I are capable of watching over our family's reading without any Jixotic assistance from him' (19 October 1928).

[11] Report in *The Times* (11 December 1928)

[12] Cf the *Nation and Athenaeum* (9 March 1929); this gave rise to a sustained correspondence in the columns of this journal, in which Gilbert Murray, Lytton Strachey, Leonard Woolf and others took part (March-April 1929).

[13] London 1929.

[14] These States were: Albania, Australia, Austria, Belgium, China, Colombia, Costa Rica, Czechoslovakia, Cuba, Denmark, Finland, France, Great Britain,

Greece, Guatemala, Hungary, Haiti, India, Italy, Japan, Latvia, Lithuania, Luxembourg, Monaco, Netherlands, Persia, Poland, the Kingdom of Serbs, Croats and Slovenes, Siam, Spain, Sweden, Switzerland, U.S.A., Uruguay and Venezuela. The Irish Free State subscribed to the agreement on 31 March 1924.

[15] See p. 3.

[16] Professor Thrift was Provost of Trinity College, Dublin from 1937 to 1942. He served on the Censorship of Publications Board from 1930 to 1936.

[17] Born 1882. General Secretary of the Irish National Teachers' Organisation 1916-1948. Leader of the Labour Party in Dail Eireann 1927-1932. Member of Seanad Eireann 1941-1944 and 1948-1951. Mr O'Connell is the only member of the Committee who is still living.

[18] Minutes of Evidence were never published but were left in the Oireachtas Library for consultation by members. In addition to examining these papers, we have also had access to the private papers of Professor Donovan; these latter include, along with all the Minutes of Evidence, the correspondence etc. of the Committee of Enquiry.

[19] These associations, etc. were: the Catholic Truth Society of Ireland; * the Irish Vigilance Association; * the Church of Ireland Young Men's Christian Association; the City of Dublin Young Men's Christian Association; the Boys' Brigade; the Irish Christian Brothers; * the Catholic Headmasters' Association; * the School Masters' Association; the Irish National Teachers' Organisation and one private person, Fr R. S. Devane, sj. (The Associations marked with an asterisk sent witnesses, who were examined by the Committee.)

[20] Cf 'Ethics of Birth Control', a leading article in *The Times* (3 June 1925) commenting on the Report on the Ethics of Birth Control issued by the National Council of Public Morals: 'the differences of opinion, not only on the ethical aspect of the question, but also on the medical, economic and ethnical aspects, which cannot be separated from it, are too great to permit a decisive verdict.'

In 1928, when criticism of the birth control clauses of the Censorship Bill was mounting, *The Standard* (25 August) recalled how the last Lambeth Conference had 'specifically condemned the practices connected with birth control' and complained (15 September 1928) at the 'liberal attitude of Protestant clergymen here' on the subject.

See also M. P. Cleary, 'The Church of Ireland and Birth Control' in *Irish Ecclesiastical Record,* fifth series, vol. xxxviii, p. 622 (December 1931).

[21] The above is taken from an unsigned statement in Professor Donovan's papers. An examination of the Minutes of Evidence in the Oireachtas Library has confirmed that it was submitted by Brother Craven, Superior General of the Irish Christian Brothers.

[22] 'It would give rise to a minimum of litigation, a maximum of noise and bustle, and fees and prosecutions, with, in the final result, a minimum of good.' However, in a letter to the Committee of Enquiry, dated 19 April 1926, Mr D. Bridgeman, Hon. Secretary of the Irish Retail Newsagents', Booksellers' and Stationers' Association, intimated that his Association entirely approved of Mr Geoghegan's bill.

[23] As regards the sale of these publications at this time, Mr Charles Eason, in the course of a letter to Professor Thrift (10 June 1926), stated that comparing the current circulation figures with those for 1919, there was a 'large falling-off' in the sales of the *News of the World*, the sales of *John Bull* had dropped by one half and those of *Sporting Times* were 'very small' (this last mentioned paper had increased in price from one penny to twopence) [RDP].

[24] A figure of 30 was given for the size of the proposed Board 'as there would be a considerable amount of reading to be done, and a large body would be necessary so that in every case there would be a panel of persons competent to favour a considered area'.

[25] Under warrants from the Minister for Justice covering some 150 known dealers in indecent wares and literature with addresses in Paris, Brussels, Berlin and elsewhere on the Continent, the Department had detained correspondence leaving or entering the country. 'I may mention that in 1923 we stopped 23 outward letters addressed to them; in 1924, 47 outward and 10 inward; and in 1926, 8 outward and no inward. That indicates that the number of people ordering indecent stuff is comparatively few and is declining.' The letters and enclosures (including money orders and bank notes) were destroyed.

[26] The current practise was as follows: 'Advertisements of contraceptives are occasionally found in the post, but this Department is advised that unless these advertisements are themselves indecent, in wording or illustration, they cannot legally be detained under existing Post Office Acts. When found they are, with the concurrence of the Minister for Justice, returned to the senders with an intimation that this Government considers them unsuitable for circulation in the Free State post, and with a warning that prosecution may follow any subsequent attempt to send them through the post.

'Contraceptives sent here from Great Britain are also being withheld from delivery as indecent articles and returned to the senders with a threat of proceedings if the offence is repeated. The senders have in every case expressed regret and promised not to offend again. This Department is, however, advised that the result of proceedings in such cases would be very doubtful. Up to 1908 prosecutions for the sending of contraceptives through the post were instituted in Great Britain and Ireland, but since 1908 the British P.O. has ceased to detain such articles owing to the reluctance of the British Courts to give a decision as to whether such articles are indecent.'

The above is a verbatim extract from the Assistant Secretary's evidence.

[27] An indication of the limited extent of police activity in this matter was given in the Dail on 15 November 1928. To the question 'Will the Minister state the number of persons and the number of charges made under the existing law dealing with indecent and obscene literature, also the number of convictions obtained for the period 6 December 1922 - 6 December 1926, and from 6 December 1926 to the present time?', the answer was: in the first period 5 persons charged, 5 convicted; in the second one charged and one convicted (*Dail Debates*, vol. 27, col. 175).

[28] The following comments in note form, made by Fr Dempsey (letter to the Secretary of the Committee, 28 November 1926), are significant:

'(1) I am inclined to think that we should let alone what is merely *vulgar*. Charlie Chaplin is often vulgar; never indecent. . . .

(3) It is not clear what machinery will bring the questionable matter before the constituted authority.

(4) Impossible to coin an effectual definition of "obscene" or "indecent".
Better leave the sense of the Authority set up to decide, and decide finally. . . .

(6) On no account should artists be allowed on the censoring Committee. We know what they do in the name of Art.

(7) Texts of classics for school use to be vigorously Bowdlerised. . . .

(9) *Something* in the way of an appeal court.'

[29] Cf *Irish Times* article on 'Censorship by the Gun' (15 September 1928) referring to an incident when several thousand copies of an English paper were burned after a train hold-up in County Sligo. Similar burnings took place in Dalkey and Killiney.

Referring to these and other such events twenty years later Senator Campbell probably overdramatised them when he said 'We know how, Sunday after Sunday, in our towns and villages, the people themselves seized these lecherous publications and publicly burned them in the market squares' (*Seanad Debates*, vol. 30, col. 980, 14 November 1945).

Evidence of a private burning was submitted to the Committee on Evil Literature by the Irish Christian Brothers. In their Statement there is mention of the treatment meted out to *Pear's Annual* 1925 because of its inclusion of the famous 'Cherry Tree' Carol: 'I at once despatched messengers to buy up all the unsold copies to be found in Dublin. The messengers returned with about 70 copies. . . . We telephoned to the *Evening Herald* for a photographer. On his arrival we set on fire all the collected specimens together with those we had in the office. The whole blaze cost us £4 10s 0d plus a gallon of paraffin.'

Before the War, some members of the Vigilance Association had taken the extreme step of burning copies of English newspapers to which they objected. The city of Limerick appears to have led the campaign. In his article 'Indecent Literature: Some Legal Remedies' in the *Irish Ecclesiastical Record*, fifth series, vol. 25, pp. 182-204, Fr R. Devane, sj recalls the 'remarkable and effective attack on the filthy Sunday cross-Channel papers in Limerick in 1911.'

[30] *The Committee on Evil Literature. Some notes of evidence*, Dublin 1927.

[31] This evidence has been mentioned above; here attention ought to be drawn especially to his proposed new definition of 'indecent': 'Whatever is opposed to common morality, offensive to chastity, immoral; whatever tends to inflame the passions or suggests thoughts of an impure or libidinous character; whatever is calculated to endanger the moral health of young people by exploiting youthful impulses.'

[32] For an earlier article advocating a tariff, cf. 'A Tariff against Filth' in *Irish Rosary*, vol. 29, pp. 631-637 (August 1925).

NOTES TO CHAPTER II

[1] *Irish Times*, 13 August 1928.

[2] 23 August 1928. Cf. leading article in the *Irish Statesman*, 27 October 1928.

[3] 13 August 1928.

[4] *The Irishman* was a Labourist weekly edited by Mr R. P. Mortished, who was later Chairman of the Labour Court, 1946-1952.

[5] Cf. the comments of Mr Sean Lemass who, while pledging the Opposition's support, acknowledged that there was plenty of room for improvement; 'In a Censorship Bill it is always much easier to go too far than not to go far enough, and we ought to be very careful to see that there would be nothing in this Bill, which by giving too much power to the Board or too much power to the Minister, would destroy public confidence in it.' Another indication of Fianna Fail attitudes is the welcome given to the elimination of the 'recognised associations' ('groups of busybodies') clause by *The Nation*, the Fianna Fail weekly newspaper founded Mr Sean T. O.Kelly in 1927 (2 March 1929).

[6] Cf. the *Irish Times'* remark that 'not one member of the Dail is satisfied with the Bill' (leading article, 25 October 1928). *The Standard* (27 October 1928) spoke of the Dail's 'unanimously favourable reception' of the Bill. One Fianna Fail Senator in particular, Senator Michael Comyn, was a more reliable supporter of Mr Fitzgerald-Kenney than were some Cumann na nGaedheal members.

[7] *Dail Debates*, vol. 26, col. 621 (18 October 1928).

[8] *The Star*, a Dublin weekly which supported Cumann na nGaedheal, rather than criticise the Bill diverted its attention to offer measures under debate at the time: cf. its mild leading article on 20 January 1929.

[9] *Dail Debates*, vol. 26, cols. 600-601 (18 October 1928).

[10] *Dail Debates*, vol. 28, col. 230 (21 February 1928).

[11] Dr Gogarty's description recalls that of the *Irish Statesman* 'Are not these associations the very bodies whose members have been breaking the laws of the Irish Free State, going into public libraries, taking out books by Shaw, Maeterlinck, Turgenieff and others and burning them without any action being taken by the Minister?' (27 October 1928). The same paper referred to the associations variously as 'preposterous' and 'ignorant and fanatical' (cf. leading article on 'Unrecognised Societies', 2 March 1929, at the time of the Dail Debate); and in its leading article on the passing of the Act (vol. 12, p. 366, 12 July 1929) it wrote 'By far the worst feature of the Bill was the provision under which the onus of setting the Censorship Board in motion was thrown on the 'recognised associations'.

[12] *Dail Debates*, vol. 28, cols. 246-247, (21 February 1929). Cf. the *Irish Statesman's* leading article of 2 March 1929, which complained that 'one of the worst things about the Bill was the assumption by many of its backers that Deputies . . . who rushed to amend the Bill were immoral and depraved persons. . . .' When the Committee State was resumed on 27 February 1929 Deputy J. J. Byrne regretted that the Minister 'has gone so far to meet the highbrow intellectuals in this section'. Professor Tierney, as one of the 'intellectuals', in turn suggested that one of the principal reasons for this outburst was that

'Deputy Byrne hopes to appear in the next issue of the *Catholic Pictorial* with a halo around his head' (*Dail Debates*, vol. 28, cols. 478z481, 27 February 1929).

[13] Cf. Æ's suggestion (in his article in the *Nation and Athanaeum*, 22 December 1928) that various associations drafted the Censorship Bill and forced it on the Minister; and, incidentally, his remark that the Catholic Hierarchy 'is very dubious about it (the Bill) indeed'.

[14] In his first (and mildest) report on the Bill, the Irish correspondent of *The Round Table* tended to discount this criticism. He wrote: 'The Bill is, in short, an attempt to steer a middle course between the quasi-intellectuals who would condemn nothing . . . and the ignorant zealots who would prevent all independence of thought and allow no foreign book of any kind to enter the country. It has already been violently attacked by both' (December 1928).

[15] Cf. 'The Censorship' by George Bernard Shaw (vol. 11, p. 206-208); 'The Censorship and Saint Thomas' by William Butler Yeats (vol. 11, p. 107-8).

An interesting view of Shaw's personal attitude to pornography was given by Mr St. John Ervine in his Appreciation in the the *Spectator* (10 November 1950): '. . . in mental cleanness he was far more fastidious than Tolstoy. During more than forty years' knowledge of him I never heard him use an improper word or tell what is called a dirty story. He himself declared that he was deeply shocked by some of the words James Joyce used in *Ulysses*. *Lady Chatterley's Lover*, if he had read it, would have horrified him.'

On the Yeats article in the *Irish Statesman*, cf. 'Mr Yeats and St Thomas' in *The Standard* (29 September 1928); on the Shaw article cf. 'Mr Shaw and Censorship', in the same paper (24 November 1928).

[16] Cf. *Irish Times*, 1 November 1928.

[17] Cf. *Irish Independent* report, 23 August 1928.

[18] 8 November 1928. Some of the *Irish Times*' readers did not take kindly to Pound's intervention. Indeed the correspondence sustained since the publication of the Bill lapsed for a while at this time when someone quoted a somewhat blasphemous poem by Pound in a letter to the paper (13 November 1928).

On the question of American censorship at the time, see Sean O Faolain's article on 'Censorship in America' in the *Irish Statesman*, vol. 11, pp. 86-8.

One Irish author writing twenty years later tried to see this criticism in perspective. Speaking of the 'Bright Young [Irish] Things' of the 'twenties he wrote: 'they felt an enormous boredom. . . . We were wrong and over-impatient—unjust also, to the men who were re-building amid the ruins. We ignored their prosaic but necessary work and concentrated our indignation on their Acts for prohibiting divorce and for prohibiting the sale of "evil literature"—measures which might have been expected from any Irish Catholic Government, and which, considering the social atmosphere of Ireland, did little more than register prohibitions that would in any case, have been effective in fact if not in form' (Arland Ussher, *The Face and Mind of Ireland*, New York, 1950).

[19] *Dail Debates*, vol. 26, cols. 595 (18 October 1928).

[20] Agreed to on 20 March 1929 (*Dail Debates*, vol. 28, col. 1529).

[21] At the Committee Stage in the Seanad Sir John Keane tried further to restrict the definition by deleting all the words after the word 'vice' but he was

unsuccessful (*Seanad Debates*, vol. 12, cols. 239-243, 25 April 1929). It was modified slightly in the 1946 Act; the word 'includes' being substituted for the phrase 'shall be construed as'.

[22] *Dail Debates*, vol. 26, cols. 829-830 (24 October 1928).

[23] *The Round Table*, vol. 19, p. 389–390, March 1929. In this, his second article on the Bill, the writer was much more critical of the measure: 'The proposed censorship will be ineffective, obscurantist and ridiculous.'

[24] *Dail Debates*, vol. 26, col. 829 (24 October 1928).

[25] *Dail Debates*, vol. 26, col. 598 (18 October 1928).

[26] Gogarty proposed the most extreme type of safeguard—that books should not come within the Censorship Board's purview at all. He twice criticised the Bill as being 'duplex'—'it should have directed itself solely against . . . contraceptive literature and nobody could object' (cf. *Seanad Debates*, vol. 12, cols. 86-92, 11 April 1929). Another point raised by Senator Gogarty was that typescripts should not come within the scope of the Act. However, he moved no amendment to this effect.

[27] *Dail Debates*, vol. 28, cols. 1529-1532 (Recommitted, 20 March 1929). Mr Fitzgerald-Kenney insisted however, that the 'final consideration' should be moral not literary: 'I know that it is not Deputy Tierney's or Deputy Law's intention that it [any of the above five matters] should be the final consideration. It may be said "This is a great literary book, no matter how indecent it is", but that is not their intention' (*Dail Debates*, vol. 28, col. 503, 27 February 1929). In order to stress this, the Minister preferred that this clause 'permit' rather than 'instruct' the Board to have regard to these matters. The Dail agreed to this, but the Seanad preferred to give the Board a specific instruction.

Two other amendments further restricted the scope of the Act in this connection. One of these, moved by Sir James Craig, had the effect of excluding from the very definition of 'book' and 'periodical publication' publications 'certified by the Board to be published *bona fide* for the information or instruction of members of the medical . . . profession' (Section 2); a Seanad amendment wrote in a similar safeguard for legal books.

[28] *Seanad Debates*, vol. 12, col. 81, 11 April 1929.

[29] *Seanad Debates*, vol. 12, col. 50, 10 April 1929.

[30] *Seanad Debates*, vol. 12, col. 58, 11 April 1929.

[31] With the intention of protecting classical works, Senator Sir John Keane at the Committee Stage proposed that the Act should be made to apply only to those books which were published after 31 December 1927. But Senator Comyn pointed out that the principle behind this amendment was wrong: that if the Censorship Board was to have authority over what was indecent and obscene it should be given that authority, and that if the amendment were carried, there would be a danger of an artificial demand for older books. The Minister, too, on the grounds that the classics were already safeguarded, refused to accept the amendment. Cf. *Seanad Debates*, vol. 12, col. 307, 25 April 1929.

[32] Sir John Keane. Born 1873. Fifth baronet, DSO 1916; DL; Barrister-at-law, Middle Temple, 1904; Senator 1922-1936; 1938-1948. He married a daughter of Sir Michael Hicks-Beach (later first Earl of St Aldwyn), Conservative Chancellor of the Exchequer.

[33] There is no doubt that Keane was not surprised at the type of books the Censorship Board was later to ban. His speeches on the Bill showed an unusually wide knowledge of modern fiction, and while many senators pooh-poohed his prophecies as to the types—and indeed names—of the books which would be banned, later events were to prove him right. It would almost seem that few members of Parliament could 'read the signs of the times', that few realised the trend that current fiction was taking.

[34] *Dail Debates*, vol. 26, cols. 626-627, 18 October 1928.

[35] *The Standard* (27 October 1928) spoke of 'one particularly gratifying' effect of this debate: 'the bogey of sectarian purpose in the Bill was effectually disposed of. Professor Thrift gave the bogey its *coup de grace*'.

[36] *Dail Debates*, vol. 26, col. 658, 18 October 1928.

[37] *Dail Debates*, vol. 26, cols. 607-608, 18 October 1928.

[38] In the other house, Senator Comyn described the distribution of birth control literature as 'political propaganda, and propaganda directed against the Irish race' (*Seanad Debates*, vol. 12, col. 99, 11 April 1929).

[39] President Tierney (in an interview) recalls that it was his experience of Dublin evening newspapers in particular which provoked him to bring in this amendment—not his dislike for the 'Imported Press'.

[40] London 1940, pp. 95 and 276.

[41] *Seanad Debates*, vol. 12, cols. 55-57, 11 April 1929.

[42] The question of majority vote on the Board also received detailed attention. The original Bill had required 4 out of 5 votes in favour of a prohibition order, but as the provision now stood (at the Seanad Report Stage), three votes would be sufficient provided that the other two members abstained, not dissented. Senator Douglas was anxious that every member—even if he missed a meeting of the Board—should have an opportunity to give his opinion: so as to ensure 'the maximum amount of uniformity in decisions of the Board.' Accordingly, an amendment was approved which ensured that all the members would have the opportunity to signify their opinion (Section 6, ss. 7): cf. *Seanad Debates*, vol. 12, col. 767 (Report Stage, 6 June 1929) and cols. 808-809 (Report Stage Resumed, 12 June 1929).

[43] *Seanad Debates*, vol. 12, cols. 814-815, 12 June 1929. See, however, p. 207 below, para. 1.

A similar amendment had been proposed in the Dail by Professor Tierney and others. After the discussion on this amendment Fitzgerald-Kenney hastened to make it clear that 'Deputy Tierney, Deputy Law, Deputy Thrift and Deputy Alton, in anything they have said and in any action they have taken in this House, have not in any way advocated birth control' (*Dail Debates*, Resumed Committee Stage, vol. 28, cols. 721-2, 28 February 1929).

[44] *Irish Independent*, 3 March 1930.

⁴⁵ No. 32 of 1930, 26 February 1930: see *Statutory Rules, Orders and Regulations*, 1922-1938, vol. v, pp. 278-285.

⁴⁶ This was in accordance with a promise the Minister made during the Seanad Second Reading that complaints would not need to be accompanied by a copy of the book for each member of the Board. The Rule also guaranteed that the cost of running the censorship would be little more than the expenses of employing a small staff of civil service officials.

⁴⁷ No. 58 of 1930, 10 July 1930: see *Statutory Rules, Orders and Regulations*, 1922-1938, vol. v, pp. 286-289.

NOTES TO CHAPTER III

¹ *Irish Statesman*, (15 February 1930). In fact, under Section 7, ss. 2 of the Act the Board could not present the Minister with a report in favour of prohibiting a book unless it was 'not dissented to by more than one and assented to by at least three members. . . .' Thus, the 'entities' could control the Board.

² W. J. O'Reilly, LLD, (born 1864) 'had been educated at Ushaw and London University. Was Resident Magistrate for Cavan (1907-1917) and for Meath (1917-1921); Privy Chamberlain of Sword and Cape to His Holiness since 1926'. W. B. Joyce, BA, FRSA, PC, was Principal of Marlborough Street Training College and Central Model Schools. He was an 'active member of library committees in Dublin and Limerick.' (He was also Hon. Treasurer of the Central Catholic Library, Dublin, an institution recently founded by Fr Browne.) Patrick Keawell, MA, was Chief Clerk of the Department of Posts and Telegraphs: cf. *Irish Statesman*, 1 March 1930.

Appendix 4 contains a list of the members of the Board during the period 1930-1945.

³ The *Catholic Mind* was ever vigilant on the censorship question and concerned itself not only with printed matter. Cf. its call for stage censorship (vol. v, p. 227, December 1934) and for control of the Dublin Broadcasting Station (vol. vi, p. 222, December 1935).

⁴ Two years later the unfortunate Mr Waugh fell foul of the *Catholic Bulletin* which severely criticised his satirical novel *Black Mischief* as advocating birth control: cf. *Catholic Bulletin*, February 1933.

⁵ In the event, both Professor Tierney and Mr Law failed to be re-elected. Professor Tierney (interviewed) does not think that this criticism was responsible for his defeat. Support for Cumann na nGaedheal slumped heavily in the 1932 and 1933 elections, in which the Party lost 5 and 8 seats respectively.

⁶ During the Dail Debates Deputy Ruttledge expressed the hope that the Press would not publish this list and was assured by the Minister that he could 'take it for granted that the Press will not publish a long list of books that are simply

obscene in their character, as it would be an advertisement for these books. I think we can safely trust the Press not to do that' (*Dail Debates*, vol. 28, col. 1536-37, 20 March 1929): a sort of censorship of censorship.

[7] Mr de Valera's Fianna Fail Party was now in power. Being much more nationalistic than the Cumann na nGaedheal government, its policies, especially the abolition of the Oath and the refusal to pay Land Annuities to the British Government, were severely criticised in the British press at the time. Regarding public support for a tariff, cf. the efforts of Cosg ar Foillseachain Gallda, below, p. 164f.

[8] August 1930. Mr St John Ervine made fun of the birth-control clauses of the Act, particularly.

[9] In his Lenten Pastoral issued the following month the Cardinal referred again to these remarks of the Pope; almost all the Lenten Pastorals in 1930 referred to the dangers of evil literature and looked forward to the operation of the Censorship of Publications Act: cf. *Irish Independent*, 3 March 1930.

[10] *Dail Debates*, vol. 50, cols. 1951-2, 22 February 1934.

[11] *Dail Debates*, vol. 60, col. 1928.

[12] Letter to Lynn Doyle (after his resignation) from the Minister published in the *Irish Press*, 13 February 1937. I am given to understand that the Minister himself was not, prior to Lynn Doyle's appointment, aware of the fact that the latter had criticised the Board and accused it of malpractices. It is possible that Mr Stephen Anselm Roche, then Secretary to the Department of Justice and an opponent of censorship, may have advised him to appoint Lynn Doyle.

[13] London, 1935.

[14] *Irish Press*, 13 February 1937.

[15] Professor Magennis did not consider Lynn Doyle as justified in resigning because he objected to the 'marked passages'. He thought that the fact that Doyle never attended a meeting of the Board gave him a one-sided view of censorship. 'I do not agree that you can detect a book merely by reading it. You have to discuss it' (*Seanad Debates*, 14 November 1945). The fact that Lynn Doyle did not attend a meeting of the Board seems to bear out the truth of the story that the others refused to sit with him. One might have expected him to attend at least one meeting, if only to get a more complete view of the workings of the censorship.

[16] One article provoked by the resignation was Fr Patrick Gannon's 'Literature and Censorship' in the *Irish Monthly*, vol. 65, pp. 434-447, June 1937. This was a relatively mild article which went as far as to advocate the institution of an appeal board; but it side-stepped the question of morality and literature by over-simplifying it: 'There is one negative precept: "Thou shalt not write porno-graphy"; and one—surely very mild—penalty, namely "If you do, your book will be denied free circulation in the Twenty-Six Counties". . . . And yet this simple measure of moral hygiene . . . has excited a passionate campaign of protest. . . .'

Another article which appeared at this time and dealt, in passing, with the censorship of periodicals was by Dr Cornelius Lucey (later Bishop of Cork) in 'The Freedom of the Press', *Irish Ecclesiastical Record*, vol. 50, pp. 584-599, December 1937.

¹⁷ In the same paper a week later (10 December 1935) a leader writer went 'in the other direction' by recommending that some control be exercised both in Ireland and in Britain over films which, though not obscene, were objectionable on other grounds: because they gave an inaccurate picture of historical figures, because they were simply vulgar and in bad taste, etc.: 'fringe' reasons for censorship, at the most.

¹⁸ The Seanad was abolished by the De Valera government in 1936. Under the 1937 Constitution it was reconstituted in a different form.

¹⁹ 12 March 1936.

²⁰ I have read this book and do not think that even the most conservative interpretation of the Act could justify its banning. It contains not one line of erotic detail; its two 'sex passages' are an example of restrained and discreet writing. Commenting on this banning in the Senate in 1942 Professor Michael Tierney said it was 'a book that is altogether repugnant to my taste, but again a book in which, on my conscience, I could not say there was anything to make it deserve to be branded as in its general tendency indecent and obscene' (*Seanad Debates*, vol. 27, col. 266, 3 December 1942).

²¹ The death of its editor, Mr D. P. Moran, in 1936 must have been largely responsible for that lack of vitality which is in evidence in issues of this periodical after that time.

²² See the *Irish Times* (6-22 January 1931), *Catholic Mind, Catholic Bulletin* and other publications for January-February 1931. When the lady in question resigned from her position the *Catholic Bulletin* devoted its cover to congratulate those responsible; it read ' WELL DONE, MAYO ' (issue for March 1931). For Mr Paul Blanshard's account of this episode, see *The Irish and Catholic Power* (Boston 1953), pp. 96-98.

²³ Some had it that they were made more complex. The activity of the Board was sufficient to provide material for a play performed in Dublin in 1943. The play 'This Book is Banned' dealt with the accidental circulation of a banned book in a county library (cf. review in the *Irish Times*, 1 July 1943).

²⁴ The figures given in the article contained two errors. Our figure of 14 read 44, and the period '24-36 months' read '24-26 months'. Some of the banning made in the 12-36 months groups may have been reprints.

²⁵ Article 40, Section 6, ss. 1, (i) of the Constitution reads as follows:

'The State guarantees liberty for the exercise of the following rights, subject to public order and morality:

'(1) The right of the citizens to express freely their convictions and opinions.

'The education of public opinion being, however, a matter of such grave import to the common good, the State shall endeavour to ensure that organs of public opinion, such as the radio, the press, the cinema, while preserving their rightful liberty of expression, including criticism of Government policy, shall not be used to undermine public order or morality or the authority of the State.

'The publication or utterance of blasphemous, seditious, or indecent matter is an offence which shall be punishable in accordance with law.'

[26] At the same time, however, another Catholic magazine, *Hibernia*, was complaining that 'our censorship is inadequate to cope with this menace (the British press) to our national heritage' (January 1941).

[27] Although the then Secretary of the Censorship Board, Mr Brian MacMahon, is quite definite that he did not supply the Committee with information, it is fairly evident that the Committee was very well acquainted with the Board's difficulties, etc. Quite possibly the Committee was assisted by Senator Wm. Magennis, a member of the original CTS censorship committee in 1926 and at this time on the Censorship Board.

NOTES ON CHAPTER IV

[1] *The Bell*, vol. 2, no. 3, June 1941, pp. 5-11.

[2] *The Bell*, vol. 3, no. 2 (November 1942) pp. 140-148.

[3] Another article in *The Bell* which deserves mention is 'In Defence of Censorship' by Dr Monk Gibbon (January 1945). The following issue contained comments by Bernard Shaw, Sean O'Casey, Mr T. C. Kingsmill Moore and Professor James Hogan. Dr Gibbon replied in the March issue.

In a letter to the writer (18 February 1962) Dr Gibbon recalls the articles in these words:

'. . . Sean O'Faolain published an article of mine which—unknown to me—he had re-named "In defence of Censorship" and had circulated in proof—again unknown to me—to G.B.S., Sean O'Casey, etc. Shaw's views didn't seem too far from mine, but O'Casey raged and stormed and said that I was a Count of the Holy Roman Empire or something of the sort. (Actually I am low Church Protestant and have very wide sympathies in other directions). . . .'

[4] This book was banned on 2 October 1942. Sections of it had been published in *The Bell* in the previous year (cf. *The Bell*, February-April 1941).

[5] *Seanad Debates*, vol. 27, col. 16, 18 November 1942.

[6] When Senator Keane began his readings from *The Tailor and Anstey* Senator Magennis appealed to the Chairman: 'I suggest . . . that before Senator Sir John Keane reads the remainder of that passage an instruction should be given to the official reporters not to record it.'

The Chairman did not comment and no senator joined in Professor Magennis' protest.

Sir John remarked: 'If the Chairman rules I will ask the Committee of Privileges to sit in regard to the matter.'

The Chairman agreed that Senator Keane is quite entitled to quote from a book which has been censored and put the facts before the House.

Senator Magennis protested again.

The Chairman then suggested that 'the Senator might use discretion as to the quotations. There is Ministerial responsibility for the Board, and the Senator may employ quotations to illustrate the argument for the motion'.

Senator Magennis: 'There is a part of the Constitution which guarantees full liberty of expression, but there is an express proviso with regard to the safe-guarding of public morals.' He asked again about the Reports.

Chairman: 'I will consider the action I should take on the matter.'

Later on in the readings Professor Magennis tried to restrain Senator Keane with 'we have had enough of this, Sir'. Other senators joined in this 'shushing' (cf. *Seanad Debates*, vol. 27, cols. 20-24, 18 November 1942).

When the Official Reports appeared they did not contain the readings: they still do not . . . not even the reference to the relevant pages in *The Tailor and Anstey* (it was from this book that most quotations were taken); neither did the newspapers quote the readings. The decision to delete the passages was taken by the Chairman and was not queried in the House afterwards (cf. *Seanad Debates*, vol. 27, cols. 121-122, 2 December 1942).

Despite the deletions there was a phenomenal demand for the *Reports* containing this debate (cf. *Irish Times*, 3 December 1942).

[7] This book has a certain sociological value; it is undoubtedly vulgar, but that is a far cry from describing it as 'suggestive of, or inciting to sexual immorality or unnatural vice'.

[8] Curiously enough, in a review of this book one month before it was banned Austin Clarke pointed to this sentence and its relation to the story as the 'one *artistic* (our italics) flaw in this book: the nature of the shock which drove Helen Archer, the beautiful, intelligent, young English girl into a Continental Order in a mood of agonised revulsion. It is an outward shock, purely pathological, and mentioned in a single euphemistic sentence' (*The Bell*, April 1941).

[9] *Seanad Debates*, vol. 27, col. 29. The Minister for Justice, Mr Gerald Boland read this book and in debate supported the Censorship Board's decision. However, he acknowledges now that he was 'on the look-out for obscenity' at the time, and that the book is not in fact obscene (interview with the author).

[10] *Seanad Debates*, vol. 27, cols. 30-33.

[11] *Seanad Debates*, vol. 27, col. 54, 18 November 1942.

[12] *Seanad Debates*, vol. 27, col. 55, 18 November 1942.

[13] During the debate the Minister complained that the *Irish Times* had been over-critical of the Board. Next day the newspaper replied: 'We are content to remind the Minister that, if we attacked the Censorship Board, it was not for its virtues but for its sins; and it is less against the Board's existence that we protest, than against its illegalities and its capacity for national insult' (19 November 1942).

[14] *Seanad Debates*, vol. 27, cols. 60-86, 18 November 1942; cols. 121-174, 2 December 1942.

[15] In his review of censorship law Professor Magennis quoted extensively in support of his case from Sir E. T. Atkinson, *Obscene Literature in Law and Practice* (London 1937) and Sir W. Joynson-Hicks (Viscount Brentford), *Do we need a Censor?* (London 1929).

[16] For Professor Magennis the position of defence was no novelty. Some years earlier, in a review in the *Daily Express*, he had described a banned book *Jackets Green* by P. Molloy as 'in its general tendency indecent'. The newspaper was

duly sued for libel by the author, and Professor Magennis was called to give evidence. In his own opinion he won hands down—cf. his references to this episode in *Seanad Debates*, vol. 27, col. 136, 2 December 1942.

[17] Professor Magennis told the House that a member of the public had complained about the book to Senator Fearon, a member of the Board at the time (*Seanad Debates*, vol. 27, col. 79). The Secretary of the Censorship Board later stated that the complainant was a Protestant. In its evidence to the Evil Literature Committee the Irish Vigilance Association had enthusiastically recommended Dr Sutherland's books on this subject.

[18] *Seanad Debates*, vol. 27, cols. 142-143, 2 December 1942.

[19] A *permissu superiorum* is given by the diocesan ordinary for printing of small religious pamphlets and also for books which are not on specifically religious subjects. For an authoritative discussion on the use of this formula as distinct from that of *imprimatur* we have been directed by a Vicar General in charge of ecclesiastical censorship in the Archdiocese of Dublin to the following article: W. Conway 'The printing of the *imprimi potest* on books, leaflets and pictures' in *IER*, Fifth Series, vol. lxxxiv, no. 6, pp. 423-424 (December 1955). On regulations for ecclesiastical censorship, see also para. 1, Appendix 8.

[20] *Seanad Debates*, vol. 27, col. 54, 12 November 1942.

[21] See below, p. 229, n. 21.

[22] *Seanad Debates*, vol. 27, col. 169, 2 December 1942.

[23] Although the length of Professor Magennis' speech must have rendered it somewhat trying there is no gainsaying that it was extremely clever. Even now, in the cold print of the Reports, one cannot fail to find it interesting, exasperating and highly entertaining. Parliamentary debates are much less colourful nowadays. As an example of the Professor at his most typical the reader is directed to that part of his speech which deals with the definition of 'indecent' and the relevance of the literary and artistic the Board should use (*Seanad Debates*, vol. 27, cols. 125-157).

[24] *Studies*, vol. 31, pp. 409-419, December 1942. In support of his argument Father Gannon quoted Mr St John Ervine as saying: 'The greater the man, the greater his ability to affect us, and if a genius chooses to be salacious he is certain to be the more effective in stirring up the silt in our natures than any common hack. I am, therefore, opposed to the canting snobs who, while willing to be rigorous with the cheap-jack, are anxious to be lenient with the genius. If there is to be hard dealing at all, let us be harder on the great men than we are on the little ones.' The Irish Censors did not spare Mr Ervine: see Appendix 2.

[25] The bulk of the information contained in these pages has been supplied to the writer by Mr Andrew Ganly, Honorary Secretary of the Council, who has given him access to its files. The Council itself existed for only about two years.

[26] These organisations were: Irish Women Citizens' Association; Women Writers Club; Writers' Guild; WAAMA (the Writers, Artists, Actors and Musicians Association)—also representing the Dublin Literary Society; Society of Intellectual Freedom; Irish Academy of Letters; Irish PEN (Dublin Centre); National Union of Journalists. The Provost of Trinity College, Dublin (Professor Alton, who had succeeded Professor Thrift in 1942), indicated that he was in

sympathy with the aims of the Council. The Women's Social and Progressive League also was represented by the Council. Delegates to the first meeting (organised by Irish PEN, Dublin Centre) were welcomed by Mr Austin Clarke, President of Irish PEN, Dublin Centre.

The Council was encouraged in its work by, among others, *The Bell* (cf. its editorial on 'The Seanad and Censorship', January 1943).

27 Composed of: Mr David Sears (Chairman), Mrs Coote, Mrs Sybil Le Brocquy, Mr A. Ganly, Mr J. Hanaghan and Mr J. M. Hone. Among others concerned in the Council were Dr Lorna Reynolds, Mr Maurice Walsh, Mr Terence de Vere White, Miss Rosamond Jacob, Mrs H. Skeffington.

28 From the minutes of the meeting (signed by Mrs Sybil Le Brocquy, 21 November 1944).

29 According to Mr G. Boland, Minister for Justice at this time, the only person ever consulted re appointment to the Board was the Catholic Archbishop of Dublin, and this only as regards a clerical member.

30 These authors included: 'Samuel Beckett, Kay Boyle, John Brophy, George Buchanan, Gerald Bullett, Joyce Cary, Austin Clarke, Vivian Connell, Reardon Connor, Elizabeth Connor, Louis Lynch D'Alton, Shaw Desmond, St John Ervine, M. F. Farrell, J. T. Farrell, Oliver St J. Gogarty, Robert Graves, Francis Hackett, James Hanley, Martin Hare, Norah Hoult, Patrick Kirwan, Maura Laverty, Stephen McKenna, George Moore, Patrick Mulloy, Eugene O'Brien, Kate O'Brien, Sean O'Casey, Jack O'Connor, E. P. O'Donnell, Sean O'Faolain, Liam O'Flaherty, Con O'Leary, Pat O'Mara, Jim Phelan, Francis Plunkett, Thomas Ryan, Bernard Shaw (Nobel Prize Winner), Hugh Shearman, L. A. G. Strong, Francis Stuart and Signe Tiksvig (Irish by marriage: Mrs Francis Hackett)'.

31 These included: Aldous Huxley, Wyndham Lewis, H. G. Wells, Hugh Walpole, H. E. Bates, Daphne de Maurier, Graham Greene, Ernest Raymond, Pamela Frankau, Somerset Maugham, Warwick Deeping, V. S. Pritchett, Noel Coward, A. J. Cronin, Bertrand Russell and Beverly Nichols.

32 If many of Senator T. C. Kingsmill Moore's remarks in the debates on the 1945 Bill have a familiar ring about them, it is because he relied heavily on this memorandum for evidence to submit against the Censorship.

A select list of the books banned under the 1929 Act is contained in Appendix 2.

33 This phrasing is very indicative of the attitude of the Council, which tended to see everything from the viewpoint of the writer. Many people would object to the suggestion that a complainant 'seeks to affect the reputation and living of an author'.

34 Senator Donal O'Sullivan, who supported the Bill, was taking an interest in the censorship question outside the Oireachtas too. Cf. *Irish Times*, 4 May 1944: report of a dinner given by the Women Writers' Club in honour of Mrs Maura Laverty whose book *Alone We Embark* had been banned. In favour of the book were good reports from 'priests', and the fact that among sixty reviews there was none which even mentioned obscenity. Senator O'Sullivan speaking at the dinner, said: 'The banning of a book without any appeal is contrary to natural justice.' Mrs Sheehy Skeffington said at this meeting that there was hardly any Irish

writer from George Bernard Shaw upwards who had not been banned 'by Professor Magennis and Co.', and that the two Universities were 'in it up to their neck.'

[35] 15 May 1944. The sudden dissolution of the Dail in May 1944 completed the Bill's eclipse.

[36] *Seanad Debates*, vol. 28, col. 1426. Mr Boland himself confesses that one of the reasons which moved him most to amend the Act was that he was extremely irritated by the *Irish Times*' custom of heading every new list of books with the following words: 'The following publications have been banned by the Minister for Justice as indecent'. . . . He also recalls how Mr Sean O'Faolain approached him in 1945 with the galley of an editorial for *The Bell* which attacked him personally. The Minister protested that this was not fair (I didn't really ban them) and the editorial was not published (*Interview*).

NOTES TO CHAPTER V

[1] On the very day of the First Reading the *Irish Times* carried a short news item to the effect that: 'A Bill may be introduced in the Dáil this week to provide for the appointment of a Book Censor', and to establish an appeal board. It quoted Mr Seán O'Faolain as saying he welcomed the idea of an appeal board and also 'the idea of a paid official, because one was then in a position to pin down a decision on an individual'. The newspapers were then, quite in the dark as to the terms of the new Bill.

On 13 October Mr O'Faolain was quoted in the *Irish Times* as saying that the Bill was 'obviously a vote of no confidence in the existing Censorship Board'.

[2] 20 October 1945.

[3] Around this time the *Round Table* did comment on another aspect of Irish Censorship not dealt with in this enquiry—the Press Censorship imposed during wartime. The Irish form of this was, it said, 'not only more drastic than that of other countries but also absurd, ostrich-like and tendentious. For example, opinions concerning the future economic policy of Ireland were altered to conform with the Government's views'. (Yet, during the war English newspapers were, strangely enough, allowed to circulate freely.)

When this censorship was lifted the *Irish Times* complained that it had been 'singled out for particular attention . . . it is difficult—indeed, it is impossible —to write with moderation about the treatment which this newspaper has received from the Censorship during recent years' (leading article, 12 May 1945). The paper then published a series of banned photographs under the title 'They Can Be Published Now'. One of these photographs was an unremarkable view of Mr P. J. Little, Minister for Posts and Telegraphs, skating in Herbert Park, Dublin.

Senator Sir John Keane took a lively interest in all matters dealing with censorship. Cf debate on his 'Censorship of Parliamentary Debates' motion, 21 and 22 February 1945 (*Seanad Debates*, vol. 29, cols. 1335-1368; and cols. 1412-1457). The motion read:

> 'That the Seanad views with concern the action of the Government in preventing the publication in the press of a report of certain proceedings of the Seanad of Wednesday, 6 December 1944, and requests information as to the grounds under which the Government claims the right to interfere with the Constitutional provision that sittings of each House of the Oireachtas shall be public.'

The Official Reports—but not the newspapers—did publish in full the proceedings referred to (these stemmed from a question about the censoring of two letters asked by Senator Sir John Keane; neither the question nor the Minister's reply gave any information prejudicial to public security). Sir John accused the Minister of '. . . by a stroke of the pen . . . putting us into secret session without consulting anybody'. Towards the end of the debate Senator Hayes pointed out that this was the first such instance since the Emergency Powers Act came into power five and a half years before. He suggested that in future the Minister should merely tell the press to hold the copy, and in the meantime consult with the House itself: 'so to preserve the privileges of the House and at the same time meet the emergency situation'. Two sections of the Constitution are relevant: Article 15, subsection 8—

(1) Sittings of each House shall be public.

(2) In cases of special emergency, either House may hold a private sitting with the consent of two-thirds of the members present, and Article 40, subsection 6. (See p. 211, n. 25).

⁴ The respective times for the Seanad Debates were: four and a half hours, eight hours and five hours.

⁵ For a summary of the provisions of the Act (which differs from the Bill only in a few details) see Appendix 3.

⁶ Mr Boland states (in an interview) that he always acted in conformity with the Censorship Board's recommendation. Incidentally he recalls how he refused to comply with a request from a Roman Catholic priest on the Board not to make a certain prohibition recommended by the Board. (The priest himself had not voted in favour of the book because he 'was afraid of scandalising the other members'!)

⁷ More specifically, he referred approvingly to the fact that some of the newspapers entering the country were special 'Irish editions'. *Dail Debates*, vol. 98, col. 326, 18 October 1945.

⁸ *Dail Debates*, vol. 98, col. 322, 17 October 1945.

⁹ This remark is relevant to the *Observer* Incident, see below, pp. 140 ff.

¹⁰ *Dail Debates*, vol. 98, col. 322, 17 October 1945.

¹² 'The 1876 Act (Customs Consolidation Act) gives them that right. . . . In case there was any question of the legality . . . we are putting it in here, but there will be no departure from the practice that has existed to this' *Dail Debates*, vol. 98, col. 516, 24 October 1945.

[13] The Minister later told the House that the vast majority of the books detained by the Customs came through the post and formed part of parcels sent to booksellers: very few came in personal baggage: *Dail Debates*, vol. 98, col. 792, 7 November 1945.

[14] In its first report on the Bill, the *Irish Times*, (12 October 1945) was sufficiently alert to see this as one of the most significant features of the Bill.

[15] *Dail Debates*, vol. 98, cols. 787–792, 7 November 1945.

[16] Senator Douglas, a member of the Fine Gael Party, was a Quaker and one of the relatively few Protestant members of the Oireachtas.

[17] *Seanad Debates*, vol. 30, cols. 934–949, 14 November 1945.

[18] *Seanad Debates*, vol. 30, col. 944, 14 November 1945.

[19] The Senator recalled how he and Canon Boylan (the then Chairman of the Censorship Board) had called on Mr Boland shortly after his appointment as Minister and how he afterwards assured his colleagues on the Board that 'now we had a Minister for Justice who was strong enough and bold enough to make any change in the legislation which experience had shown to be necessary'. According to Mr Boland (in an interview with the author) this meeting was not as amicable as the Senator would make out. In fact, Mr Boland objected to the Senator's strictness with regard to the censorship of books and told him so very clearly. There is little doubt that Professor Magennis exerted considerable influence on the Board even before he became Chairman.

[20] *Seanad Debates*, vol. 30, col. 947, 14 November 1945.

[21] Section 8 states: 'The Minister may at any time, after consultation with the Board, by order revoke any prohibition order theretofore made by him.'

During the Report Stage Senator Magennis repeated this assertion: 'I regard it as a violation of justice to say that there was no appeal.' *Seanad Debates*, vol. 30, col. 1263, 12 December 1945.

[22] The book referred to was Sean O'Faolain's *Bird Alone*.

[23] There is apparent ambiguity in the Senator's remarks on the effectiveness of censorship. Thus, when referring to the 'black market' in banned publications he told the House that there was hardly 'a man you meet who would not tell you that the Censorship Act is a fiasco'. (*Seanad Debates*, vol. 30, col. 1179) and yet went on to assert his faith in the Censorship Act as 'a safeguard of the Irish race against contamination and depravity' (*loc cit*).

[24] *Seanad Debates*, vol. 30, col. 948, 14 November 1945. The reasons he gave for the 'failure' of the Act agree to the letter with the criticism made by the CTS Committee in 1937.

[25] *Seanad Debates*, vol. 30, col. 951, 14 November 1945. It will be remembered that the Catholic Truth Society's draft Bill (see above page 19) favoured this procedure. Senator Magennis acted on the committee which drew up this Bill.

[26] A notice in the *Iris Oifigiuil* was the only official source from which booksellers might learn of a new prohibition order and this gazette is not a publication which booksellers are addicted to reading.

[27] *Seanad Debates*, vol. 30, col. 951–952, 14 November 1945.

[28] *Seanad Debates*, vol. 30, col. 952, 14 November 1945. The Dublin literary world was not inclined to view the Bill as a panacea. Cf report in the *Irish Times*

(2 November 1945) of a dinner in honour of Miss Kate O'Brien at which criticism was offered to the Bill and doubts were raised 'as to whether the Appeal Board would remedy the obvious defects'.

[29] Professor Magennis told the House that he had drawn up a Bill privately for the Minister. 'In my Bill the Censorship Board was one of the parties to the appeal, or they could delegate someone among their number to represent them and he could be heard on behalf of the finding'. But it is doubtful whether the Senator had written in a similar right for the author or publisher. Mr Gerald Boland, interviewed by the author, does not recall having seen this draft Bill. According to him Professor Magennis submitted only a series of 'suggestions'.

An unsuccessful attempt has been made to locate the private papers of Professor Magennis, if such exist.

[30] An amendment to this effect was passed at the Report Stage. See also p. 151 for *Irish Times* comment on this amendment.

When the Seanad amendments were being discussed in the Dail (*Dail Debates*, vol. 99, cols. 582–589) it was explained to the deputies that the reason these words were deleted was to make justifiable the banning of collections of short stories, some of which stories might be objectionable. For discussion on this point and a fine example of Professor Magennis' confused subtleties, see *Seanad Debates*, vol. 30, col. 961, 14 November 1945, and cols. 1140–1154, 29 November 1945.

[31] *Seanad Debates*, vol. 30, cols. 965–975, 14 November 1945.

[32] *Seanad Debates*, vol. 30, cols. 965–975, 14 November 1945.

[33] *Seanad Debates*, vol. 30, cols. 975–983, 14 November 1945.

[34] It was Senator Mrs Concannon who once pronounced a veritable eulogy on Professor Magennis, in the course of which she said: 'There is no man in Ireland to whom we owe so much as Professor Magennis.' (*Seanad Debates*, vol. 28, cols. 57–60, 18 November 1942).

[35] On this point Senator Professor M. J. Ryan mentioned how copies of the *Modern Law Review* addressed to him had been held up by the Customs: he suggested that the officials had been perturbed by the description 'Modern'.

[36] Senator Magennis had a ready answer to this, explaining it in terms of Civil Service bureaucracy.

[37] On 28 and 29 November 1946. The *Irish Press* and *Irish Times* published lengthy reports of the Committee stage debate of the days previous, but these provoked no exchanges in the correspondence columns of these newspapers.

[38] On 12 December 1946.

[39] The equivalent clause in the 1929 Act (Section 2) read: 'the word "indecent" shall be construed as including suggestive of, or inciting to sexual immorality or unnatural vice or likely in any other similar way to corrupt or deprave.'

[40] Many senators objected to the amendment on the grounds that a precedent would thereby be created of quoting from the Constitution in an Act of Parliament.

[41] See p. 211, n. 25.

[42] To prove his point Professor Magennis quoted liberally from legal textbooks.

[43] *Seanad Debates*, vol. 30, col. 1032–1033, 28 November 1945.

[44] Sir John was suffering from an eye complaint at this time.

[45] See Appendix 4.

[46] On this point see p. 184.

[47] *Seanad Debates*, vol. 30, col. 1067, 28 November 1945. Cf also *Dail Debates*, vol. 98, col. 512, 24 October 1945.

[48] *Seanad Debates*, vol. 30, col. 1081–1083, 28 November 1945. Among the 35 members of the Academy at this time were: Elizabeth Bowen, Austin Clarke, Padraic Colum, Lord Dunsany, St. John Ervine, Oliver Gogarty, Stephen Gwynn, Sir Shane Leslie, the Earl of Longford, Robert Lynd, Frank O'Connor, Peadar O'Donnell, Sean O'Faolain, Liam O'Flaherty, Eugene O'Neill, Seamus O'Sullivan, Lennox Robinson, Bernard Shaw, Walter Starkie, James Stephens and L. A. G. Strong. Cf. *Thom's Directory of Ireland for the Year* 1945, Dublin 1945, p. 474.

[49] *Seanad Debates*, vol. 30, col. 1085, 28 November 1945.

[50] *Seanad Debates*, vol. 30, col. 1259–1260, 12 December 1945.

[51] Sir John Keane expressed the desire at the Report Stage that the House would not ask for more than five members to act in this capacity: 'I know that in many instances in which I have been pursuing the most commendable purposes I found great difficulty in finding even one person to support me' *Seanad Debates*, vol. 30, col. 1238, 12 December 1945.

[52] *Seanad Debates*, vol. 30, col. 1346, 13 December 1945.

[53] Among the amendments which were accepted were: (1) a new subsection to Section 8 to the effect that 'the Appeal Board may act for all purposes notwithstanding the existence of one vacancy in their membership' (this was consequent on the increase in the size of the Board from three to five); (2) an addition to Section 8, ss 1, whereby the lodgement of an appeal had to be made within twelve months after the operative date or twelve months after the date on which the prohibition order took effect (whichever was the later): this replaced a clause which would have permitted appeal at any time; (3) a Government-Magennis amendment in the form of a new subsection to Section 9 whereby the word 'advocating' (. . . the unnatural prevention of conception, etc.) should be construed to include an advertisement or notice of any publication which advocated the forbidden procedures (apart from a mild comment by Senator Johnston, *Seanad Debates*, vol. 30, cols. 1158-1159, there was no criticism of the birth control clauses in the Dail or Seanad Debates on the 1946 Bill)—this made the clause more restrictive than the equivalent one in the 1929 Act; (4) a provision (Section 9, ss 3, a, b and c) which varied the duration of the ban for newspapers and weeklies, and for monthlies and quarterlies (rather than the procedure under the 1929 Act whereby there was a ban for only three months in respect of all types of periodicals); (5) the introduction of a new subsection to Section 5 (subsection 3) to the effect that 'an officer of customs and excise shall not detain under this section a book, not being merchandise, which is carried by or forms part of the personal baggage of an incoming traveller': a notable modification.

Among other amendments withdrawn or negatived during the Seanad debates were the following: (1) a change in Section 4 requiring the Minister to appoint not 'so many persons as he thinks necessary to be officers and servants of the Censorship Board and the Appeal Board' but 'so many persons as the boards consider necessary' (Senator Magennis); (2) a provision which would have required the Board to 'read and examine' every book duly referred to it (Senator Kingsmill-Moore)—it was pointed out that it was quite unnecessary for censoring purposes to read completely books which advocated the unnatural prevention of conception, etc. (3) an addition which would *require* rather than simply permit the Censorship Board to inform the author or publisher that his book was under consideration (Senator Douglas); (4) a proposal to give the Chairman of the Censorship Board a casting vote (Senator Magennis); (5) another amendment of Senator Douglas' enabling members of the Oireachtas to import banned books (the Minister preferred that they use the permit apparatus); and (6) a requirement that the Minister consult with the Board regarding the making of statutory regulations.

[54] *Seanad Debates*, vol. 30, col. 1378, 13 December 1945.

[55] I have been unable to trace the text referred to.

[56] On 2 February 1946 the Seanad received a message from the Dail to the effect that it agreed to all the amendments made by the Upper House, and on 13 February 1946 the Bill became law. The Dail discussion of the Seanad amendments is contained in *Dail Debates*, vol. 99, cols. 582–589, 7 February 1946.

[57] No. 254 of 1946: (6 July 1946) see *Statutory Rules, Orders and Regulations*, vol. xxxvi (1946–1947), p. 455–473.

[58] See above, pp. 78f.

[59] *Seanad Debates*, vol. 33, cols. 794–798, 29 January 1947.

[60] *Seanad Debates*, vol. 33, cols. 1097–1100.

[61] Cf. Censorship of Publications Act 1946, Section 8, ss. 1.

[62] No. 42 of 1947 (see *Statutory Rules, Orders and Regulations*, vol. xxxvi (1946–1947), p. 477.

[63] For appeal statistics, see Figure 4, p. 132.

NOTES TO CHAPTER VI

[1] Mr Joyce, a solicitor, had been a member of the CTS committee of enquiry on censorship: see p. 77.

[2] It is not known whether Professor Wigham was offered the position of chairman.

[3] Published in the *Irish Times*, 6 July 1949.

[4] As the Secretary pointed out on another occasion, the marked passages

system (which could suggest that more importance be given to offensiveness than to other qualities) was decided on at a conference presided over by the Minister for Justice on 2 February 1930, when the first statutory regulations were devised (letter, *Irish Times*, 15 May 1953). The Secretary added that 'not dissenting was a distinguished professor of Trinity College, Dublin, who later became Provost' and had sat on the Evil Literature Committee, in the Dail, and for seven years on the Censorship Board. He was referring to Professor Thrift.

[5] *Irish Times*, 14 July 1949.

[6] *Irish Times*, 18 July 1949.

[7] *Irish Times*, 21 July 1949.

[8] Mr O'Flynn was at this time managing director of a Dublin contracting firm. He was also very active in youth work in Dublin and active in the Knights of St Columbanus.

[9] These figures may be compared with certain contemporary U.S. statistics which have come to my notice. Mr Paul Blanshard in *The Right to Read: the battle against censorship* (Boston 1955, p. 184) reports: 'Detroit has a full-blown police censorship bureau with twelve employees who devote their energies chiefly to seamy magazines, comics and paperback books.' In one three-year period this bureau ' "removed" more than 2,700 books and "withheld" 154. In 1951 they screened 726 book titles, 394 different magazines and "withheld" 454,000 copies of banned publications'. It used the 'marked passages' method of examination.

[10] During this particular year the Board banned over 80% of the books it examined. This industry may be compared *mutatis mutandis*, with the work of the full-time Film Censor around this time. The following figures are taken from his annual Reports.

YEAR	FILMS EXAMINED	REJECTED	CUT	PASSED
1954	1,525	33	211	1,281
1955	1,381	52	308	1,021
1956	1,431	51	204	1,176
1957	1,403	54	213	1,118

[11] 5 July 1956; 25 August 1956.

[12] A County Cork solicitor.

[13] Graduate of Trinity College, Dublin, company director and man of wide literary interests.

[14] *Irish Times*, 5 October 1957. Mr Gore Grimes was quoted as saying 'Avoiding the larger issue as to whether censorship of publications control by the State is desirable, I believe that those who have studied the Censorship Act carefully would agree that it is difficult to improve. It is not the Act, but the administration, and the fact that for a great number of years no lawyer was on the Board, which have resulted in the absurdities which have arisen.'

[15] *Irish Times*, 18 December 1957. For information on the Association see p. 228, n. 10.

[16] Now Mr Oscar Traynor, for the Fianna Fail Party had been returned to power in March 1957.

[17] Professor Pigott's press statement (*Irish Independent*, 5 December 1957).

[18] Professor Pigott justified his action of adjourning the meeting *sine die* on the grounds that the power to do so is the normal prerogative of any chairman.

[19] Professor Pigott's press statement.

[20] In the *Irish Times* on 7 December 1957 Mr Sean O'Faolain, President of the Irish Association for Civil Liberty, was quoted as saying that Professor Pigott 'resigned in a huff because he failed to bully the Minister for Justice into allowing him to interpret the Act in his own way'. To this Professor Pigott replied (10 December 1957): 'Far from resigning in a huff, I did not resign at all—I was actually pushed off the Board. The Civil Liberties Association has now complete control.'

[21] News of this disagreement was one of the very few items which appeared in *The Times* on Irish censorship. The report (5 October 1957) announced the new appointments and stated that the situation had become 'inflammatory' after the Board was reconstituted the previous December, and that the Minister for Justice had asked Professor Pigott to resign.

[22] *Dail Debates*, vol. 170, cols. 377–379, 10 July 1959.

[23] It was precisely such a change that Mr Sean O'Faolain called for in March 1956 when addressing the University Philosophical Society at Trinity College: 'The machinery of the Censorship of Publications Act does not need much alteration, but the attitude of mind of the censors themselves does. . . . The Irish Censorship of Publications Act is a sensible Act and could do a lot of good in the control of pornography . . . (but) those who administer the Act run roughshod over it' (*Irish Times*, 24 February 1956).

[24] In a reply to a question on 20 May 1958, the Minister gave a full statistical account of the rate at which the Board had been working since October 1957, and of the number and source of complaints reaching the Board during that period (*Dail Debates*, vol. 168, cols. 278–279).

[25] In 1958 the only notable new books banned were:

Behan, Brendan   *Borstal Boy* (11 November)
De Montherlant, Henry *Desert Love* (7 October)
Metalious, Grace   *Peyton Place* (6 May)

[26] Professor Pigott's press statement (*Irish Independent*, 5 December 1957).

[27] Professor Pigott's press statement.

[28] The sections included in brackets in this and following quotations were published in Professor Pigott's statement to the press. The word '*might*' was not emphasised in the press statement.

[29] Professor Pigott's press statement.

[30] 'The Minister for Justice received me in June last and I pointed out to him the impasse which had arisen and the difficulty of operating the Act where the question of the literary merit of a book was in question, because it was on the question of literary merit of these books that the difficulty arose. . . .

'I suggested to the Minister that he would either have to ask these two gentlemen to resign, or ask me to resign. . . .'

[31] Extract No. 1, reads: 'The Minister for Justice, who introduced the Censorship of Publications Bill in the Dail, stated that literary, artistic, or scientific merit in a book should not be the final consideration, and that he knew that those who sought to introduce the subsection had no such intention. (*Dail Debates*, vol. 28, No. 2, col. 503). Speaking in the Dail, the Minister also mentioned the inadvisability of having 'somebody representing an interest, like the people who think that nothing can ever be immoral in art, and that anything which is artistic must be allowed into the country, added on (as a member of the Board) as a deadweight to *retard the efforts* (Professor Pigott's italics) of all the others'. . . . In the Seanad, the Minister, after quoting the terms of this same Section 6, Sub-section 2, stated: 'There are certain matters which the Board may, but need not of necessity take into consideration. I think they should always take them into consideration, but they may not be final considerations when they make up their minds' (*Seanad Debates*, vol. 12, No. 1, col. 50).

[32] Extract No. 2 reads as follows: 'Speaking in the Dail the Minister said, in discussing border-line cases: "Those will cause the Committee (meaning the Board) a great deal of trouble, only those. There are certain books the Committee will have only to skim through and say 'those cannot come in'. Then there are books they will have to weigh up very gravely" (vol. 28, No. 1, col. 114). And again, from what we must consider the authoritative statements of the Minister for Justice: "There are books which are so blatantly indecent and known to be indecent, that it would be unnecessary for the members of the Board to read every line of them. Should the members of the Board, for instance, be compelled to read every line of *Ulysses*, a book which has been universally condemned?" (vol. 28, No. 2, cols. 495 and 496).'

[33] It is also clear that Mr Comyn was not prepared to accept the Attorney General's opinion re 'omnibus editions'. He continued to press his point that the Board should form a fresh opinion on an omnibus edition which contained a banned book.

[35] *Irish Times*, 6 December 1957. Cf. the *Church of Ireland Gazette*, 13 December 1957, which put it rather succinctly: 'The current tiff between Professor Pigott and two members of the Board would seem to have its origin in conflicting interpretations of the intention of the Act towards what might be described as responsible works.'

[36] The address was published in *The Cross* (a monthly published in Dublin by the Passionist Fathers), May 1960.

[37] This address was not widely reported in the press. It was one of the few severe criticisms made of the new Board.

[38] Cf. *The Irish and Catholic Power*, p. 88: 'It is evident that age, dignity and popular approval have something to do with the release of a work from detention.' Mr Blanshard also suggests, *loc. cit.*, that 'some members of the Appeal Board are sensitive to ridicule'.

[39] *Irish Times*, 27 July 1946. In the course of his letter Mr O'Connor suggested that as a ninetieth birthday present to Bernard Shaw 'the Government remove the ban on his *The Black Girl in Search of God*.'

[40] *Irish Times*, 10 August 1946.

[41] 24 August 1946.

[42] Dr Pyle's plea was not heard until it was almost too late: cf. p. 114.

[43] Cf. his letter of 26 August 1946.

[44] *Irish Times*, 3 January 1948.

[45] 19 January 1948.

[46] *Irish Times*, 28 January 1948. In private and in public Frank O'Connor complained bitterly of this; he pointed to the fact that few Irish libraries contain any one of these books, mentioning in particular *The Tailor and Anstey* which was unbanned at this time, but of which a copy could not now be bought for ten pounds. This book was later reprinted.

[47] Cf. *The Spectator*, 28 November 1952, which spoke of the Board as 'a more enlightened group of citizens'.

[48] *The New Statesman and Nation*, vol. xlv, No. 1159, 23 May 1953, p. 606. There were only two lawyers on the Board at the time.

[49] *Irish Times*, 2 January 1956. The Appeal Board may not have been responsible for this: the periodicals referred to had probably been banned for periods of three to six months only.

[50] Cf. in the *Irish Times*, 24 February 1956, report of a debate at the Trinity College, Dublin, Philosophical Society, at which Dr Pyle complained that only one newspaper (the *Irish Times*) published lists of banned books—he thought that more applications for revocation orders would be forthcoming if the lists were made readily available to a wider public. He suggested that at least one author should be on each Board; and mentioned that one difficulty the Appeal Board had when examining periodicals was that often it did not see the same issues of the periodicals as were seen by the Censorship Board. (On this last point, see p. 236, n. 23.

[51] Cf. *Annual Reports* of the Censorship of Publications Appeal Board, 1946–1953.

[52] Cf. Mr Michael Campbell's survey (*Irish Times*, 14 March 1959), carried out among seven sales managers of British publishing firms. This revealed the highest conceivable sale of a cloth-bound book in Ireland to be around the 4,000 mark (not fiction, but a book of special Catholic or Irish interest). As for novels, Irish authors get markedly greater support than foreign writers, but all this means is that the highest sale for an Irish novel (clothbound) is about 750 copies (which may mean only about £50 royalties to the author).

[53] *The Bell*, Editorial, July 1947.

[54] 1 October 1948. Cf. also 'Smuggled Culture' by Brian Inglis in the *Spectator*, 28 November 1952.

[55] One former member of the Censorship Board has, in private, suggested that in the event of a successful appeal, the Censorship Board should view the Appeal Board's decision in the same light as a judge would the decision of a higher court. Incidentally, the same member would put criticism of a Censorship Board decision on the same level as that of a court decision, and considers that the Censorship Board should not reply to criticism of its decisions. ('I'm the censor, not you. I'm doing the job as well as I can, and if you were censor I suppose you would do the same. It's me the Minister has appointed, not you'.)

[56] The *Reports* were addressed to the Minister; before 1946 the Censorship Board was in an advisory capacity, and so not expected to submit such reports.

[57] With regard to recent bannings the *Register* is of little help: usually it is at least a year out of date. It is also published only sporadically.

[58] Cf. for example, the *Church of Ireland Gazette:* Editorial, 19 August 1955, and *Irish Times*, 13 August 1955.

[59] Cf. the alacrity with which the Film Censor's *Reports* appeared: that for 1954—on 7 February 1955; for 1955—on 24 January 1956; for 1956—on 30 January 1957; for 1957—on 11 February 1958.

[60] These letters appeared in the daily and Sunday papers. It was never the policy of the Board to reply to criticisms made in periodicals, despite the fact that it received severe criticism from the *Bell*, the *Leader*, the *Spectator*, the *New Statesman and Nation*, etc.

[61] *Irish Times*, 3 June 1954. This complaint was made at the time of the Secretary's exchanges with Mr Paul Blanshard (see p. 147f.).

[62] 12 July 1954.

[63] *Irish Times*, 12 July 1954.

[64] *Irish Times*, 1 May 1953. Cf. a letter to the same paper, 4 May 1953.

[65] Dublin *Evening Mail*, 15 February 1944.

[66] I am informed that the Minister for Justice instructed some officials, the Secretary to the Censorship Board among them, not to issue press statements etc.

[67] Cf. 'Mr Blanshard's Ireland' in *The Tablet*, 7 May 1955, in which the writer suggested, possibly for this reason, that 'it is likely that Southern Protestants, on the whole, are more restive under the censorship than most of the overwhelming Catholic majority'.

[68] However, an article in the *New Statesman and Nation* at the same time did suggest that 'all Protestants who take the responsibility of parentage seriously have a real grievance in the total ban on all contraceptives' (29 January 1949). There are instances of birth-control literature being suppressed in England. Cf. 'Banning Books', an article by C. R. Rolph in the *New Statesman and Nation*, 18 November 1950.

[69] 10 July 1946.

[70] Cf. letter to the *Irish Times*, 15 May 1954. Incidentally, Blanshard made out in this book (p. 95) that 'the attempted bannings of current magazines for printing favourable judgements on birth control has recently been reduced to an absurdity because of the flood of such favourable comments in popular periodicals.' In fact, however, few periodicals have been banned on birth control grounds (see Figure 5, p. 134).

[71] 30 June 1949; the *Irish Catholic* agreed wholeheartedly with the ban. *Christus Rex* in its review of the Report (vol. 3, p. 20, October 1949) wrote in the following terms: 'But while thus expressing appreciation of the extremely valuable contribution to our knowledge of an uncommonly complex problem, one must also express disappointment at the absence of any evidence of the influence of Christian belief in such an important document of a country that is professedly Christian.'

[72] 5 November 1949.

[73] Published by the *Irish Times* in pamphlet form under the same title, Dublin 1950.

[74] *Irish Independent* (cf. 2 April 1956) referred to 'impounding'. This newspaper did not interest itself in the incident at all. The same was true of the *Irish Press*.

[75] See *Irish Times*, 7 April 1956.

[76] *Irish Times*, 11 April 1956. 'Suspicious', 'unsolved' and 'totalitarian' were the terms the *Church of Ireland Gazette* used to describe the goings-on (13 April 1956).

[77] *Seanad Debates*, vol. 45, cols. 1761–1765.

[78] 28 April 1956. Cf. also comment in its issue for 14 April 1956.

[79] 20 April 1956.

[80] The quotation is taken from the transcript of the proceedings of the Meeting, in private papers of Professor J. J. Pigott.

For the purposes of comparison, part of the *Irish Times*' report (23 April 1956) reads as follows:

> 'The man whose privilege and profit it was to collect this paper at Collinstown Airport had a fear inserted in his mind as to the possible consequence of distributing it, that the Act provided for a possible penalty of £50, and for a period of imprisonment. That man, an honest, decent citizen, was unable to get anyone to tell him whether he could remove the papers in safety, and he decided not to move them.'

[81] In an editorial (13 April 1956) *The Standard* criticised the *Irish Times* for jumping to the conclusion that the Board was responsible, and for not apologising when the Board disowned having any part in the affair.

[82] *Irish Times*, 3 April 1956. Another letter (28 March 1951) criticised the banning of a book called *Modern Marriage* 'simply because it does not conform to the views of one section of the people.'

NOTES TO CHAPTER VII

[1] Support for the Censorship Board was, of course, clearly implied in the movements described in the third section of this chapter. And, as was pointed out earlier, opposition to censorship would have been a very fragile affair were it not for the support which that opposition received from the *Irish Times*.

[2] Mgr J. Deery, during his period as Chairman of the Board, was reported as saying that 'he never knew a book to be banned on the strength of one extract, except where the offensive passage was extremely long and very dirty' (*Irish Times*, 25 February 1956). Professor J. J. Pigott, in a letter to the *Irish Times*, 13 January 1958, said: 'The Censorship Board has been charged with banning

books on single episodes and even for a single phrase; that, I can tell you, for the period I was on the Board, is an absolute lie.'

[3] London, 1954. With a foreword by H. Montgomery Hyde. An earlier edition was published in Boston 1953. This is the volume we quote from.

[4] Boston, 1951.

[5] *Irish Times*, 25 May 1954.

[6] Another colourful incident which took place during this year (1954) was the 'Kavanagh Case'. Mr Patrick Kavanagh sued *The Leader* for publishing (11 October 1952) an article which he considered libellous. This article stated that his book *The Great Hunger* had been banned. (Another book of his *Tarry Flynn* had been banned and unbanned). For an amusing account of the affair cf. Mr Jack White's article, 'The Kavanagh Case' in the *Spectator*, 5 March 1954.

[7] Cf. *Irish Times'* report, 25 February 1956.

[8] In his *The Face and Mind of Ireland* (1950) Mr Arland Ussher had suggested that 'what the Censorship Board seems to be really after is books which have a non-Catholic, "pagan" mentality'.

[9] In an editorial (2 March 1956) the *Church of Ireland Gazette* stated that while it agreed with the Censorship Act 'it was patently obvious, from the published report of the lecture, that the approach of the Chairman of the Censorship Board was the Roman Catholic approach.' It called for a Board 'more representative of the community as a whole', and wanted its method of working made public.

[10] Cf. letter, *Irish Times* (9 October 1948) from Mr Sean O'Faolain, Lord Killanin and Professor Felix Hackett.

The Association has two main purposes: 'To hold a watching brief for the ordinary citizen in all matters which concern his individual rights, and to cultivate a wider public understanding and appreciation of civil liberties' (cf. *Thom's Directory of Ireland*, 1960, vol. 2, p. 445). Vice-Presidents of the Association have included: Mr C. J. Gore-Grimes, Professor J. W. Moody, Mr Sean O'Faolain, Dr Bethel Solomons, Professor W. B. Stanford, the Earl of Wicklow and Professor Desmond Williams.

[11] First announced in a letter by Mr Roger McHugh to the *Irish Times*, 29 March 1956. The following is an extract from the petition form: 'I consider that the number of works having general literary merit banned is so great as to demand investigation. I am in favour of censorship being applied to pornography, but question the widespread banning of books of literary merit found acceptable in other democratic countries where the Christian faith is practised.' In the accompanying letter, the Association expressed itself as concerned with 'the undesirable banning of publications of recognised literary merit', but did not question 'the necessity of some form of censorship'. The aim of the petition was to induce the Taoiseach to examine the working of the censorship 'with a view to reconciling the protection of morals with the reading habits and interests of the educated public in Irish society'.

[12] Mr O'Faolain was a leading light in the Association and was very much concerned in the stepping-up of criticism of the Board in the first months of 1956.

Cf. his address to the University Philosophical Society of Trinity College (reported in the *Irish Times*, 24 February 1956). In the course of this address he stated that 'the machinery of censorship does not need much alteration, but the attitude of the censors themselves does. . . .' The Censorship Board was not an evangelical body. Fostering ignorance by protecting alleged innocence could be one of the greatest instruments for the corruption of youth ever introduced.

His article 'Indecent or Obscene' (*Irish Times*, 1 March 1956) echoes the same idea and complains that 'the Minister of Defence, speaking for the Minister for Justice, assured the annual general meeting of the party machine (Fianna Fail) a few weeks ago that the Government fully agreed with the Board'.

[13] The quotations which follow are taken from a transcript of the meeting found among the papers of the late Professor Pigott. The fullest newspaper report is to be found in the *Irish Times*, 23 April 1956.

[14] *Irish Times*, 18 May 1957.

[15] 6 June 1957: he refers presumably to Joyce's *Ulysses*. The point brought up by Dr Gibbon—the influence of reading on conduct—is of course important, and is not as generally accepted nowadays as say thirty or forty years ago. Cf. 'Obscenity, Literature and the Law' by Norman St John-Stevas in the *Dublin Review*, Summer 1956, and letters in the *New Statesman and Nation* (13 and 20 May 1954). In the article cited Mr St John-Stevas criticised the Irish censorship, *en passant*.

[16] Maria Duce (after 1955 known as 'Firinne') is a right-wing Catholic organisation which gained the reputation of being anti-Jewish. It criticised many aspects of Irish political and social life, notably Article 44 of the Constitution which, it thought, did not give adequate political recognition to the Catholic Church.

[17] *Irish Times*, 8 June 1957.

[18] Or were, as the *Irish Times* saw it (6 December 1957), 'confining it to its proper and reasonable function, which is the prohibition of "indecent and obscene" publications'.

[19] For the reasons for the deletion, see above p. 269, n. 30.

[20] *Irish Times*, 7 December 1957.

[21] But not until one correspondent quoted for him the *Register* as on 31 December 1950: 'item No. 1426 on p. 65, which reads: 'Laws of Life', Halliday Sutherland—Date of prohibition order, 8 October 1941. Edition or editions to which the prohibition order relates—ALL' (*Irish Times*, 7 January 1958).

At the end of the controversy Dr Skeffington wrote privately to Professor Pigott commending him on 'doing the big thing' and expressing the hope that they would agree to differ without bitterness. The Professor preserved this letter together with a copy of his graciously phrased—even touching—reply.

[22] *Irish Independent*, 13 January 1958.

[23] *Irish Independent*, 24 March 1958.

[24] 28 November 1952.

[25] 23 May 1953.

[26] 13 February 1954.

[27] *Bookseller*, 27 March 1954.

[28] Cf. *Irish Times* report, 11 January 1956.

[29] *Obscenity and the Law*, with an introduction by Sir Alan Herbert, London, 1956, pp. 177–188: 'The Irish Censorship. An Experiment.' With the exception of Queensland, where a censorship board was established in 1954, Ireland was, he said, the only English speaking country with book censorship machinery. Appendix vii of this book contains a full list of proceedings re obscene publications in England and Wales under the Obscene Publications Act 1857 and for common law misdemeanour.

[30] 12 April 1956. In an article on 'Obscenity, Literature and the Law' in the *Dublin Review* (Summer 1956) the same writer dealt more mildly with the Irish censorship and pointed out that in Southern Ireland there was almost universal agreement on certain moral principles, and that this fact enabled a censorship to be imposed which would be intolerable in England.

[31] The first-mentioned is published by the Jesuits, while the other three are edited at St Patrick's College, Maynooth, the National Seminary, which is a recognised College of the National University of Ireland. *Studies* and *Christus Rex* are quarterly; the other two are monthly.

[32] Bi-monthly (later monthly), monthly, fortnightly and monthly respectively. In recent years *Hibernia* has become a general magazine of current affairs.

[33] Bi-monthly, weekly, weekly, respectively. The *Irish Rosary* stopped publication in December 1962.

[34] 'Faith and Fiction' by Thomas Halton, vol. 4, No. 8, pp. 427–432 (August 1953).

'Censorship and Literature' by John Courtney Murray, vol. 7, No. 11, pp. 679–691 (November 1956).

'Censorship and Moral Classification of Films', by Peter Connolly, vol. 8, No. 2, pp. 110–114 (February 1957).

Statement from the Irish Bishops on Indecent Publications, vol. 9, No. 3, pp. 193–194 (March 1958).

[35] 'Censorship' by Peter R. Connolly, MA (Oxon.) in *Christus Rex*, vol. xiii, No. 3, pp. 151–170 (July 1959).

[36] Pp. 54–55: 'In the present century the first thirty years saw only four literary names added . . . and the next thirty saw only three fresh names— Gide, Sartre and Moravia. It may be significant that the last three illustrate not so much simple obscenity as a doctrinaire brand, a "moral" propaganda which (in another phrase of the Code) "subverts the foundations of religion and right morals"; for Gide justifies and recommends a homosexual cult and Moravia insinuates more obliquely a total moral inertia. . . .

'As declared by the Holy Office in 1943, Church law, having prohibited *ex professo* obscene books as a class, leaves the specifying of particular titles to the bishops of each country or diocese . . . a practice to which, as we know, these local authorities are not wildly addicted.'

See also Appendix 8.

[37] Publication suspended in September 1954. Regarding *Hibernia*, reference is made elsewhere to its comment on censorship, see pp. 162 and 164.

[38] 16 July 1949.

[39] 11 June 1955.

[40] 14 April 1956.

[41] 25 January 1958. The legislators in 1929 had rejected this possibility but in 1966 I understand a popular woman's journal received a semi-official assurance that it would not be prosecuted if it serialised a novel by Edna O'Brien which was on the banned list.

[42] *Irish Catholic*, 29 December 1949.

[43] 'We have no hesitation in commending the work of the association to every Irish Catholic' (Editorial, 23 May 1953). See also, in a review of Benedict Kiely's *Modern Irish Fiction* (22 December 1950), criticism of the censorship.

[44] The *Irish Times* (17 April 1950) published a letter announcing the formation of a National Protest Committee—'to request that action be taken to restrict undue imports of papers, periodicals and books, and thereby give protection to Irish publishers, journalists, writers, etc.' It would appear that the Committee did not function for very long.

[45] In an editorial on 'Defence of the Mind' the *Irish Catholic* (20 April 1960) said that 'much good is done in this respect through the operation, however cumbersome it may be, of the censorship of publications, but a more effective barrier must be imposed'.

[46] The value of imported periodicals had risen from £90,000 for the year 1944 to £289,000 in 1949 (cf. *Irish Times*, 13 April 1950). The increase was not as dramatic as would appear, for the 1944 figure was artificially low due to war conditions and purchasing power had decreased. Cf. also correspondence on 'The Imported Press' in the *Irish Times* at the beginning of May 1949.

[47] March 1949. Fr Devane wrote in favour of a tariff and made a passing reference to Ireland's 'half-hearted attempt to protect ourselves against indecency (by no means the gravest danger) by a system of censorship'; but most of his article dealt with the education of Catholic journalists. Lord Killanin was in favour of increasing taxation on 'purely entertainment value magazines' printed in England. The following year *Hibernia* published another (unsigned) article, on 'The Imported Press' (February 1950) which concluded with the rallying-cry 'Let the year see Ireland liberated from the alien press, from black ink as once from black-and-tans!'

[48] *The Imported Press: a national menace: some remedies* by R. S. Devane, SJ, Dublin 1950.

[49] 6 October 1950.

[50] 8 February 1951 (leading article). For criticism of the movement cf. *The Leader*, 1 July 1950.

[51] Cf. *Irish Independent*, 3 August 1953.

[52] The phenomenon of the horror comic was not only an Irish one; in Britain too it was very current at this time: in February 1955 the British Government introduced the Children's and Young Persons' (Harmful Publications) Bill, which later became law. For correspondence on this Bill, cf. the *Spectator*, February–March 1955.

Cf. *Evening Herald*, 9 September 1954. Horror comics published in periodical form could of course be prohibited under the existing Acts on the grounds that they devoted too much space to matters dealing with crime.

[53] *Dail Debates*, vol. 147, col. 19, 27 October 1954.

[54] Soon yet another pressure group was to be started: the Irish League of Decency. Cf. *Irish Independent* report of its first meeting at which it called for 'rigorous enforcement of the Censorship of Publications Act and for revocation of the 'right of appeal' clauses (11 July 1955). However, this body was ineffective.

[55] *Irish Independent*, 3 November and 17 November 1954.

[56] Cf. *The Standard*, leading articles on 12 and 19 November 1954.

[57] During the correspondence an English reader wrote to the *Irish Times* to point out that many horror comics available there were printed in Rathmines, Dublin (an accusation which duly provoked letters from printers in that district disowning responsibility for such scandalous behaviour) cf. *Irish Times*, 3 and 5 November 1954.

[58] Around this time a Dublin newsagent was successfully prosecuted for publishing obscene libels (cf. *Irish Times*, 8 February 1955). The publications in question were three (unbanned) horror comics: *The Further Adventures of Belle*, *The Snatch Kid* and *The Flagellant's Paradise*.

[59] Report in the *Irish Times*, 4 December 1957. At the same time ecclesiastic authorities in Northern Ireland were protesting at the type of books available in Belfast.

[60] The booksellers claimed that hucksters, not they, were responsible for selling these publications (*Irish Times*, 7 December 1957).

[61] Cf. *Standard*, 6 December 1957 (Editorial); *Irish Catholic*, 12 December 1957 (Editorial), 2 January and 16 January 1958 (letters), 9 January (article); *Evening Herald*, 14 January 1958; *Hibernia*, January 1958; *Irish Independent*, 6 February 1958; *Sunday Independent*, 8 and 15 December 1957, 5 and 26 January 1958.

[62] The present Dublin City Librarian, Miss Mairin O'Byrne, recalls that she made a private survey of bookstalls, etc. at the time (not simply respectable bookshops), and is firmly convinced that the alarm was exaggerated. She also paid a visit to Belfast where, she agreed, the situation was one to get worried about. On 31 March 1958, in a leading article, 'New Curb on Evil Literature' commenting on the publication of the *Report of the British Select Committee on the Obscene Publications Bill*, the *Irish Independent* wrote: 'In some quarters (in Ireland) there has been a tendency to foster the notion that the recent campaign against these evil imports was either unnecessary or unduly alarming, but so complacent an attitude loses all semblance of reality when it is seen that Britain itself has become worried by the activities of vendors of pornography.'

[63] 31 December 1957.

[64] The private papers of the late Professor J. J. Pigott contain an interesting letter from a priest in Co. Kerry, dated 10 February 1958.

'Thanks for your very interesting and informative letter. I took it to N. and he read it to the Bishop. Of course it is treated as confidential. I thought that it would be best to go to higher quarters for action. I do know that a resolution was sent from C.Y.M.S. Tralee. The B[ishop] has ordered all priests in the diocese to preach on evil literature on 2nd Sunday in Lent, and I do feel he won't let the matter rest there. Of course the Bishops have issued a letter, as you know. You have every reason to be proud of the part you played in the matter [he probably refers to the *Irish Times*' controversy between Professor Pigott and Dr Sheehy Skeffington which took place in December 1957-January 1958]. . . .'

It will be remembered that Professor Pigott made public his reasons for resigning from the Censorship Board because he felt that the new Board was neglecting its duty under the Act. Mr Comyn, a new member of the Board, stated at the time that the change in the Board made no difference re its treatment of the publications at which the protest was aimed. He was also reported as saying that 'books meant for young people had got to be judged by a wholly different standard' than those meant for adults (cf. *Irish Times*, 7 December 1957).

⁶⁵ Some initiative in book control was taken by the newsagents themselves: cf. a report in the *Irish Independent* (20 January 1958), mentions that 'Many Dublin booksellers have now refused to take any publications of an American publishing house, because they consider that some of the books with this company's imprint are indecent.'

⁶⁶ Cf. *Irish Independent*, 22 January 1958. The newsagents' statement went on: 'Before the situation becomes even more confused, we suggest the licensing of all importers of books and the application of sanctions against those who repeatedly work against the aims of the Censorship Board.'

⁶⁷ *Irish Times*, 16 December 1957. Two months later the Association reiterated its full support for the Censorship Board. Cf. report of the Presidential Address to the Association, *Irish Independent*, 27 February 1958.

⁶⁸ Cf. *Irish Independent* report, 29 December 1957.

⁶⁹ The statement was reported and commented on by all the daily papers, the *Irish Independent* gave it its leading article on 1 February 1958.

⁷⁰ Dr Cornelius Lucey, Bishop of Cork, dealt with this subject in his Lenten Pastoral for 1958. He said that 'the voice of the Censorship Board was a very inadequate substitute for the voice of the individual Catholic conscience', and warned parents against assuming that the Censorship Board 'does all the work' (cf. *Irish Times*, 17 February 1958). Regarding the Bishop's views on censorship, see the *Irish Times*, 9 March 1956 and 8 May 1962.

⁷¹ *Dail Debates*, vol. 165, col. 36.

⁷² *Dail Debates*, vol. 165, cols. 344–345. The figures given were:

YEAR	BOOKS	PERIODICALS
1954	31	1
1955	48	36
1956	41	51
1957	52	21

The Minister also supplied the following figures for the last seven months of 1957:

MONTH	BOOKS	PERIODICALS
June	0	0
July	2	1
August	0	0
September	0	0
October	1	1
November	25	1
December	8	6

[73] *Dail Debates*, vol. 165, cols. 645–646.

[74] Around this time one member of Galway Corporation 'whose memory goes back longer than anyone else's in public service' recalled that over 50 years ago, when evil literature found its way into the city, a special vigilance committee was formed and was so successful that the trade was wiped out in them, and suggested that vigilance organisations be organised again (cf. *Irish Independent*, 7 March 1958).

[75] *Dail Debates*, vol. 166, cols. 34–35. Mr Traynor stated that it was unnecessary to introduce a system of licensing 'because the principal distributors are well known to the trade and to my Department'.

[76] *Dail Debates*, vol. 168, cols. 278–179 (20 May 1958).

[77] *Dail Debates*, vol. 170, cols. 377–379.

[78] As early as January, we find items in the papers mentioning holdups of book consignments by the customs. Cf. *Evening Herald*, 20 January 1958.
The Minister's reply to a question from Mr J. Blowick (*Dail Debates*, vol. 167, col. 1230, 1 May 1958) indicated that the Customs had increased the number of books they sent to the Board as compared with the months of November and December 1957.

[79] On 11 September 1958 the *Irish Times* reported on the result of the campaign, mentioning that 'customs officials appeared to have been given instructions to make a 100% examination (according to one bookseller "they virtually open every parcel")'.

[80] Statistics are not available of the number of prosecutions under the Censorship of Publications Act at this—or any other—time. Four cases have come to my notice: The first resulted in a fine of £10 for keeping 22 prohibited books for sale, and £10 for exposing a prohibited book for sale (cf. *Irish Times*, 30 November 1956). In February 1957 a fine of £10 was imposed for selling two prohibited books (cf. *Irish Times*, 12 February 1957). The third prosecution resulted in a fine of £20 for each of the following offences: selling four prohibited periodicals, selling three prohibited periodicals, keeping prohibited periodicals for sale (cf. *Irish Press*, 23 May 1957). In April 1958 a fine of £35 was imposed for selling two books (cf. *Irish Times*, 16 April 1958). The shop assistant was fined £1 for aiding and abetting.

234

NOTES TO CHAPTER VIII

[1] For convenience sake, future references to 'author' should be taken as applying also to 'editor', unless otherwise stated.

[2] Customs officials; the former Secretary to the Boards; booksellers; literary editors of Dublin newspapers; Irish authors; and others.

[3] With the exception of a few resignations, all disagreements between the Minister and the Board have taken place discreetly within the Government Offices. Never has the Minister criticised a Board in public—and never has he given a public directive to a Board (as requested, for example, by the Irish Association for Civil Liberties in 1956).

[4] It is convenient to mention here that the Censorship Board maintains no contact with any British agency involved in book control, much as the police, customs, Home Office or Director of Public Prosecutions (information given by a Secretary to the Board).

[5] The Council of Action on Censorship (1942–1944) appears (incorrectly) to have regarded the Secretary of the Board as responsible for many of these complaints. Among its papers is a proposal that 'the Secretary should not look for books' (this proposal was in substitution of another to the effect that 'A new Secretary to the Censor is essential'): cf. private papers in the possession of Mr Andrew Ganly.

[6] A member of the Censorship Board has little time for 'reading around his course'. However, if he receives a casual complaint about a book from a member of the public (not a crank) he will often go out of his way to bring the book before the Board himself.

[7] The point has been made that the *practice* of the Customs in England has been to exclude goods which are *obviously* indecent or obscene (indecent photographs is the typical example). But a more thorough examination is certainly permitted by the Act. See p. 30.

[8] Apart from the fact that the bookscale was established to stop leakages in the censorship system, the Customs officer has no special *duty* to examine these parcels.

For some years there was an import duty on novels of about one penny per copy, but although this did mean that all books imported were counted, it did not mean that they were subjected to a more vigorous examination than that given by the bookscale.

[9] Since examination by the Censorship Board delays the delivery of consignments, the books are sent to Dublin Castle—presumably to avoid unnecessary delay in the delivery of books which senior officials consider harmless.

[10] It has been reported that an English book club was requested by residents of the Republic to forward their books to a Belfast address, but the publishing company received so many such requests that it was not able to cope with them. The same company reported that 'one of their members, a Belfast resident, had written to them not to forward books on the Dublin censored list. He said he regarded himself as a member of the Republic, and that he wished to observe its laws, (cf. *Irish Times*, 20 December 1956).

[11] Even less watch is kept on banned periodicals cf. *Irish Independent* report (24 September 1953) of a debate on censorship of publications during the annual Conference of the Library Association of Ireland, in which a complaint was made that banned periodicals entered the country easily through the post.

[12] Shortly after the *Lady Chatterley's Lover* case in England I asked various friends (university students) to write to the Minister for Justice for permission to import one copy of this book. Permission was refused.

[13] Booksellers handle permits only on behalf of individuals to whom these have been granted. A 'special course of study' is the most usual reason for which permits for many copies of the same book are granted.

[14] Cf. *Irish Times* report; 13 January 1958. See also an article on 'Censorship' in *The Leader*, 11 June 1955, where the appointment of three full-time censors drawn from the senior ranks of the Civil Service is proposed. This article discusses the problem of the size of the Board's task.

[15] The British Home Office, for example, is careful to see that none of its officials is left for too long a period in the department for examining obscene publications.

[16] If a Board decides against prohibiting a particular book (in a bound edition, for example) it may of course re-open the case at a later date and issue a prohibition order (affecting perhaps only the paperback edition).

[17] Some publications manage, for different lengths of time, to avoid publishing consecutive issues to which the Board will be likely to object. They distribute their doubtful issues in such a way that the Board finds it difficult to establish clearly that they are objectionable.

[18] Under the 1929 Act all first prohibition orders had a duration of three months; thus a ban weighed heavier on publications of frequent periodicity.

[19] The Act provided that Oireachtas appeals did not require to be accompanied by a deposit. A statutory rule made in 1947 (Statutory Rules, 1947, No. 42) removed the requirement re six copies which had been imposed by the Principal Regulations made the previous year. (See above, p. 114).

[20] A simple arrangement would be to provide that the Censorship Board keep a library which would contain every book ever banned.

[21] See *Statutory Rules and Orders*, 1946, No. 254, vol. xxxvi, p. 455.

[22] At this point it is opportune to point out that there has been some criticism of the practice of closing the Courts when cases of obscene libel are being examined. Cf. remarks of Mr Noel Peart, SC at a meeting of Trinity College, Dublin (*Irish Times*, 5 March 1955).

[23] As has been mentioned elsewhere, the Appeal Board does not examine the same three issues of the periodical as were examined by the Censorship Board. Aware of this, a publisher may 'clean up' the paper in question before approaching the Appeal Board, or after his prohibition order runs out.

[24] Cf. article in the *Times Pictorial* (8 December 1956) giving some examples of the kind of variation which arose between Irish and English editions of the

same paper. See also *Irish Catholic* (8 September 1955), editorial on 'The Two-Faced Press', which contained an additional objection that the English editions of certain papers carry no Irish news and, in particular, do not give adequate coverage to the Partition question.

[25] Letter to the author from the Secretary to the Department of Justice, 21 November 1961. The Office of Censorship keeps no statistics of prosecutions.

[26] Many booksellers of course refuse to stock certain books on principle. Another reason for conservatism is that the most important clients of the bigger booksellers are librarians, who are notably cautious in their selection. For praise of censorship by newsagents cf. *Irish Press*, 25 February, 1965.

[27] The Censorship Board never gives any indication that a particular book is before it; this is only known if a prohibition order is made. Only the consignors know that their books have been forwarded to the Board.

Appendix I

Part I Preliminary

Section 1: SHORT TITLE

Section 2: DEFINITIONS: including a clause to the effect that 'the word "indecent" shall be construed as including suggestive of, or inciting to sexual immorality or unnatural vice or likely in any other similar way to corrupt and deprave'; and definitions of 'book' and 'periodical publication' so phrased that any printed publication must fall under one or other of these heads, the only exception being *bona fide* publications for the information or instruction of members of the legal or medical profession.

Part II Censorship of Publications

Section 3: ESTABLISHMENT OF CENSORSHIP OF PUBLICATIONS BOARD: which shall consist of five 'fit and proper persons' (including a Chairman) appointed by the Minister for Justice for a term of three years and eligible for reappointment. The Minister may remove from office any member who neglects to attend meetings or who becomes unfit in his opinion to be a member of the Board.

Section 5: MEETINGS AND PROCEDURE OF THE BOARD: times of meetings to be fixed by the members; the Board may act notwithstanding a vacancy in their number.

Section 6: PROHIBITION ORDERS IN RESPECT OF BOOKS: the Minister may refer to the Board any complaint made to him, and the Board shall examine the publication and (ss. 3) 'shall have regard to all or any of the following matters . . . (a) the literary, artistic, scientific or historic merit or importance and the general tenor of the book or the particular edition of a book which is the subject of such a complaint, (b) the language in which such book or edition is printed or produced, (c) the nature and extent of the circulation which, in the opinion of the Board, such book or edition is intended to have, (d) the class of reader in Saorstat Eireann which, in the opinion of the Board, may reasonably be expected to read such book or edition, and (e) any other matter relating to such book or editions which appears to the Board to be relevant.' The Board may communicate with the author, editor or publisher and take into account their representations, if any. The Board may examine a book on their own initiative. The Minister may prohibit the sale and distribution of a book which the Board consider 'in its general tendency indecent or obscene' . . . or which 'advocates the unnatural prevention of conception or the procurement of abortion or miscarriage or the use of any method, treatment or appliance for the purpose of such prevention or miscarriage.' The decision of the Board recommending prohibition must not be dissented to by more than one and must be assented to by at least three members. A prohibition order made under this section shall apply to every edition of such book, unless it is limited to one or more particular editions or unless certain editions are excluded by an amending order.

Section 7: PROHIBITION ORDERS IN RESPECT OF PERIODICAL PUBLICATIONS: the same procedure shall operate as for books, *mutatis mutandis*. Periodicals may be prohibited which 'have usually or frequently been indecent or obscene . . . or . . . have advocated the unnatural prevention of conception, (etc.) . . . or have devoted an unduly large proportion of space to the publication of matter relating to crime. Such prohibition order shall continue in force for three months provided no such prohibition order has been previously made (in which case, the implication is, the order becomes permanent).

Section 8: REVOCATION AND AMENDMENT OF PROHIBITION ORDERS: the Minister after consultation with the Board may at any time revoke a prohibition order or amend such order so as to exlude any particular edition.

Section 9: PUBLICATION OF PROHIBITION ORDERS: the orders shall have effect as from the date of their publication in the *Iris Oifigiuil*.

Section 10: OFFENCES IN RELATION TO PROHIBITED PUBLICATIONS: the importing, selling, keeping for sale, advertising, distributing, etc. of a prohibited publication renders the offender liable to a fine not exceeding fifty pounds and/or to imprisonment with or without hard labour of any term not exceeding six months. The Minister may permit any person to import, sell, distribute etc. any prohibited book.

Section 11: REGISTER OF PROHIBITED PUBLICATIONS: is prepared and kept by the Minister and shall be made available to the public.

Section 12: SEARCH WARRANT IN RESPECT OF PROHIBITED BOOKS, etc.: conditions etc. for same.

Section 13: CUSTOMS AND POSTAL RESTRICTIONS: Minister for Posts and Telegraphs may arrange to prevent the importation of prohibited publications by post; the Customs authorities are given an equivalent power.

Part III Reports of Judicial Proceedings

Section 14: RESTRICTIONS ON PUBLICATION OF REPORTS OF JUDICIAL PROCEEDINGS. It shall be unlawful to print or publish 'any indecent matter the publication of which would be calculated to injure public morals' or 'any indecent medical, surgical or physiological details the publication of which would be calculated to injure public morals. Limitation on matter of reports of judicial proceedings for divorce etc.

Section 15: PENALTIES IN RELATION TO ABOVE.

Part IV Miscellaneous and General

Section 16: PROHIBITION OF PUBLICATIONS ADVOCATING CONTRACEPTIVES: the publishing, selling, distributing of such publications is made a statutory offence. The mere publication of an advertisement relating to such publications is not an offence provided such advertisement is not and could not reasonably be supposed to be itself an advocacy of any such matter. The Minister for Posts and Telegraphs may make regulations to prevent the sending or delivery of such publications by post.

Section 17: AMENDMENT OF THE INDECENT ADVERTISEMENTS ACT, 1889.

Section 18: PROHIBITION OF SALE OF INDECENT PICTURES.

Section 19: SEARCH WARRANT IN RESPECT OF INDECENT PICTURES: subsection (3) repeals the Obscene Publications Act of 1857.

Section 20: REGULATIONS: provision for the Minister for Justice to make regulations regarding the manner and form in which complaints are to be made to him under this Act, the procedure of the Censorship of Publications Board; etc.

Section 21: EXPENSES.

Appendix 2

A SELECTION OF BOOKS PROHIBITED 1930-1946

Compiled from the *Register of Prohibited Publications* (*As on* 31 *December* 1943) and from the *Irish Oifigiuil*. The date given is that on which the prohibition order was published in the *Iris Oifiguil*. An asterisk indicates that the book was later the subject of a revocation order.

ANDERSON, Sherwood	Horses and Men (27 January 1931)
BATES, H. E.	4 titles
BECKETT, Samuel	More Pricks than Kicks (23 October 1934)*
BLOOM, Ursula	Rose Sweetman (24 November 1933)
BOCCACIO, Giovanni	Pasquerella and Madonna Babetta (14 August 1934)
BROCKWAY, Fenner	Purple Plague (30 March 1937)
BROMFIELD, Louis	6 titles, inc. The Rains Came (8 Dec 1939)
CALDWELL, Erskine	5 titles, inc. God's Little Acre and Tobacco Road (20 March 1934) (15 December 1933)
CARY, Joyce	3 titles
CASANOVA	My Life and Adventures (20 Sept 1932)
CHEVALIER, Gabriel	2 titles, inc. Clochemerle (1 September 1936)
CLARKE, Austin	The Bright Temptation (20 Sept 1932)*
	The Singing Men at Cashel (5 May 1936)*
COLETTE	5 titles, inc. Cheri, The Last of Cheri (7 April 1931)
COWARD, Noel	To Step Aside (19 December 1939)
CROSS, Eric	The Tailor and Anstey (2 October 1942)*
DALTON, Louis Lynch	Rags and Sticks (17 May 1938)
DEEPING, Warwick	I Live Again (20 November 1942)
DE MONTHERLANT, Henri	The Lepers (12 July 1940)
DU MAURIER, Daphne	I'll Never be Young Again (1 Nov 1932)
DURRELL, Laurence	Pied Piper of Lovers (17 December 1935)
ELLIS, Havelock	5 titles
ERVINE, St. John	Sophia (13 February 1942)
FARRELL, James T.	Studs Lonigan (17 July 1936)
FAULKNER, William	7 titles, inc. Sanctuary and As I Lay Dying (27 October 1931) (17 December 1935)
FRANCE, Anatole	A Mummer's Tale (27 November 1936)*
FREUD, Sigismund	Collected Papers (vol. II) (11 August 1944)*

GIBBONS, Stella	2 titles, inc. Cold Comfort Farm
	(1 November 1932)
GOGARTY, O. St. John	Going Native (23 January 1942)
GORKI, Maxim	Bystander (7 April 1931)*
GRAVES, Robert	Claudius the God and His Wife Messalina
	(25 September 1936)*
	I, Claudius (25 September 1936)*
	Wife to Mr Milton (11 August 1942)*
GREENE, Graham	Brighton Rock (14 February 1939)*
	It's a Battlefield (11 February 1938)*
	Stamboul Train (18 October 1938)*
HALL, Radclyffe	2 titles, inc. The Well of Loneliness
	(13 May 1930)
HARRIS, Frank	Bernard Shaw (22 December 1931)
HEMINGWAY, Ernest	A Farewell to Arms (31 March 1936)*
	Fiesta (12 September 1941)
	For Whom the Bell Tolls (10 June 1941)*
	To Have and Have Not (11 February 1938)*
HEYER, Georgette	2 titles
HUXLEY, Aldous	After Many a Summer (9 February 1940)*
	Antic Hay (12 August 1930)*
	Brave New World (8 March 1932)*
	Brief Candles (11 July 1930)*
	Eyeless in Gaza (1 September 1936)*
	Point Counter Point (13 May 1930)*
ISHERWOOD, Christopher	Goodbye to Berlin (13 June 1939)
JAMES, Norah C.	6 titles, inc. Strap-Hangers (17 July 1934)
JOHNSON, Pamela Hansford	2 titles
JOYCE, James	Stephen Hero (10 November 1944)*
KEYES, F. Parkinson	1 title
LAVERTY, Maura	Alone We Embark (28 December 1943)*
LAWRENCE, D. H.	Lady Chatterley's Lover (22 March 1932)
LEWIS, Sinclair	2 titles, inc. Elmer Gantry (27 January 1931)
LLEWELLYN, Richard	How Green Was My Valley (12 July 1940)*
MACKENZIE, Compton	1 title
MALRAUX, Andre	The Royal Way (14 February 1936)*
	Storm in Shanghai (*La Condition Humaine*)
	(10 March 1936)*
MANN, Thomas	The Transposed Heads (13 February 1942)*
MANNIN, Ethel	9 titles
MARSHALL, Bruce	Delilah Upside Down (8 April 1941)
	The Uncertain Glory (19 July 1935)
	Yellow Tapers for Paris (8 October 1943)
MAUGHAM. Somerset	6 titles, inc. Cakes and Ale (7 Nov 1930)
MEAD, Margaret	Coming of Age in Samoa (15 August 1944)*
	Growing Up in New Guinea (15 Aug 1944)
MOORE, George	A Storyteller's Holiday (20 January 1933)*
MORAVIA, Alberto	Wheel of Fortune (11 March 1938)

MUGGERIDGE, Malcolm — Autumnal Face (26 January 1932)*

NABOKOFF, Vladimir — Camera Obscura (14 February 1936)

O'BRIEN, Kate — Land of Spices (6 May 1941)*
Mary Lavelle (29 December 1936)

O'CASEY, Sean — I Knock at the Door (16 May 1939)*
Pictures in the Hallway (8 May 1942)*
Windfalls (4 December 1934)

O'CONNOR, Frank — Dutch Interior (12 July 1940)*

O'FAOLAIN, Sean — Bird Alone (1 September 1936)*
Midsummer Night Madness (22 April 1932)

O'FLAHERTY, Liam — 5 titles

O'HARA, John — Appointment in Samarra (19 July 1935)
Hope of Heaven and Other Stories
(16 May 1939)

PROUST, Marcel — Remembrance of Things Past:
Vol. 9 (The Captive) Pt. 1 (9 April 1943)*
Vol. 10 (The Captive) Pt. 2 (9 April 1943)*
Vol. 11, Pt. 2 (Sweet Cheat Gone)
(9 April 1943)*
Vol. 12 (Time Regained) (9 April 1943)*

SADE, Marquis de — Justine, of the Misfortunes of Virtue
(21 January 1936)

SHAW, Bernard — Adventures of the Black Girl in her Search
for God (5 May 1933)

SHOLOKHOV, Mikhail — And Quiet Flows the Don (28 Sept 1934)
The Don Flows Home to the Sea
(17 January 1941)
Virgin Soil Upturned (14 February 1936)

SPENDER, Stephen — The Burning Cactus (9 June 1936)

STEELE, Allen and
HANCOCK, Joan (Editors) — Modern Irish Short Stories (3 March 1944)

STEINBECK, John — The Grapes of Wrath (9 February 1940)*
To a God Unknown (16 August 1935)*

STROHEIM, Eric von — Paprika (21 January 1936)

TOYNBEE, Philip — A School in Private (27 March 1942)

UNAMUNO, VALLE INCLAN,
IBANEZ, AYALA, BAROJA,
AZORIN, etc. — The Spanish Omnibus (22 April 1932)

WALPOLE, Hugh — 3 titles

WELLS, H. G. — 4 titles

The above selection from the 1,700 (approx.) books prohibited in the period has been made paying special attention to well-known authors, Irish authors and certain books whose prohibition caused particular controversy.

All the books included in the list (with the exception of those by Havelock Ellis and Ethel Mannin) were prohibited on the grounds of indecency. Of the total number of books banned between 1930 and 1945 approximately $12\frac{1}{2}\%$

were prohibited on the grounds that they advocated the unnatural prevention of conception or the procurement of abortion.

Of the books whose titles are given in the list those marked by an asterisk were later removed from the *Register of Prohibited Publications* after a successful appeal to the Censorship of Publications Appeal Board.

The following short list of titles may indicate the nature of some other books banned:

> Lady Chatterley's Second Husband
> Nuns in Jeopardy
> Nicer to Stay in Bed
> A Lover would be Nice
> The Virgin's Progress
> Strip-Tease Murders
> Women as Pets
> Flaming Sex
> Kept Man
> Naked Truth About Nudism

PROHIBITIONS PER YEAR

Year	No.	Year	No.
1930	47	1938	133
1931	99	1939	142
1932	118	1940	122
1933	120	1941	129
1934	118	1942	117
1935	152	1943	134
1936	171	1944	73
1937	106	1945	60

Appendix 3

A SUMMARY OF THE CENSORSHIP OF PUBLICATIONS ACT, 1946

Section 1: DEFINITIONS: including the definition of the word 'indecent' as 'includes suggestive of, or inciting to, sexual immorality or unnatural vice or likely in any other similar way to corrupt or deprave'; and definitions of 'book' and 'periodical publication' so that any printed publication must fall under one or other of these heads.

Section 2: THE CENSORSHIP OF PUBLICATIONS BOARD: consists of five members (including a chairman), appointed by the Minister for Justice for a term of five years and eligible for reappointment. The Minister may remove from office any member who becomes 'unfit' or who neglects to attend meetings of the Board. The Board may act notwithstanding a vacancy in their membership.

Section 3: THE CENSORSHIP OF PUBLICATIONS APPEAL BOARD: consists of four ordinary members and a chairman who is a judge or a practising barrister or practising solicitor of not less than seven years' standing; appointed by the

Minister for a term of three years. In other respects the provisions regulating the Board are the same as those for the Censorship Board.

Section 4: OFFICERS AND SERVANTS OF THE CENSORSHIP BOARD AND OF THE APPEAL BOARD.

Section 5: REFERENCE OF BOOKS TO THE CENSORSHIP BOARD BY CUSTOMS OFFICIALS: an official may detain any book (other than one, not being merchandise, which forms part of the personal luggage of an incoming traveller) which, in his opinion, ought to be examined by the Board.

Section 6: EXAMINATION OF BOOKS BY THE CENSORSHIP BOARD: the Board may examine any book they wish to, having regard to '(a) the literary, artistic, scientific or historic merit or importance, and the general tenor of the book: (b) the language in which it is written; (c) the nature and extent of the circulation which, in their opinion, it is likely to have; (d) the class of reader which, in their opinion, may reasonably be expected to read it; (e) any other matter relating to the book which appears to them to be relevant'; and may communicate with, and take into account, any representation made by the author, editor or publisher.

Section 7: PROHIBITION ORDERS IN RESPECT OF BOOKS: shall be made by the Censorship Board if it is of the opinion that a book is indecent or obscene, or 'that it advocates the unnatural prevention of conception or the procurement of abortion or miscarriage or the use of any method, treatment or appliance for the purpose of such prevention or procurement'.

Section 8: APPEALS TO THE APPEAL BOARD IN RESPECT OF PROHIBITED BOOKS: the author, editor or publisher or any five members of the Oireachtas acting jointly, may appeal at any time within twelve months after the operative date or after the date on which the order took effect; only one appeal shall lie to the Board for each book; the appellants may apply once for a variation order for any edition of the book published after the date of the prohibition order.

Section 9: PROHIBITION IN RESPECT OF PERIODICAL PUBLICATIONS: the Censorship Board shall examine recent issues of the periodical and shall prohibit the sale and distribution thereof if they are of the opinion that the said issues '(a) have usually or frequently been indecent or obscene, or (b) have advocated the unnatural prevention of conception . . ., or (c) have devoted an unduly large proportion of space to the publication of matter relating to crime.' A periodical publication shall be deemed to 'advocate' if it contains any matter or advertisement which 'advocates'. First prohibition orders shall remain in force for three to twelve months, depending on the periodicity of the publication.

Section 10: APPLICATIONS TO THE APPEAL BOARD IN RESPECT OF PROHIBITED PERIODICAL PUBLICATIONS: the appellants are the same as for books (see Section 8 above). Three months must lapse between the failure of one appeal and lodgement of another in respect of the same periodical.

Section 11: PROCEDURE OF THE CENSORSHIP BOARD: meetings to be held as occasion requires; four members constitute a quorum; prohibition orders shall not be made unless three at least vote in favour and not more than one votes against.

Section 12: PROVISIONS AS TO APPEAL AND APPLICATIONS TO THE APPEAL BOARD: the Board meet as occasion requires; four members constitute a quorum;

revocation must be supported by three at least; an appeal by an author, editor or publisher must be accompanied by a deposit of five pounds which will be refunded if the appeal is not deemed frivolous.

Section 13: PUBLICATION OF ORDERS: the Censorship Board shall order that every prohibition order and every order of the Appeal Board shall be published in the *Iris Oifiguil* and shall take effect on the day on which it is published.

Section 14: PROHIBITION OF SALE AND DISTRIBUTION OF PERIODICAL PUBLICATIONS: to sell, expose, offer, advertise or keep for sale, or distribute, or offer or keep for distribution a prohibited publication renders one liable to a fine not exceeding fifty pounds, to imprisonment with or without hard labour for a term not exceeding six months or to both such fine and imprisonment and, in any case, to forfeiture of the relevant prohibited publication.

Section 15: PROVISIONS: to the effect that all prohibition orders in force before the operative day continue to be in force and are treated in the same manner as are new orders.

Section 16: REGISTER OF PROHIBITED PUBLICATIONS: is prepared and kept by the Censorship Board; shall contain title, author, publisher and date of each order; shall be made available to the public. It shall be the duty of every customs officer when examining luggage of incoming travellers to exhibit on demand a list of prohibited publications. Entry in the *Register* shall be conclusive evidence that a publication is banned.

Section 17: SEARCH WARRANTS.

Section 18: RESTRICTION OF IMPORTATION OF PROHIBITED PUBLICATIONS: importation is forbidden unless in accordance with permit.

Section 19: PERMITS: may be granted by the Minister for the purposes of the Act subject to such conditions as he thinks fit to impose; permits in force before the operative date shall continue to be in force.

Section 20: REGULATION.

Section 21: DEPOSITS AND FEES.

Section 22: EXPENSES.

Section 23: REPEAL of Part 11 and section 20 of the Censorship of Publications Act 1929.

Section 24: SHORT TITLE AND COLLECTIVE CITATION.

Appendix 4

MEMBERSHIP OF THE CENSORSHIP BOARD 1930-1964

FIRST BOARD (appointed 13 February 1930): Patrick Canon Boylan, MA, DD, DLITT (Chairman); W. E. Thrift, MA, FTCD, TD; W. J. O'Reilly, LLD; W. B. Joyce, BA, FRSA, PC; P. J. Keawell, MA; R. Donovan, BA, DLITT (replaced Keawell resigned as from 13 February 1932).

SECOND BOARD (appointed 18 February 1933): Boylan (Chairman); O'Reilly; Donovan; Thrift; Joyce; Senator Professor William Magennis (for Donovan deceased, as from 9 May 1934).

THIRD BOARD (appointed 11 February 1936): Boylan (Chairman); Thrift; O'Reilly; Joyce; Magennis; W. R. Fearon, DSC, FTCD (for Thrift resigned as from 20 November 1936); R. A. Montgomery: Lynn Doyle (for Joyce resigned as from 1 January 1937); Denis J. Coffey, MA, MB, DLITT (for Montgomery as from 28 September 1937); W. J. Williams, MA (for O'Reilly as from 15 October 1937).

FOURTH BOARD (appointed 11 February 1939): Boylan (Chairman); Magennis; Fearon; Coffey; Williams.

FIFTH BOARD (appointed 11 February 1942): Magennis (Chairman); Rev J. P. Camac, BA, CC (for Boylan); Coffey; Fearon; Williams; J. T. Wigham, MA, FRCSI (for Fearon as from March 1944).

SIXTH BOARD (appointed 15 February 1945): Magennis (Chairman); Coffey; Williams; Wigham; Rev J. Deery, MA, CC; B. F. Shields, MA, DECONSC (for Coffey deceased, as from 20 July 1945).

SEVENTH BOARD (appointed 27 March 1946): Magennis (Chairman); Deery (replaced Magennis deceased as Chairman from March 1946); C. J. Joyce, MA, Solicitor; Shields; Wigham; J. J. Pigott, MA, H DIP IN ED (substitute for Magennis as from 1 April 1946); J. D. Smyth, BSC, PHD (for Wigham as from 2 February 1949); District Justice T. G. O'Sullivan (for Smyth as from 16 August 1949); Dr P. T. Breathnach (for Shields as from 14 September 1950).

EIGHTH BOARD (appointed 13 February 1951): Deery (Chairman); O'Sullivan; Pigott; Joyce; Breathnach; C. J. O'Reilly, MA (for Breathnach deceased, as from 28 June 1951); D. J. Flynn, MECONSC (for Joyce as from 7 May 1952).

NINTH BOARD (appointed 13 February 1956) [last=last meeting attended; first =first meeting attended]: Deery (Chairman, last 8 June 1956); O'Sullivan (last 9 March 1956); Pigott (replaced Deery as Chairman, last 8 May 1957); O'Flynn (last 8 May 1957); O'Reilly (last 8 May 1957); A. F. Comyn, BA (as from 5 December 1956); R. R. Figgis, BA (as from 5 December 1956); Judge J. C. Conroy, SC (Chairman, first 28 October 1957); Miss Emma Bodkin, ACA (first 28 October 1957); F. T. O'Reilly (first 28 October 1957).

TENTH BOARD (appointed 12 February 1962): Conroy (Chairman); O'Reilly; A. A. Rochford (replaced Comyn as from 12 February 1962); F. C. Connolly (replaced Figgis as from 12 February 1962); ex-Chief Justice C. A. Maguire (replaced Bodkin as from 2 April 1962); A. Gibney (replaced Maguire as from 16 December 1963); M. Binchy (replaced Connolly as from 21 December 1964).

Appendix 5

MEMBERSHIP OF THE CENSORSHIP OF PUBLICATIONS APPEAL BOARD 1946-1967

FIRST BOARD (appointed 15 April 1946): Mr Justice Kevin O'Hanrahan Haugh (Chairman); James Hogan, MA, DLITT; W. F. Pyle, PHD, FTCD; R. Hayes, LRCSI, LRCPI, DLITT; Henry B. O'Hanlon.

SECOND BOARD (appointed 13 April 1949): Haugh (Chairman); Pyle; Hayes; O'Hanlon; Liam O Briain, MA (for Hogan).

THIRD, FOURTH, FIFTH, SIXTH, SEVENTH BOARDS (7 February 1952–12 February 1967): during this period the only change was the replacement of Hayes by Professor Jeremiah J. Hogan, MA, DLITT on 7 October 1954.

Appendix 6

A SELECTION OF BOOKS PROHIBITED DURING THE YEARS 1946–1966 INCLUSIVE

Compiled from the Register of Prohibited Publications; with the date on which the prohibition order was published in the *Iris Oifigiuil*.

AMIS, Kingsley	Lucky Jim (16 April 1954)
	That Uncertain Feeling (20 June 1956)
BALZAC, Honoré de	Ten Droll Tales (13 February 1953):
	particular edition published in USA
BATES, H. E.	Various titles
BECKETT, Samuel	Watt (22 October 1954)
	Molloy (20 January 1956)
BELL, Sam Hanna	December Bride (11 April 1952)
BRAINE, John	Room at the Top (17 June 1958)
BRODERICK, John	The Pilgrimage (31 March 1961)
BROPHY, John	Numerous titles
BURTON, Sir Richard	The Book of the Thousand and One Nights
	(21 July 1959): particular edition
CONNELL, Vivian	September in Quinze (1 August 1952)
	The Hounds of Cloneen (15 June 1961)
CONNOLLY, Cyril	The Rock Pool (15 August 1947)
DE MONTHERLANT, Henri	Desert Love (7 October 1958)
DOLCI, Danilo	To Feed the Hungry (12 June 1962)
FORESTER, C. S.	The African Queen (20 June 1951)
GENET, Jean	The Thief's Dinner (22 December 1961)
	Our Lady of the Flowers (October 1965)
GIDE, André	Fruits of the Earth (15 February 1952)

GOGARTY, O. St John	Mr Petunia (2 August 1946)
GRAVES, Robert	King Jesus (14 January 1947)
HELLER, Joseph	Catch 22 (13 November 1962)
HEMINGWAY, Ernest	Across the River and into the Trees (17 November 1950)
	The Sun Also Rises (14 November 1952)
HUXLEY, Aldous	Ape and Essence (10 May 1949)
	The Devils of Loudon (14 November 1952)
	The Genius and the Goddess (15 July 1955)
HYDE, H. Montgomery	Roger Casement (9 June 1964)
KAZANTZAKI, Nikos	Zorba the Greek (10 October 1952)
KENYATTA, Jomo	Facing Mount Kenya (19 June 1953)
KOESTLER, Arthur	The Age of Longing (15 May 1953)
	Arrow in the Blue (13 February 1953)
McCARTHY, Mary	The Group (21 January 1964)
MACKEN, Walter	Quench the Moon (6 July 1948)
	I am Alone (17 February 1950)
	The Bogman (20 June 1952)
MAILER, Norman	Barbary Shore (16 May 1952)
	The Deer Park (5 April 1957)
	The Naked and the Dead (12 August 1958)
MANN, Thomas	The Holy Sinner (1 August 1952)
	The Black Swan (19 November 1954)
	The Confessions of Felix Krull (18 Nov '55)
METALIOUS, Grace	Peyton Place (6 May 1958)
MOORE, Brian	Wreath for a Redhead (19 December 1952)
	The Lonely Passion of Judith Hearne (11 February 1958)
MORAVIA, Alberto	Numerous titles
MURDOCH, Iris	The Flight from the Enchanter (15 June 1956)
	A Severed Head (20 February 1962)
NABOKOV, Vladimir	Laughter in the Dark (17 November 1950)
	Lolita, vols. I and II (20 January 1956)
O'FLAHERTY, Liam	Land (2 August 1946)
O'HARA, John	Various titles
SPARK, Muriel	The Bachelors (23 December 1960)
QUIGLY, Isabel	The Eye of Heaven (18 February 1955)
SARTRE, Jean Paul	The Age of Reason (21 March 1947)
	The Diary of Antoine Roquentin (14 June 1949)
	Intimacy and other stories (28 July 1950)
	Iron in the Soul (13 October 1950)
	The Chips are Down (Les Jeux Sont Fait) (15 June 1951)
SELBY Jr., Hubert	Last Exit to Brooklyn (April 1966)
SIMENON, Georges	Numerous titles
STRONG, L. A. G.	The Hill of Howth (19 June 1953)

THOMAS, Dylan	Adventures in the Skin Trade (21 October 1955)
	A Prospect of the Sea and other stories and prose writings (17 February 1956)
TOMELTY, Joseph	The Apprentice (16 October 1953)
UPDIKE, John	Rabbit, Run (20 February 1962)
WHEATLEY, Denis	Numerous titles
WILLIAMS, Tennessee	The Roman Spring of Mrs Stone (20 February 1951)
	Cat on a Hot Tin Roof (16 March 1956)

Appendix 7

NOTES ON CONTROVERSIES, 1946–1966

These notes are arranged in a roughly chronological order and in so far as possible do not cover controversies already mentioned in the text.

1946

FRANK O'CONNOR, *The Midnight Court*: an anthology of translations of Irish poetry including 'The Midnight Court' ('Cuirt an Mheadoin Oidche') by Bryan Merriman (d. 1805). Banned in May 1946: the only banning to date of a book published in Ireland. Described by O'Connor as 'a Rythmical Bacchanalia from the Irish' the poem concerns a dream about a slanging-match between a young girl complaining that the fine young men of the time will marry old women, and an old man complaining of the untrustworthy nature of young brides (he has been presented with a son on his wedding night). There is a voluble attack on marriage, and another on clerical celibacy. O'Connor himself has described the poem as 'a great paean in praise of bastards', saying that 'the bastard is used as a symbol of natural innocence' (cf. *New Statesman and Nation*, 13 April 1946). The ban was followed by lengthy correspondence in the *Irish Times*, July–August 1946. An appeal lodged by the publisher, Mr Maurice Fridberg, in 1946 was unsuccessful.

Another English translation of the poem, made by Mr Arland Ussher in 1926, with a preface by W. B. Yeats, was not banned. In 1948 a new edition of the poem in the original Irish was published in Dublin by subscription. Mr Eamon de Valera and Mr Sean T. O'Kelly were among the subscribers. The same poem suffered printer's censorship when published in *Poetry Ireland* (cf. *Irish Times*, 18 July 1949).

Kings, Lords and Commons, a new anthology by Frank O'Connor was banned when it appeared in 1961: the ban was automatic, because the book contained 'The Midnight Court' and it was the poem itself which had been banned in 1946. In December 1961 the prohibition order on *Kings, Lords and Commons* was revoked after an appeal was lodged by five members of the Oireachtas (cf. news-report and leading article in the *Irish Times*, 9 December 1961). There is a curious case here of two appeals being admitted in respect of the one text; presumably a variation of the internal rule on 'omnibus editions' permitted this appeal. The case deserves further investigation as to whether it constitutes a precedent.

The Common Chord and *Traveller's Samples*, two other books by Frank O'Connor were also banned during this period (on 19 December 1947 and 20 April 1951, respectively).

SINCLAIR LEWIS, *Cass Timberlaine*: banned 7 June 1946. Mentioned in correspondence at various times.

1947
JOHN STEINBECK, *The Wayward Bus*: banned 19 December 1947; *Cannery Row*: banned and unbanned; *Tortilla Flat* and *Burning Bright*: banned 15 February 1952; *East of Eden*: banned 19 December 1952; *The Pastures of Heaven, Cup of Gold* and *The Pearl*: banned 16 April 1954; *The Short Novels of J. S. Steinbeck*: banned 19 November 1957.

1948
GRAHAM GREENE, *The Heart of the Matter*: banned June 1948; appeal successful. *The End of the Affair*: banned 20 November 1951; appeal in 1955 unsuccessful. *England Made Me*: banned 18 July 1955; appeal successful. *The Quiet American*: banned 21 January; appeal successful.

1949
GEORGE ORWELL, *1984*: banned 15 July 1949. Protest in the *Irish Times*, 6 March 1956. Figured in the Pigott-Skeffington correspondence (December 1957–January 1958). See also *Irish Times* (leading article, 13 September 1958).

1950
APULEIUS, *The Golden Ass*: an edition published by Penguin Books was banned on 19 May 1950. Correspondence in the *Irish Times*, May–June 1950. Robert Graves, the translator, writing from Mallorca, described the Irish censorship as 'the fiercest literary censorship this side of the Iron Curtain—and I do not except Spain' (*Irish Times*, 22 June 1950). Paul Blanshard in *The Right to Read* (p. 145) mentions that the US Customs ban on this work was lifted as late as 1931.

1952

JAROSLAV HASEK, *The Good Soldier Schweik*: banned 10 October 1952. Protest in the *Spectator* (28 November 1952). The book first appeared in English 20 years earlier. As for most translations, the ban was confined to all English editions.

1953

STANLEY KAUFFMAN, *The Philanderer*: banned 19 June 1953. This book was the subject of an interesting prosecution in London (cf. C. R. Rolph, 'The Philanderer Case' in the *New Statesman and Nation*, 10 July 1954). *The Tight-rope*: the same book, under this title, was banned 29 July 1958.

1955

FRANCOISE SAGAN, *Bonjour Tristesse*: banned 17 June 1955; *A Certain Smile*: banned 5 February 1957 (both 'all English editions').
MARCEL PROUST, *Remembrance of Things Past*: banned April 1943 (vols. 9, 10, 11, 12); revocation 1950. *Jean Santeuil*: banned November 1955. Dr Monk Gibbon in the course of a letter to the *Irish Times* (23 November 1955) asked: 'Is it just pruriency or stupidity, or a kind of sub-conscious malice that accounts for the fact that once an author's name has appeared on the list his chances of reappearance there seem to be enormously increased?' The ban was lifted in January 1956.

1956

NICHOLAS MONSERRAT, *The Tribe that Lost its Head*: it was reported in the *Irish Times* (7 December 1956) that while the Censorship Board was not functioning (due to vacancies in its number) Dublin booksellers had by common consent withdrawn this book from circulation. It was banned on 6 April 1957 (in the second list issued by the newly consti-tuted Board). Various other books by the same author have been banned.

1957

JOSEPH MC CABE, *Twelve Years in a Monastery*: banned in 1957; a letter in the *Irish Times* (4 June 1957) suggested that it had been banned on religious grounds; appeal successful.
DANIEL DEFOE, *Roxana*: the 'Giant Edition No. 24' published by Royal Books, New York, was banned on 17 December 1957. According to the *Irish Times* (19 December) this particular edition was prohibited 'because of the nature of the resumé and picture which was on the cover'. Mr Sean O'Faolain appears to have for once agreed with the Board: 'the publisher of the edition in question' he wrote 'deserves nobody's sym-

pathy' (*Irish Times*, 23 December). This ban was reported in *The Times*, an honour which it shared with few other prohibitions.

AUSTIN CLARKE, *The Singing Men of Cashel* (banned in 1936) figured in the Pigott-Skeffington correspondence (*Irish Times*, December 1957–January 1958); *The Bright Temptation*: the 1932 ban was lifted in October 1954; *The Sun Dances at Easter*: banned, 10 October 1952; an appeal in 1955 failed.

1958

MARGARET MEAD, *Growing Up in New Guinea*: banned 15 August 1955. An American edition was banned on 9 September 1958 and a shocked letter appeared in the *Irish Times* (15 September) warning that this ban on a sociological study was the 'thin end of the wedge' and asking '*Will Coming of Age in Samoa* be next?'; *Coming of Age in Samoa*: banned 11 August 1944: successful appeal in April 1953; *Male and Female*: banned, 15 May 1953.

BRENDAN BEHAN, *Borstal Boy*: banned, 11 November 1958; ban reported in *The Times* the following day. The book was published on 20 October 1958; Dublin booksellers have stated that many copies were sold before the ban. The publishers (Hutchinson), in their publicity for the book abroad, made advertising capital out of the ban. According to one member of the Board, the censors 'just got by' on obscenity.

1960–1966

EDNA O'BRIEN, one of the most colourful figures of recent censorship controversies. All her books have been banned and appear to grow in permissiveness as the years go by. (Censorship has possibly aided this process.) *The Country Girls* (21 June 1960); *Girl with Green Eyes* and *The Lonely Girl* (12 June 1962); *Girls in their Married Bliss* (15 December 1964); *August is a Wicked Month* (7 December 1965) (this book came under bans also in Australia, Rhodesia and South Africa); *Casualties of Peace* (December 1966).

In October 1965 a Dublin shiny began a serial of *The Country Girls* apparently by privately clearing the way with the Minister for Justice—a type of licensing for which there was no precedent. In April 1966 Peter Connolly, Professor of English at Maynooth College, the national seminary, praised her literary ability and 'cheerful natural rural ribaldry', obtaining a bouquet from the *Irish Times*. In May 1966 the *Sunday Independent* reported that widespread changes in existing censorship laws were planned (this had been demanded two months earlier in the Dail). Meanwhile the Roman Catholic Bishop of Cork called for stricter censorship laws, suggesting that the Censorship Board be scrapped and the prosecution method be revived (*Irish Times*, 16 May 1966).

PETER LENNON published four articles in *The Guardian* (8–11 January 1964) dealing with Irish censorship formal and informal. Often mistaken in his facts and tendentious in his judgements. See also his letter in the *Evening Press* (11 February) replying to criticism by John Jordan and Peter Connolly in *Hibernia* (February). The original articles were published in the Irish provincial press and in *TCD Miscellany* (1 May 1964). Lennon also intervened in the McGahern controversy.

JOHN MC GAHERN was the first Irish writer to receive the AE Memorial Award (1962), for the opening chapters of his novel *The Barracks*. Early in May 1965 his second book *The Dark*, a shocking, sensitive and vivid account of a country boy growing up, was detained by the Customs; it was banned the following month. In February 1966 it became known that in October 1965, on his return from a sabbatical year to the Dublin school at which he taught, he had been dismissed from his job. He claimed that he had been dismissed because of *The Dark*; the clerical authorities who managed the school did not see fit to give reasons for their action. See also 'McGahern Affair' by O. Sheehy Skeffington in *Censorship*, Vol. 2, No. 2, pp. 27–30 (Spring 1966).

Appendix 8

THE INDEX LIBRORUM PROHIBITORUM AND THE CANONS OF THE CODE OF

CANON LAW RELATING TO BOOKS

Given that the great majority of the population of the Republic of Ireland is Roman Catholic and that Church has a long tradition of censorship it has often been alleged that Irish censorship is catholic-inspired. This short Appendix indicates Church law on reading but it should be stressed (i) that custom has always been in some instances at variance with law; (ii) that subsequent to the Second Vatican Council the *Index* has been suppressed; and (iii) that the Code of Canon Law is at present under revision.

Two sections of the Code of Canon Law refer to books. Canons 1384-1394 deal with prior censorship of books written by Catholics. All Catholics, lay as well as clerical, are bound to submit to ecclesiastical censorship any writings dealing with theological, moral and related subjects (*c.* 1385). Priests are bound to submit everything they write:

'Vetantur clerici saeculares sine consensu suorum Ordinariorum, religiosi vero sine licentia sui Superioris maioris et Ordinarii loci, libros quoque, que de rebus profanis tractent, edere, et in diariis, foliis vel libellis periodicis scribere vel eadem moderari' (*c.* 1386, 1). (On this matter cf. J. G. McGarry, 'The exercise of authority over religious publications' in *The Furrow*, January 1967).

The second section (*c.* 1395–1405) deals with the prohibition of books. Individual Catholics have a duty to denounce to their diocesan Ordinary or to the Holy See books which they consider pernicious (*c.* 1397, 1). The prohibition of a book implies that it may not be published, read, kept, sold, translated or in any way communicated to others (*c.* 1398, 1). Among the categories of books forbidden are: translations of Scripture published or made by non-Catholics; books which defend heresy or schism; books which purposely attack religion or good morals; books which favour any type of superstition; books which declare duelling, suicide or divorce to be licit; books 'qui res lascivas seu obscenas ex professo tractant, narrant aut docent' (*c.* 1399). Permission to read prohibited books may be obtained from the diocesan Ordinary if sufficient reason is given (*c.* 1402).

All the above are prohibited in a general way. Thus if the reader thinks that a particular book falls into any of these categories he is forbidden to read it. In addition to this general prohibition certain books were specifically forbidden, usually by inclusion in the *Index Librorum Prohibitorum.*

The continuous history of the *Index* dates from 1559 although even in the early Church there are cases of lists of prohibited reading. A Congregation of the *Index* maintained a separate existence until 1917 when it was fused with the Holy Office (now called the Congregation for the Doctrine of the Faith). On 14 June 1966 the congregation suppressed the *Index* but stated that 'its significance and moral value remain in full vigour in the sense that it calls the attention of the christian conscience to its duty to avoid reading books which are dangerous to faith and morals'. Moreover, from now on it is the duty of bishops and episcopal conferences, in agreement with the Sacred Congregation for the Doctrine of the Faith, to control publications by condemning those which are bad and promoting those which are good. The Holy See reserves to itself the right to intervene directly and publicly only in extreme case. Diocesan Ordinaries very rarely prohibit the reading of specific bookss.

The last edition of the *Index*, published in 1948, contained a preface explaining its purpose, most of the relevant Canons, and also an Instruction from the Holy Office (dated 3 May 1927) to archbishops and bishops concerning sensual and mystico-sensual writings 'quarum quidem scriptionum incredibiliter fecunda sunt haec tempora quotidieque maior ubique copia diffunditur' (p. xxix).

The great majority of the 5,000 books included in the *Index* were published in the seventeenth and eighteenth centuries. For the most part theological, biblical and philosophical works, they are almost all out of print. Among well-known authors and works on the list were (*oo* signifies *opera omnia*):

> Bentham; Bergson; Sir Thomas Browne (*Religio Medici*); Benedetto Croce (*oo*); Gabriele D'Annunzio; Daudet; Defoe (*Political History of the Devil*); Dumas—*pater et filius* (*Omnes fabulae amatoriae*); Flaubert (*Madame Bovary*); Anatole France (*oo*); Gentilis (*oo*); Gibbon (*Decline and Fall*); Hobbes (*oo*); Hugo; Hume (*oo*); Locke; Maeterlinck (*oo*); Charles Maurras; J. S. Mill; Samuel Richardson (*Pamela*); Proudhon (*oo*); Renan; Georges Sand; Stendhal (*Omnes fabulae amatoriae*); Sterne (*A Sentimental Journey*); Voltaire; Zola (*oo*).

Between 1948 and 1966 new prohibitions included:

> Jean-Paul Sartre (*oo*, 27 October 1948); Alberto Moravia and André Gide (*oo*, 2 April 1952).

The dangers and difficulties inherent in prior and post-publication censorship in a civil context are also to be verified in ecclesiastical censorship and are heightened in a situation where authority is exercised without due regard to personal rights and administrative law.

Bibliography

The list of secondary works does not include the more important books which were the object of prohibition orders (these are included in various appendices), neither is it meant to be exhaustive, especially because most of the material used came from primary sources. In recent years there have appeared a considerable number of books on different aspects of censorship. Many of these have been markedly propagandist in character and may well eventually be seen as harmful to the cause of the right to read.

MANUSCRIPT

The private papers of the Council of Action on Censorship (in the possession of Mr Andrew Ganly)

The private papers of the late Professor Robert Donovan (in the possession of Mr P. F. Donovan): these papers include the minutes of evidence taken before the Committee on Evil Literature

The private papers of the late Professor J. J. Pigott (in the possession of Mrs J. J. Pigott)

GOVERNMENT PUBLICATIONS (BRITISH AND IRISH)

Dail Debates (from 1922)

Seanad Debates (from 1922)

Parliamentary Debates (Official Report): House of Commons and House of Lords (UK)

Censorship of Films Act, 1923

Censorship of Films (Amendment) Act, 1925

Censorship of Publications Act, 1929

Censorship of Publications Act, 1946

Customs Consolidation Act, 1876 (UK)

Dublin Police Act, 1842 (UK)

Judicial Proceedings (Regulation of Reports) Act, 1926 (UK)

Indencent Advertisements Act, 1889 (UK)

Obscene Publications Act, 1857 (UK)

Obscene Publications Act, 1959 (UK)

Post Office Act, 1908 (UK)

Annual Estimates

Appropriation Accounts
Iris Oifigiuil
Oireachtas Eireann Bills
Minutes of Evidence taken before the Select Committee on the Obscene
    Publications Bill, (HMSO), 1958
Register of Prohibited Publications (as published in various years)
*Annual Reports of the Censorship of Publications Board and the Censorship
    Appeal Board*
Report of the Committee on Evil Literature, 1927
Report of the Royal Commission on the Press, (HMSO) 1949
Report of the Select Committee on the Obscene Publications Bill, (HMSO)
    1958
Statutory Rules, Orders and Regulations

REFERENCE WORKS
Books prohibited in Ireland under the Censorship of Publications Act
    (published in various years by Eason, Dublin)
Essay and General Literature Index, New York
Flynn, W. J., *Oireachtas Companion and Saorstat Guide* (continued as
    Free State Parliamentary Companion), Dublin
Halsbury, *The Laws of England*, London 1910.
Irish Catholic Directory, Dublin
Legal Diary, Dublin
Reader's Guide to Periodical Literature, New York
Subject Index to Periodicals, London
Who's Who in the Seanad Election, Dublin 1925
Thom's Directory of Ireland

SPECIAL ARTICLES
AE, 'The Censorship in Ireland', *Nation and Athenaeum*, xliv, pp.
    435–436 (22 December 1928)
Connolly, Peter R., 'Censorship', *Christus Rex*, xiii, pp. 151–170 (July
    1959); 'The Moralists and the Obscene', *Irish Theological Quarterly*,
    xxxii, 2, pp. 116–128 (April 1965)
Devane, R. S. (SJ), 'Indecent Literature: some legal remedies', *IER*,
    fifth series, 25, pp. 182–204 (February 1925)
Gannon, Patrick (SJ), 'Literature and Censorship', *Irish Monthly*, 65,
    pp. 434–447 (June 1937); 'Art, Morality and Censorship', *Studies*,
    33, pp. 409–419 (December 1942)
Gibbon, Monk, 'In Defence of Censorship', *The Bell*, 9 pp. 313–322
    (January 1945)

Harmon, Maurice, 'The Era of Inhibition: Irish Literature 1920–60', *The Emory University Quarterly*, xxii, pp. 18–28 (Spring 1966)

'Ineffective Censorship', *Catholic Truth Quarterly*, 1, No. 11, pp. 2–5 (January–March 1940)

'Ireland' in *Censorship*, No. 1, Autumn 1964, pp. 16–18.

Murphy, C. B., 'Sex, Censorship and the Church', *The Bell*, 2, No. 6, pp. 65–75 (September 1941); 'Censorship: Principle and Practice', *The Bell*, 3, pp. 293–301 (January 1942)

Murray, J. Courtney (sj), 'Censorship and Literature', *The Furrow*, 7, pp. 679–691 (November 1956)

O'Faolain, Sean, 'Standards and Taste', *The Bell*, 2, No. 3, pp. 5–11 (June 1941)

Shaw, G. Bernard, 'The Censorship', *Irish Statesman*, 11, pp. 206–208 (17 November 1928); with Sean O'Casey, T. C. Kingsmill Moore, James Hogan, 'Censorship', *The Bell*, 9, pp. 395–409 (February 1945).

NEWSPAPERS AND PERIODICALS

The Bell, Dublin
British national newspapers
The Bookseller, London
Catholic Bulletin, Dublin
Catholic Mind, Dublin
Catholic Truth Quarterly, Dublin
Catholic Voice, Cork
Censorship, London
Church of Ireland Gazette, Dublin
Christus Rex, Maynooth
Cork Examiner
Doctrine and Life, Dublin
Dublin Review, London
Encounter, London
Evening Mail, Dublin
The Furrow, Maynooth
Hibernia, Dublin
Irish Catholic, Dublin
Irish Ecclesiastical Record, Dublin
Irish national and provincial newspapers
The Irishman, Dublin
Irish Monthly, Dublin
Irish Rosary, Dublin

Irish Statesman, Dublin
Irish Worker, Dublin
An Leabharlann, Dublin
The Leader, Dublin
The Nation, Dublin (1927–1931)
Nation and Athenaeum, London
New Statesman and Nation, London
An Phoblacht, Dublin
An Realt (*The Star*), Dublin
The Round Table, London
The Spectator, London
The Tablet, London

SECONDARY WORKS

Aristotle, *Politics*, (Ernest Barker trans.), London 1948
Atkinson, Sir E. Tindal, *Obscene Literature in Law and Practice*, London 1936
Bailey, K. C., *A History of Trinity College, Dublin, 1892–1945*, Dublin 1947
Blanshard, Paul, *The Irish and Catholic Power: an American interpretation*, London 1954; *The Right to Read: the battle against censorship*, Boston 1951
Bromage, Mary, *De Valera and the March of a Nation*, London 1956
Craig, Alec, *Banned Books of England*, London 1937; *The Banned Books of England and Other Countries*, London 1962
CTS Committee (issued by), *The Problem of Undesirable Printed Matter*, Dublin 1927
Devane, R. S. (SJ), *Evil Literature: some suggestions* (with a Foreword by Sir E. Cecil), Dublin 1927; *The Committee on Evil Literature: some notes of evidence*, Dublin 1927; *The Imported Press: a national menace*, Dublin 1950
Dicey, A. V., *Introduction to the Study of the Law of the Constitution*, (8th ed.), London 1915
Doolan, AE (OP), *Order and Law*, Dublin 1954
Doyle, Lynn, *The Spirit of Ireland*, London 1935
Gardiner, Harold (SJ), *Norms for the Novel*, New York 1953; *Catholic Viewpoint on Censorship*, New York 1958
Haight, A. L., *Banned Books*, London 1955
Herbert, A. P., *Uncommon Law*, London 1935
Hoggart, Richard, *The Uses of Literacy*, London 1957

Joynson-Hicks, Sir W., *Do We Need a Censor ?*, London 1929

Kelly, John M., *Fundamental rights in the Irish Law and Constitution*, Dublin, 1961.

Maritain, Jacques, *Art and Scholasticism*, London 1930

McCracken, J. L., *Representative Government in Ireland*, London 1958

Mansergh, Nicholas, *The Irish Free State: its government and politics*, London 1934

Milton, John, *Areopagitica*, 1644

Murphy, Fergus, *Publish or Perish*, Cork 1951

O'Faolain, Sean, *The Irish*, West Drayton 1948

O'Sullivan, Donal, *The Irish Free State and its Senate*, London 1940

Pieper, Joseph, *Leisure, the basis of culture*, London 1952

Rolph, C. H., *Does Pornography Matter*, London 1961

Rolph, C. H., (ed.) *The Trial of Lady Chatterley*, London 1961

Stevas, N. St John, *Obscenity and the Law*, London 1956

Ussher, Arland, *The Face and Mind of Ireland*, London 1949

Index